Preparing Mathematics
and Science Teachers
for Diverse Classrooms

Promising Strategies for Transformative Pedagogy

Preparing Mathematics and Science Teachers for Diverse Classrooms

Promising Strategies for Transformative Pedagogy

Edited by

Alberto J. Rodriguez
San Diego State University

Richard S. Kitchen
University of New Mexico

LAWRENCE ERLBAUM ASSOCIATES, PUBLISHERS
2005   Mahwah, New Jersey   London

Lawrence Erlbaum Associates, Inc., Publishers
10 Industrial Avenue
Mahwah, New Jersey 07430

Cover design by Kathryn Houghtaling Lacey

Library of Congress Cataloging-in-Publication Data

Preparing Mathematics and Science Teachers for Diverse Classrooms: Promising Strategies
for Transformative Pedagogy, by Alberto J. Rodriguez and Richard S. Kitchen.
    p.   cm.
    Includes bibliographical references and indexes.
    ISBN 0-8058-4679-4 (cloth: alk. paper) — 0-8058-4680-8 (pbk : alk. paper).

Copyright information for this volume can be obtained
by contacting the Library of Congress.

Books published by Lawrence Erlbaum Associates are printed on acid-free paper,
and their bindings are chosen for strength and durability.

Printed in the United States of America
10 9 8 7 6 5 4 3 2

*For my father whose unwavering faith
in me became my compass.*

*For children, Chantelle and Brandon, whose rich
dreams and aspirations give the future a ladder
on which to climb.*

*For Cathy Z. whose love and support make facing
demanding challenges possible . . . and possible to face more.*

—ARJ

*For Janet, Olivia, and Sophia
whose love and faith have inspired me
and brought joy to my life.*
—RSK

Contents

Foreword

Preparing Prospective Mathematics and Science Teachers to Teach for Diversity: Promising Strategies for Transformative Action is an outstanding contribution to the field of teacher education, especially mathematics and science education. It achieves a milestone in the field of multicultural education and transformative teaching. It is a major piece of work, and a rich asset for those concerned with mathematical and scientific learning for students who have historically been under represented in advanced mathematics and science classes. Visits to the honor math and science classes in high schools across the country reveal few students of color, especially African American, Latinos and Native American. Also, students of color are behind in basic math and science knowledge and skills. For example, in 1996, 58% of 4th graders, 61% of 8th graders, and 60% of 12th graders who were eligible for free or reduced-priced lunch scored below basic level in mathematic achievement, compared to 26% of 4th graders, 29% of 8th graders, and 26% of 12th graders who were ineligible (Reese, Miller, Maddeo, & Dossey, 1997).

Important too, is that *Preparing Prospective Mathematics and Science Teachers to Teach for Diversity: Promising Strategies for Transformative Action* comes at a time when, state standards, discussions of alternative certification, testing, portfolio assessment, and the No Child Left Been Act are driving the discourse in teacher education. Much of this discourse, however, is lacking in knowledge and understanding of how to prepare teacher candidates to constructively and successfully engage marginalized students in science and math at the elementary and middle grades. Rodriguez, Kitchen and the chapter authors, however, provide valuable ideas and insights here, as they engage in "highly qualified teacher" preparation. By highly qualified teachers, I mean teachers who do not believe that students of color are the major cause (a "blame the victims" ideology) of their own academic difficulty in school; or that they are anti-intellectual. Highly qualified teachers know their subject matter, and have learned culturally relevant pedagogical instructional strategies, and according to Martin Haberman's observation must have "great commitment, greater courage, and even more persistence" to teach students from diverse backgrounds.

This book is an excellent contribution for teacher educators' concern with integrating theory and practice, while they contend with their teacher candidates' ideology that is too often (unconsciously) moored in systems of reason that are racist, sexist, classist, homophobic, as well as supported by false notions of rugged individualism and benign neglect regarding issues of diversity and the need for transformative action. Rodriguez, Kitchen and their colleagues successfully meet the challenge they have set in writing this book. They "provide both a theoretical basis and practical strategies to counter teachers' resistance to teaching for diversity (i.e., resistance to teaching in cultural and gender inclusive ways) as well as to counting teacher resistance to teaching for understanding (i.e., resistance to using student-centered and inquiry-based pedagogical approaches)."

Each chapter author(s) has crafted an excellent piece of scholarship that illuminates how they confront the resistance their teacher candidates bring to the teaching of mathematics and science to culturally diverse students. Chapter authors explain how they teach their teacher candidates to recognize, challenge and critique their own perspectives and beliefs, as well as explain and point out the social practices and instructional structures that produce and sustain inequalities in science and mathematic instruction. Also, and indeed of major significance, chapter authors explain the strategies they use to help teacher candidates to embrace a socio-transformative framework, and to teach for diversity and understanding in science and mathematics classrooms. Additionally, as they explain how to prepare mathematics and science teachers, they point out how the interconnecting relationship among their teacher-candidates' ideology, power, and resistance becomes a web of influence that impedes their progress to learn how to teach all children, unless it is interrupted.

As teacher educators, we too often hear teacher candidates protest that science and mathematics are the subject areas that should be free of any form of critical or transformative pedagogy because of the neutral or fact-based construction of the disciplines. This argument also contends that because of the so-called objective nature of science and mathematics, multiculturalism and/or transformative pedagogy cannot be an informative and illuminating dimension of the science and mathematic teachers' education discourse. *Preparing Prospective Mathematic and Science Teachers to Teach for Diversity* disrupts this narrow thinking, and analyzes and critiques the resistance that attempts to hold it in place. More significantly, it includes theoretical frames and practical strategies that counter teachers' resistance to teaching for diversity, and offers culturally relevant way of teaching that are located within a constructivist and inquiry-based paradigm.

As a former mathematics and science teacher in a middle school in Chicago, and as a teacher educator who is committed to preparing teacher candidates to successfully teach *all* children, I applaud the insights that each chapter author(s) brings to the teaching of mathematics and science. Their observations, for example, about using students' home culture, language and experiences can greatly inform the strategies that teachers use to teach culturally diverse students. This book will help teacher educators who are reluctant to engage in transformative pedagogy to see how it can be done, as well as to gain understanding of why they should undertake this assignment. Rich descriptions of successful strategies, and the variability in approach that chapter authors use to discuss teaching for diversity and understanding, engages the reader chance in discovering a plan or approach of interest. Additionally, the conception of teaching that Rodriguez, Kitchen and their colleagues present will support teacher educators' efforts to critique poor and less engaging science and mathematics teaching, as they compare and contrast much of what such teaching has become: the use of teacher-proof materials, prepackaged methods and procedures, and standardized evaluation.

Meier, in her widely praised book *The Power of Their Ideas*, argues that in order for education in the United States to be transformed so that all students receive a quality education that will help them to become capable of participating and sustaining our democratic principles and values, the work force of teachers must do three things: "change how they view learning itself, develop new habits of mind to go with their new cognitive understanding, and simultaneously develop new habits of work—habits that are collegial and public in nature, not solo and private as has been the custom in teaching" (p. 140). Each chapter author does this, and more: as they instruct their students to view the learning of mathematics and science differently; they lead them to develop a new cognitive way of understanding and new work (teaching) habits.

Malcolm X argued that without a "struggle there is no change." *Preparing Prospective Mathematics and Science Teachers to Teach for Diversity* chapter authors take you inside their struggle for change, and make clear

how resistance to change can be overcome. For those concerned and committed to developing highly qualified teachers, who will really "Leave No
Student Behind," this book is a must-read.

Carl A. Grant
University Wisconsin–Madison
November 2003

Preface

The purpose of this book is to provide a theoretical basis and practical strategies to counter teacher resistance to teaching for diversity (resistance to teaching in culturally and gender inclusive ways) and to teaching for understanding (resistance to using student-centered and inquiry-based pedagogical approaches). A critical component of teaching for diversity includes creating classroom environments that support the mathematical and scientific learning of all students, particularly students who have historically been underrepresented in advanced mathematics and science courses (e.g., females and student from diverse cultural backgrounds). A critical component of teaching for understanding involves using constructivist, inquiry-based, and intellectually stimulating pedagogical approaches to support the learning of all students as suggested by national curriculum standards. Throughout this book, authors discuss both teaching for diversity and teaching for understanding.

Teacher educators from across the United States present rich narratives of their experiences in helping prospective and practicing teachers learn to teach for diversity and understanding in a variety of science and mathematics contexts. Most of the existing research documenting teachers' resistance to learning to teach for diversity and understanding has focused on describing prospective and practicing teachers' struggles to work with diverse learners in specific school contexts. These rich descriptions have been very informative, and have often included the researchers' interpretations of how various sociocultural, institutional, and historical factors influence teachers' perceptions of themselves as agents of social change. What is needed now is mathematics and science teacher educators' accounts of successful strategies they use that are specifically focused on preparing teachers to teach mathematics and science for diversity and understanding. In the chapters that follow, teacher educators describe research projects that they have undertaken toward this goal. Some present cases from their methods course while others have written more conceptual chapters. Some chapters include with practical activities that teacher educators and practicing teachers can utilize with their students.

This book is the direct result of an interactive symposium that took place at the 2001 Annual Meeting of the American Educational Research Association (AERA). Alberto Rodriguez and Richard Kitchen organized the interactive symposium so that teacher educators in science and mathematics could gather, share practical strategies about teaching for diversity and understanding, and initiate a professional network dedicated to teaching for transformative social action. The variety of submissions received from science and mathematics education scholars from across the country in response to our initial invitation to participate in the symposium demonstrated that teacher educators were using a variety of effective strategies to manage teachers' resistance to learning to teach for diversity and understanding. Many of the contributors to this volume attended the symposium. We would like to express our sincere appreciation to their long-term commitment to this project and patience to bring this book to fruition. Each chapter received at least one blind peer review, and underwent several revisions until we felt that we had a theoretically strong and coherent manuscript.

We are convinced that the creative approaches offered by the science and mathematics educators whose chapters were selected for this project will add to a better understanding of how to make the notion of "science and mathematics for all" more than just a catchy slogan. Another goal is to share strategies for managing teachers' resistance to learning to teach for diversity and understanding. There is a need for synthesis of how teacher educators are responding to teachers' resistance. This volume begins to address these issues by providing a compendium of promising pedagogical strategies used by teacher educators in a variety of contexts. Finally, we hope this book may provide possible solutions and begin critical dialogues that will inspire and encourage others to take the unavoidable, yet necessary, risks associated with teaching for transformative social action. It is our hope that teacher educators, graduate students, administrators, and practicing teachers will find the ideas presented in this book to be particularly valuable.

OVERVIEW

In chapter 1, Alberto Rodriguez provides the theoretical framework for the chapters that follow. In chapter 2, Rodriguez describes his use of a sociotransformative constructivism (sTc) framework to address both resistance to ideological change and pedagogical change. In all chapters, the authors address resistance to ideological change (RIC) and/or resistance to pedagogical change (RPC).

In chapter 3, Richard Kitchen discusses how he approaches resistance to ideological change by increasing his students' cultural understanding through a visitation to an American Indian cultural event and by incorporating socially and politically relevant model lessons in his secondary mathematics methods course.

In chapter 4, Marianne Barnes and Lehman Barnes address resistance to pedagogical change by contrasting different pedagogical approaches. The teacher/participants in their project also engage in an action research project aimed at improving teaching practices and increasing understanding of students' cultural backgrounds and learning modes.

In chapter 5, Jacqueline Leonard and Scott Dantley describe their work with prospective teachers in their mathematics and science methods courses, respectively. In mathematics, Leonard addresses prospective teachers' resistance to ideological change by sharing how storybooks with characters from diverse backgrounds can be used to make mathematical concepts in the storybooks more socially and culturally relevant. Prospective teachers across the methods courses visit urban classrooms to observe high-level thinking and reasoning skills in mathematics. Dantley tackles resistance to pedagogical change in his science methods courses by engaging prospective teachers in inquiry-based experiments followed by a metacognitive discussion of how they learned during the experiment.

In chapter 6, Aurolyn Luykx, Peggy Cuevas, Julie Lambert and Okhee Lee address ideological resistance as they describe how participants in a professional development institute explore students' home communication patterns and interaction styles as a means to engage with academic content, their peers, and with the teacher.

In chapter 7, Thea Dunn describes how prospective teachers in her courses write autobiographies based on experiences in mathematics courses. In so doing, they engage in ideological reflection as they examine the social, cultural and pedagogical factors that influenced whether their experiences were positive or negative.

In chapter 8, Pauline Chinn addresses ideological change as she examines the nexus of culture and learning in students' understanding of science concepts.

In chapter 9, Joy Moore engages prospective teachers in ideological change as they complete critical assessments of their learning through journals and reflection in a culturally relevant mathematics content course.

In chapter 10, Randy Yerrick discusses how he models effective teaching in local and diverse school contexts. In so doing, he provides examples of how he engages prospective teachers in both ideological and pedagogical change.

In chapter 11, Jacque Ensign addresses ideological change by highlighting stories of culturally responsive teaching and encouraging prospective teachers to author their own stories of success in their classrooms.

Lastly, in chapter 12, Carol Brandt approaches both ideological and pedagogical resistance by having prospective teachers of science conduct research on individually selected projects of relevance. Her goal is to give prospective teachers an opportunity to make the traditional, impersonal, detached science text more personal, socially relevant and accessible.

ACKNOWLEDGMENTS

The authors would like to acknowledge the thoughtful support and guidance provided us by the prospective and practicing teachers we have taught at our respective universities. Many of the teachers who participated in classes and workshops conducted by the book's authors have taken the notion of "teaching for diversity" to heart and are actively engaged in the process of providing their students with access to challenging content and instruction in mathematics and science. We have learned a great deal from prospective and practicing teachers as they have provided us with ideas and feedback to our work. Excerpts from prospective and practicing teachers' journals, reflective papers, activities, interviews, and class dialogues are included in many of the book's chapters. We are grateful to all of these teachers for their willingness to engage in a variety of learning activities that were constructed as a means to model and/or provide examples of inclusive instructional strategies.

We would like to thank our editor, Naomi Silverman and her assistant Lori Hawver for their consistent, timely, and valuable feedback as the project progressed. We also appreciate reviews of the book completed by Angela Calabrese Barton, Teachers College, Columbia University; Jeffrey Frykholm, University of Colorado; Okhee Lee, University of Miami; and Francine Roy, University of Rhode Island. We appreciate the reviewers' insightful comments and suggestions for strengthening the manuscript. Finally, we would like to thank Professor Carl Grant for his kind foreword. We are deeply honored to have Professor Grant, one of the pioneers of multicultural education in this country and abroad, introduce this book.

1

Teachers' Resistance to Ideological and Pedagogical Change: Definitions, Theoretical Framework, and Significance

Alberto J. Rodriguez
San Diego State University

In my methods classes, students are required to write short reaction papers based on the assigned readings before we discuss them in class. They are expected to explain how the articles they read resonate (or not) with their own experiences as students and as individuals, as well as with their emerging teaching orientations. Consider the following excerpt from a reading reaction paper written by Luisa, a Latina prospective teacher. Luisa was one of five Latinas in an elementary science methods class with 17 other female students and 1 male student (who were of Anglo ethnic backgrounds):

> I also believe that it is important for educators and teachers, as well as everyone, to embrace diversity and multiculturalism. A few weeks ago, I heard some of my peers discussing multiculturalism, and they were saying that they thought it was so "annoying" that the education department promoted multiculturalism, and that it was stupid, and when they wrote papers they wrote what their professors wanted to hear, not what they really felt. I thought it was sad, and a little scary, that these people are our future teachers and they thought the "whole diversity and multicultural thing was annoying and stupid." It made me think that there are plenty of educators out there who also think like this, and there are even more children who will become the students of these teachers who will suffer because of their ignorance.

After having taught for more than a decade in postsecondary institutions in various cities in Canada and the United States, I have often heard and read comments like the ones Luisa mentions in the preceding quotation. A few times, the comments are directed at me and meant to be personal because I am a Latino concerned with issues of social justice. One prospective teacher from the U.S. Midwest once wrote in his course evaluation, "Dr. Rodriguez is jamming multicultural education down our throats because he has a chip on his shoulder."

Comments of this nature reflect some of the prospective teachers' fears, frustrations, and anxieties as they attempt to make sense of what it means to be an effective teacher in a pluralist society. Whereas many prospective teachers embrace the goals of the teacher education programs in which they are enrolled, others (like the ones just mentioned) often resist learning to teach for diversity (i.e., teaching in more culturally responsive, gender-inclusive, and socially relevant ways) and/or resist learning to teach for understanding (i.e., using constructivist, inquiry-based, and intellectually stimulating pedagogical approaches).

In this book, we (the authors in this volume including myself) recognize that the use of the term *resistance* has some limitations, because it is not always easily apparent what the intentions of the individual might be. Prospective teachers may purposely refuse to teach for diversity and understanding for a variety of reasons, which are discussed later, or they may simply avoid using more inclusive, multicultural, and student-centered approaches because they feel that they lack confidence and/or skills. In any of these cases, we prefer to use the term resistance because it involves the individual's *agency,* or conscious choice to take action or not, and in doing so become authors of their own texts. We also prefer to use the term resistance because it provides a better construct for exploring the prospective teachers' thinking and professional growth, as they strive to align their belief systems and notions of good teaching with the expectations of their teacher education programs, programs that, in turn, are expected by teacher accreditation organizations, national and state boards of education, and national and state curriculum standards to prepare teachers as well-rounded professionals who are culturally inclusive and effective facilitators of knowledge in our pluralist society (Sleeter, 2001).

How then can teacher educators respond—and in essence positively counter—prospective teachers' resistance to teach for diversity and for understanding? What are some examples of promising pedagogical strategies that teacher educators could use in their courses to help prospective teachers meet the expectations of their teacher education programs, supervising teachers, and state and national standards? How can teacher educators better prepare prospective teachers to meet the challenges of helping increase the achievement and participation of all students in mathematics and science?

We tackle these questions head-on by providing rich narratives of our experiences in helping prospective teachers learn to teach for diversity and understanding in a variety of science and mathematics contexts.

Hence, the first goal of this chapter is to provide a broad description of multicultural education and social constructivism as the two theoretical frameworks that link all of the chapters together. The second goal is to provide an advanced organizer for the other chapters by listing a compendium of the various pedagogical strategies used by the authors in either their science or mathematics methods courses. We hope that this advanced organizer will provide a quick reference guide for readers and encourage them to find out more about how to implement these strategies in their own teaching contexts.

Also, it is important to note that the authors of this volume may use different ethnic terms to refer to individuals' cultural backgrounds. For example, I prefer to use the term *Anglo,* because this relates to the individuals' ethnic and linguistic origins rather than their skin color. Although there is no perfect way to describe ethnic diversity, I believe these terms are more inclusive than using colonial and skin color–based categories such as black, white, red, brown, and yellow. Using individuals' ethnic and cultural terms is a way to celebrate our rich cultural diversity instead of color coding it into colonial categories. Thus, readers may find the use of the following terms throughout this book, *underrepresented or diverse students, First Nations* (Native Americans), *African or African American* (Black), *Latina/o* (Hispanic), and *Anglo* (White).

In the next section, to facilitate discussion of the theoretical frameworks that guide the contributing authors' work, and how these relate to the construct of teacher resistance, two broad categories of teacher resistance are presented (Rodriguez, 1998a).

RESISTANCE TO LEARNING TO TEACH
FOR DIVERSITY AND UNDERSTANDING

When the word *resistance* is used as a key term for conducting a bibliographical search in the Educational Resources Information Center (ERIC) database (http://askeric.org/plweb=cgi/fastweb?search) something really interesting happens. A list containing more than 6,900 documents is produced! This clearly indicates that at least in the last three decades the term resistance has been a key subject of study in education. This is also apparent when the word *teacher* is added to the same ERIC search. The result is a list of 2,574 documents dealing with teacher education and resistance in a variety of ways (e.g., teachers' resistance to teaching for diversity, students' resistance to learning the prescribed curriculum, resistance to dominant discourses, and so on).

It is odd, however, that the construct of resistance is not as predominant a topic in either the chapter titles or indices of important syntheses of educational research like those found in the *Handbook of Research on Multicultural Education* (Banks & Banks, 1995), the *Handbook of Research on Teaching* (Richardson, 2001),[1] or the *Handbook of Research on Science Teaching and Learning* (Gabel, 1994). So, though teacher resistance to teaching in culturally and gender-inclusive ways (teaching for diversity), as well their resistance to teaching using student-centered and inquiry-based approaches (teaching for understanding), may be addressed in these handbooks or syntheses of educational research in one way or another, there is a need to make more predominant and more clear what educational researchers and educators mean by *resistance* in teacher education. Most important, there is a need to provide a synthesis of how teacher educators are responding to teachers' resistance. This volume begins to address these issues by providing a compendium of promising pedagogical strategies used by teacher educators in a variety of contexts.

The urgency to explore more effective ways to prepare teachers to teach for diversity and understanding is even more apparent when we consider the pervasive educational inequalities in our schools. These inequalities continue to prevent many traditionally underrepresented students from fully participating and finding academic success in science and mathematics classrooms (Rodriguez, 1998a, in press; Secada et al., 1998).

It is no wonder that in recent years, national standards and professional organizations in science and mathematics require that teachers be prepared to teach in more culturally sensitive and responsive ways (National Council of Teachers of Mathematics [NCTM], 1989, 2000; National Research Council [NRC], 1996). Similarly, the National Council for the Accreditation of Teacher Education (NCATE) requires teacher education programs to include courses on multicultural education and/or provide activities and experiences aimed to increase the prospective educators' teaching abilities and dispositions to work with culturally diverse students. In the United States, 25 out of 50 states and the District of Columbia require prospective teachers to complete multicultural education requirements (usually in the form of a university course) before certification (Sleeter, 2001). Even national teacher organizations, like the National Science Teachers Association (NSTA), have put forward position statements that explicitly explain the importance of preparing teachers to teach for diversity. For example, one of the NSTA's goals is to make certain that ethni-

---

[1]One small exception is found in chapter 44, where resistance to official and unofficial classroom discourses is briefly discussed.

cally diverse children have "access to quality science education experiences that enhance success and provide the knowledge and opportunities required for them to become successful participants in our democratic society" (NSTA, 2000).

More recently, the *No Child Left Behind* (NCLB) act states that the gap in student achievement in the United States must be eliminated within 12 years, and that schools must make adequate yearly progress toward this goal (The White House, 2002). The NCLB act also mandates that schools failing to make adequate progress will be put in either the "identified for improvement category," or be reorganized under an improvement plan. Whereas this new national policy evokes many questions regarding the significant financial and professional development support necessary to meet the prescribed goals within 12 years, we cannot avoid the obvious question: What role should (or must) teacher education programs play in helping prepare new generations of teachers to meet the challenges posed by the NCLB act? This takes us back to the core of this volume. If national policies and teacher education programs are expecting that teachers be well prepared to teach effectively in diverse school contexts, how can teacher educators manage teachers' resistance to teaching for diversity and understanding? In this book, we provide a variety of suggestions for addressing this important question.

So, what is multicultural education, and why do some prospective teachers resist learning to teach for diversity?

RESISTANCE TO IDEOLOGICAL CHANGE

The oppressor is solidary with the oppressed only when he stops regarding the oppressed as an abstract category and sees them as persons who have been unjustly dealt with, deprived of their voice, cheated in the sale of their labor . . . To affirm that men are persons and as persons should be free, and yet do nothing tangible to make this affirmation a reality, is a farce. (Freire, 1989, p. 34)

This statement by Paulo Freire is at the crux of what it means to work for social justice in our everyday lives, and it also illustrates why perhaps the most difficult type of teacher resistance to manage is resistance to ideological change (resistance to teaching for diversity). This is defined as the resistance to changing one's beliefs and value system. Some prospective teachers who show resistance to ideological change might articulate a kind of "rugged individualism" by stating that what all students need to do is "to work hard enough" to be successful in science and/or mathematics or in life in general (Rodriguez, 1998b). They might also state that the

students' language abilities, gender, ethnic backgrounds, or socioeconomic status do not matter, as long as they work hard enough. In addition, as mentioned previously, teachers may show resistance to ideological change not because they disagree with this orientation, but because
they may lack the awareness, confidence, and/or knowledge and skills to
implement more culturally responsive and socially relevant curriculum.

Since the early 1970s, research on multicultural education has been
aimed at raising awareness about equity issues in all areas of education
(Grant, 1999). Banks and Banks (1995) described multicultural education
"as a field of study designed to increase educational equity for all students
that incorporates, for this purpose, content, concepts, principles, theories,
and paradigms from history, the social and behavioral sciences, and particularly from ethnic and women studies" (p. xii). Similar definitions have
been put forward for multicultural mathematics and science education in
an effort to make more explicit the importance of increasing the participation of underrepresented students in these curriculum areas. A second
goal has been to increase underrepresented students' academic achievement and career opportunities in science, mathematics, engineering, and
technology (Atwater & Riley, 1993; Rodriguez, 1998a).

A growing body of research on multicultural education in the past four
decades has increased our understanding of the sociocultural, historical,
institutional, curricular, and economic factors that influence the achievement and participation of underrepresented students in mathematics and
science. Similarly, many studies have also described the strong resistance
prospective and in-service teachers wield against learning to teach for diversity—against ideological change—and against the notion that *all* children can learn (Ahlquist, 1991; Cochran-Smith, 1991, 1995; Goodwin,
1994; Jordan, 1995; McIntosh, 1989; Rodriguez, 1998a, 2002; Scott, 1995;
Sleeter, 2001; Sweeney, 2001; Tatum, 1992). The bulk of these studies have
focused on documenting teachers' resistance to ideological change and/
or the difficulties they encounter in trying to transfer what they learned in
the university context about teaching for diversity to their school teaching
contexts. Most of these studies provide rich descriptions and are very informative, but what is needed is more explicit suggestions for how to
counter prospective teachers' resistance to ideological change in positive
and effective ways. Educators, policymakers, and researchers face a
sociocultural conundrum when they expect prospective teachers (who are
mostly members of the culture of power) to teach science and mathematics in culturally relevant ways to students who are increasingly from diverse ethnic and socioeconomic backgrounds (Mendoza Commission,
2000).

This is one of the challenges that the authors in this volume wish to
meet by describing their promising *strategies of counterresistance*, that is,

pedagogical strategies designed to positively address prospective teachers' difficulties, concerns, and/or direct opposition to the notion that all educators can (and should) create multicultural and gender-inclusive learning environments where all students feel supported to learn.

RESISTANCE TO PEDAGOGICAL CHANGE

Another conundrum educators, policymakers, and researchers face is the pedagogical challenges embedded in helping prospective teachers learn to teach science and mathematics using inquiry-based and constructivist approaches. The contributing authors of this book also address this issue by describing a variety of promising strategies they have used to counter prospective teachers' resistance to pedagogical change, that is, resistance to learning to teach for understanding due to avoiding, refusing, or feeling unable to change one's perception of what constitutes being an effective teacher. So, teachers who show resistance to pedagogical change would state that they prefer to lecture, to assign individual work to students, and/or that students must "get the content" first before they can be allowed to do any kind of activity or experiment. There is also the possibility that teachers may show resistance to pedagogical change because they lack the confidence and/or knowledge and skills to move away from the models of transmissive teaching to which they have become accustomed after 16 or so years of schooling (Lortie, 1975).

Unfortunately, resistance to pedagogical change is hardly discussed in the science and mathematics education literature (Banks & Banks, 1995; Fosnot, 1996; Gabel, 1994; Richardson, 2001), but it is clearly reflected in the lack of impact teacher education programs have had on how teachers teach for the last two decades (Anderson, 1994; Carter, 1990; Glenn, 2000; Kagan, 1992; Sleeter, 2001; Weiss, Banilower, McMahon, & Smith, 2001; Zeichner & Gore, 1990). Also, Rodriguez's previous work with prospective and cooperating teachers documents the challenges teachers encounter as they are exposed to constructivist, student-centered learning in collaborative professional-development research projects (1993, 1994, 1998b, 2002).

So, what is constructivism and how is this framework connected to multicultural education and issues of social justice in this book?

CONNECTING MULTICULTURAL EDUCATION'S TENETS WITH SOCIAL CONSTRUCTIVISM

The most predominant theory of learning guiding the work of teacher educators and researchers for the last four decades appears to be *individual constructivism* (Gabel, 1994; Pfundt & Duit, 1991). This theoretical framework is based on the work of the French developmental psychologist, Jean Piaget (1977). In general terms, individual constructivism suggests that learners are not empty vessels waiting to be filled with knowledge by the teacher. Instead, each student brings into the classroom a set of tools (schema) with which they construct meaning as they interact with their environment and with others (Fosnot, 1996; Tobin, 1993). Even though this theoretical framework has been very fruitful in terms of increasing our understanding of children's alternative (naive) conceptions about natural phenomena (e.g., heat, temperature, velocity, states of matter, the human body, and so on; Gabel, 1994), it seems to have mainly benefited the members of the research community. That is, this theoretical framework has augmented the knowledge base of the science and mathematics research communities, but it has had very little impact on how teachers teach and, consequently, on how children learn.

This is quite evident in the pervasive gap in students' mathematics and science achievement across the United States (Rodriguez, in press), as well as in various studies and reports on teachers' practices as mentioned earlier. For example, a recent report by the Horizon Research Group indicates that after observing 364 lessons taught by K–12 teachers from various parts of the United States, fewer than 1 in 5 lessons were intellectually rigorous (Weiss, Pasley, Smith, Banilower, & Heck, 2003). Furthermore, 66% of the teachers observed used inadequate or low-level questioning strategies. They also found that in 66% of the classrooms observed, students were engaged in what Weiss and her colleagues called "inadequate sensemaking," that is, teachers not helping students make relevant connections with the key concepts being covered in the lesson. In only 16% of the classrooms, the research team found teachers actively engaging students in more meaningful understanding of the subject matter and in high-level questioning.

To add to this situation, the science and mathematics education community have recently been strongly criticized by other science and mathematics organizations for failing to make more meaningful connections between academic research and school practice. For example, Bruce Alberts, the NRC's president, exclaimed, "It is poignantly clear that research has not had the kind of impact on education that is visible in medical practice, space explorations, energy, and many other fields" (NRC, 1999, p. vii). These sentiments are also echoed in the influential Glenn Commission's report, *Before It's Too Late: A Report to the Nation From the National Commission on Mathematics and Science Teaching* (Glenn, 2000).

In my view, two of the reasons that research based on individual constructivism has not had a greater impact on teaching and learning in today's schools are its technorational approach and its detachment from the sociocultural and economic factors that affect how teachers are prepared to teach, how they teach, and how children from diverse ethnic and socioeconomic backgrounds learn. This may also explain why *social constructivism,* based on the work of the Russian psychologist, Lev Vygotsky (1978), has been gaining more interest among researchers and teachers educators who see learning as a socially constructed process, a process mediated by sociocultural, historical, and institutional codes (Steffe & Gale, 1995; Wertsch, 1991; Wink & Putney, 2002). Whereas individual constructivists may focus on the individual child's cognitive schema for constructing new knowledge in active participation with others (Fosnot, 1996; Tobin, 1993), social constructivists are more concerned with how the sociocultural, historical, and institutional contexts mediate the opportunities afforded to individuals to construct new meaning together. This is why language in use plays such an important role for social constructivists. Language is "more than a symbolic system through which we make meaning. Language also carries with it the meanings and intentionality of those who came before us" (Wink & Putney, 2002, p. 30). Therefore, social constructivism is neither exogenic (primarily concerned with the external) nor endogenic (primarily concerned with the internal) worlds of the individual (Gergen, 1995). Social constructivism moves away from essentializing Western dichotomies by focusing on the complexity of language both as a tool to negotiate and construct meaning through interaction with others and as a cultural tool to gain access to, and grow within, a community of practice (e.g., a school or university classroom, an ethnic or cultural group, a profession, a professional organization, etc.).

Social constructivist and multicultural education theoretical frameworks inform the work of the authors in this volume; therefore, it is evident that the strategies being proposed here to enhance the professional preparation of teachers will in turn enhance the academic achievement and participation of all students. The premise is that if beginning teachers feel more confident and able to teach for diversity and understanding, it follows that their students will benefit. Of course, more empirical field-based research is needed to systematically investigate how prospective teachers transfer and adapt over time what they learned from the university context to their school contexts.

CONCLUSION: HELPING TEACHERS LEARN TO TEACH FOR DIVERSITY AND UNDERSTANDING

Though each contributing author in this volume describes his or her own theoretical orientations, I have broadly described in this chapter the two theoretical frameworks that link all the chapters together, multicultural education and social constructivism. The authors put various interpretations and applications of these frameworks forward in an effort to explain the pedagogical strategies they use to respond to or counter prospective teachers' resistance. To facilitate discussion of the various types of strategies that can be used to respond, I have suggested that teacher resistance can be categorized into resistance to ideological change (resistance to teaching for diversity) and resistance to pedagogical change (resistance to teaching for understanding). The use of the term resistance is not without its limitations, but it seems that this is the most appropriate term to use to account for an individual's agency, that is, the conscious choice individuals have to act (or not) in response to the difficulties and/or contradictions they encounter as they attempt to reconcile their ideological and pedagogical orientations with the expectations of teacher education programs and the realities of teaching in today's diverse schools.

This chapter closes with a compendium of the various strategies discussed in this book (see Table 1.1). We hope that readers will use the compendium as an advanced organizer and as a quick reference guide for future use in their own teaching contexts.

REFERENCES

Ahlquist, R. (1991). Position and imposition: Power relations in a multicultural foundations class. *Journal of Negro Education, 60,* 158–169.

Anderson, R. D., & Mitchener, C. P. (1994). Research on science teacher education. In D. L. Gabel (Ed.), *Handbook of research on science teaching and learning: A project of the National Science Teachers Association* (pp. 3–37). Toronto: Macmillan.

Atwater, M. M., & Riley, J. P. (1993). Multicultural science education: Perspectives, definitions, and research agenda. *Science Education, 77*(6), 661–668.

Banks, J. A., & Banks, C. A. (1995). *Handbook of research on multicultural education.* New York: Macmillan.

Carter, K. (1990). Teachers' knowledge and learning to teach. In W. R. Houston (Ed.), *Handbook of research on teaching education* (pp. 291–310). New York: Macmillan.

Cochran-Smith, M. (1991). Learning to teach against the grain. *Harvard Education Review, 61,* 279–310.

Cochran-Smith, M. (1995). Color blindness and basket making are not the answers: Confronting the dilemmas of race, culture, and language diversity in teacher education. *American Educational Research Journal, 32,* 493–522.

Dewey, J. (1938). *Experience and education.* New York: Macmillan.

Fosnot, C. T. (1996). *Constructivism: Theory, perspectives, and practice.* New York: Teachers College Press.

Freire, P. (1989). *Pedagogy of the oppressed.* New York: Continuum Publishing.

Gabel, D. (Ed.). (1994). *Handbook of research on science teaching and learning.* Toronto: Macmillan.

Gergen, K. J. (1995). Social construction and the educational process. In L. P. Steffe & J. Gale (Eds.), *Constructivism in education* (pp. 17–39). Hillsdale, NJ: Lawrence Erlbaum Associates.

TABLE 1.1

A Compendium of Promising Strategies to Respond to Teachers' Resistance to Ideological and Pedagogical Change

Type of Resistance	Type of Counter Pedagogical Strategy	Description	Subject Area	Contributor	Chapter
RIC	Using sociotransformative constructivism (sTc) to address controversial issues and the science education standards	Use a videotaped program on controversial issues (e.g., evolution vs. creationism; personal beliefs vs. curriculum standards) to engage students in a dialogic conversation about their own positions and of how to address controversial issues in the classroom.	Science	Alberto J. Rodriguez	2
RPC	Using sTc to demonstrate learning for understanding through hands-on, minds-on experiences	Prospective teachers make learning centers and have school children visit the centers in an open-exhibition, hands-on type environment.	Science		
RIC	Building cultural understanding by visiting culturally diverse communities	Take prospective teachers on field trips to culturally different communities (e.g., a Pueblo Indian community) and have students participate in community activities and write about their experiences as a part of a methods course assignment.	Math	Richard Kitchen	3
RIC and RPC	Modeling lessons that are socially and politically relevant	Examine anti-affirmative-action admissions policies at major universities and the consequences for students.	Math/ Statistics		
RPC	Contrasting different pedagogical approaches through hands-on activities	Have participants compare the value of inquiry-based science teaching by performing the same activity (building of foam tower) using three different approaches: following worksheet instructions; semi-open inquiry-based activity; and open inquiry-based activity.	Science	Marianne Barnes & Lehman Barnes	4

(Continued)

11

TABLE 1.1
(Continued)

Type of Resistance	Type of Counter Pedagogical Strategy	Description	Subject Area	Contributor	Chapter
RIC and RPC	Conducting teacher action research projects	Action research project could be on any topic aimed at improving teaching practice and better understanding of students' cultural backgrounds and learning modes.	Science		5
RIC	Using multicultural storybooks with a mathematics theme	(Leonard) Prospective teachers learn how storybooks with characters from diverse backgrounds can be used to make mathematical concepts in the storybooks more culturally and socially relevant.	Math	J. Leonard & Scott Dantley	
RIC and RPC	Observing diverse students succeed in mathematics	Visit urban classrooms to observe high-level thinking and reasoning skills in mathematics.			
RPC	Conducting inquiry-based experiments	(Scott) Prospective teachers conduct a ball-and-ramp experiment to determine how far the cup will travel after the marble is released. This is followed with a metacognitive discussion of how participants learned from the experiment.	Science		
RIC and RPC	Making connections between the students' home language and science instruction	Participants explore how students' home communication patterns and interaction styles play important roles in how they engage with academic content, their peers, and the teacher.	Science	A. Luykx, P. Cuevas	

RIC and RPC	Writing autobiographies based on experiences in mathematics courses	Prospective teachers write and share autobiographies based on their former experiences with mathematics, reflecting on the following: were these experiences positive or negative and why? What were the social, cultural, and/or pedagogical factors that influenced whether their experiences were positive or negative? Did they learn mathematics for understanding?	Math	Thea Dunn	7
RIC and RPC	Examining the nexus of culture and learning in students' understanding of science concepts	Prospective teachers conduct in-depth interviews with students from diverse backgrounds to investigate their prior knowledge of science concepts and the source of that knowledge.	Science	Pauline W. U. Chinn	8
RPC	Critical assessment of one's own learning through journals and reflection in a culturally relevant mathematics content course	Prospective teachers keep a critical reflection journal on how they and their peers solve mathematics problems in a culturally relevant mathematics content course. Prospective teachers are encouraged to become more aware of how diverse learners may approach solving mathematics problems in diverse ways.	Math	Joy Moore	9
RPC	Modeling effective teaching in local schools	Methods instructor models effective teaching in local and diverse school contexts, videotapes lesson, and then engages prospective teachers to critique the lesson.	Science	Randy Yerrick	10

(Continued)

13

TABLE 1.1
(Continued)

Type of Resistance	Type of Counter Pedagogical Strategy	Description	Subject Area	Contributor	Chapter
RIC	Sharing stories of successful culturally responsive teaching	Highlight stories of successful culturally responsive teaching from the literature and encourage prospective teachers to author their own stories of success in their classrooms.	Math	Jacque Ensign	11
RPC	Creating new and socially relevant texts	Prospective teachers conduct research on individually selected projects of relevance and present results to the class. This approach gives students an opportunity to make the traditional, impersonal, detached science text more personal, socially relevant, and accessible. For example, prospective teachers chose to do their projects on specific illnesses that were either present in their family or that they could inherit.	Science	Carol Brandt	12

Note. **RIC** = resistance to ideological change; **RPC** = resistance to pedagogical change.

Glenn, J. (2000). *Before it's too late: A report to the nation from the National Commission on Mathematics and Science Teaching.* Washington, DC: U.S. Government Printing Office.

Goodwin, A. L. (1994). Making the transition from self to other: What do preservice teachers really think about multicultural education. *Journal of Teacher Education, 45,* 119–131.

Grant, C. A. (1999). *Multicultural research: A reflective engagement with race, class, gender and sexual orientation.* London: Falmer Press.

Jordan, M. L. R. (1995). Reflections on the challenges, possibilities and perplexities of preparing preservice teachers for culturally diverse classrooms. *Journal of Teacher Education, 46,* 369–374.

Kagan, D. (1992). Professional growth among preservice and beginning teachers. *Review of Educational Research, 62,* 129–169.

Lortie, D. (1975). *School teacher.* Chicago: University of Chicago Press.

McIntosh, P. (1989, July/August). White privilege: Unpacking the invisible knapsack. *Peace & Freedom,* pp. 10–12.

The Mendoza Commission. (2000). *Land of plenty: Diversity as America's competitive edge in science, engineering and technology* (Report of the Congressional Commission on the Advancement of Women and Minorities in Science, Engineering and Technology Development). Washington, DC: Author.

National Council of Teachers of Mathematics. (1989). *Curriculum and evaluation standards for school mathematics.* Reston, VA: Author.

National Council of Teachers of Mathematics. (2000). *Principles and standards for school mathematics.* Reston, VA: Author.

National Research Council. (1996). *National science education standards.* Washington, DC: National Academy Press.

National Research Council. (1999). *Improving student learning: A strategic plan for educational research and its utilization.* Washington, DC: National Academy Press.

National Science Teachers Association. (2000). NSTA position statement on multicultural education. Retrieved June 30, 2003 from http://www.nsta.org/159epsid=2/

Pfundt, H., & Duit, R. (1991). *Bibliography: Students' alternative frameworks and science.* Kiel, Germany: IPN.

Piaget, J. (1977). *The principles of genetic epistemology: Toward a theory of knowledge.* Harmondsworth, England: Penguin.

Richardson, V. (2001). *Handbook of research on teaching.* Washington, DC: American Educational Research Association.

Rodriguez, A. J. (1993). "A dose of reality": Understanding the origin of the theory/practice dichotomy in teacher education from the students' point of view. *Journal of Teacher Education, 43,* 213–222.

Rodriguez, A. J. (1994). *Managing the dilemmas of learning to teach: An exploration of the strategies used by preservice science teachers.* Unpublished doctoral dissertation, University of British Columbia, Vancouver, B.C., Canada.

Rodriguez, A. J. (1998a). Busting open the meritocracy myth: Rethinking equity and student achievement in science. *Journal of Women and Minorities in Science and Engineering, 4(2&3),* 195–216.

Rodriguez, A. J. (1998b). Strategies for counterresistance: Toward sociotransformative constructivism and learning to teach science for diversity and for understanding. *Journal of Research in Science Teaching, 36(6),* 589–622.

Rodriguez, A. J. (2002). Using sociotransformative constructivism to teach for understanding in diverse classrooms: A beginning teacher's journey. *American Educational Research Journal, 39(4),* 1017–1045.

Rodriguez, A. J. (in press). *Turning despondency into hope: Charting new paths to improve students' achievement and participation in science education.* Tallahassee, FL: Southeast Eisenhower Regional Consortium for Mathematics and Science (SERVE).

Scott, R. M. (1995). Helping teacher education students develop positive attitudes toward ethnic minorities. *Equity & Excellence in Education, 28*(2), 69–73.

Secada, W., Chavez-Chavez, R., Garcia, E., Muñoz, C., Oakes, J., Santiago-Santiago, I., & Slavin, R. (1998). *No more excuses: The final report of the Hispanic dropout project.* Washington, DC: U.S. Department of Education.

Sleeter, C. E. (2001). Epistemological diversity in research on preservice teacher preparation for historically underserved children. In W. Secada (Ed.), *Review of research in education 2000–2001* (Vol. 6, pp. 209–250). Washington, DC: American Educational Research Association.

Steffe, L. P., & Gale, J. (1995). *Constructivism in education.* Hillsdale, NJ: Lawrence Erlbaum Associates.

Sweeney, A. E. (2001). Incorporating multicultural and science-technology-society issues into science teacher education courses: Successes, challenges and possibilities. *Journal of Science Teacher Education, 12,* 1–28.

Tatum, B. D. (1992). Talking about race, learning about racism: The application of racial identity development theory in the classroom. *Harvard Educational Review, 62*(1), 1–24.

Tobin, K. (1993). *The practice of constructivism in science education.* Hillsdale, NJ: Lawrence Erlbaum Associates.

Vygotsky, L. S. (1978). *Mind in society: The development of higher psychological processes.* Cambridge, MA: Harvard University Press.

Weiss, I. R., Banilower, E. R., McMahon, K. C., & Smith, P. S. (2001). *Report of the 2000 national survey of science and mathematics education.* Chapel Hill, NC: Horizon Research.

Wertsch, J. V. (1991). *Voices of the mind: A sociocultural approach to mediated action.* Cambridge, MA: Harvard University Press.

Wink, J., & Putney, L. (2002). *A vision of Vygotsky.* Boston: Allyn & Bacon.

Zeichner, K. M., & Gore, J. M. (1990). Teacher socialization. In W. R. Houston (Ed.), *Handbook of research on teaching education* (pp. 329–348). New York: Macmillan.

2

Using Sociotransformative Constructivism to Respond to Teachers' Resistance to Ideological and Pedagogical Change

Alberto J. Rodriguez
San Diego State University

Though my research and teaching agenda are also highly influenced by advancements in multicultural education and social constructivism, as a Latino committed to science education and social justice issues, I have struggled with the disconnection between these two fields of study. In other words, multicultural education is a theory of social justice that seeks to raise our awareness about equity issues, but it provides little guidance on how to implement the multiple social and institutional changes needed to help all students have access to an equitable and socially relevant education. On the other hand, social constructivism is a theory of learning that helps us understand how learning is socially constructed and mediated, but it provides little guidance on how to raise the awareness of teachers and learners so that they can use the newly constructed knowledge toward more socially transformative goals.

In my view, the missing construct here is *power.* Because power imbues human interactions, I believe that this is the construct that links multicultural education's tenets (as a theory of social justice) with social constructivism (as a theory of learning). Therefore, elsewhere (Rodriguez, 1998), I articulate *sociotransformative constructivism* (sTc) as an alternate theoretical framework that supports the notion that knowledge is socially constructed and mediated by institutional, historical, and social codes, but at the same time sTc seeks to engage the learners in (de)constructing the structures of power from which those established codes spring. An example of a cultural code is the pervasive notion that men are usually the ones expected to pursue science and mathematics careers. An example of a historical code is the fact that women continue to dominate the teaching profession at the elementary level and men at the secondary level. An example of an institutional code is tracking, that is, a form of institutionalized racism that prevents traditionally underrepresented students from enrolling in advanced courses. So, educators interested in following an sTc orientation would see the established curriculum as a site for learning the subject matter in socially relevant and empowering ways—a site where existing contexts can be collaboratively transformed to meet social justice goals. In this fashion, power is deconstructed and utilized for what it is. Power is the currency of social change.

Sociotransformative constructivism is more than a theory of learning; it is a theory of teaching and learning. That is, sTc requires teachers to make issues of power, social justice, and social reproduction as much integral parts of the curriculum as the subject matter. This does not imply that a prescribed set of pedagogical strategies or one-model-fits-all is possible or favorable. What it does mean is that the strategies and ideas presented in this chapter, like the others compiled in this volume, could add to the repertoire of those interested in helping teachers learn to teach for diversity and understanding. To this end, the four elements that constitute sTc are discussed in more detail as follows. The elements are: *the dialogic conversation, authentic activity, metacognition,* and *reflexivity.* Each of these is closely connected to one another, and they are enacted neither in any particular order nor in certain stages. These elements take place through the natural social interaction of all participants in the learning environment. This discussion is followed by two examples of how sTc can be used in a science methods class to respond to prospective teachers' resistance to ideological and pedagogical change.

WHAT MAKES SOCIOTRANSFORMATIVE CONSTRUCTIVISM "TRANSFORMATIVE"?

The Dialogic Conversation

Sociotransformative constructivism draws from the work of Vygotsky (1978) in terms of his useful explanations of the complex interplay between social contexts and learning. However, when it comes to the analysis of the individual's agency to transform these contexts through direct action (or chosen inaction—resistance), Vygotsky's ideas fall short. Wertsch (1991), for instance, suggested that for someone interested in formulating a "Marxist psychology, [Vygotsky] made precious little mention of broader historical, institutional, or cultural processes such as class struggle, alienation, and the rise of commodity fetishism" (p. 46). It is especially at this juncture that I find Mikhail Bakhtin's work most helpful (1981, 1986). Bakhtin (1986) advanced Vygotsky's ideas by describing the multivoicedness of meaning construction:

> Our speech, that is, all of our utterances (including creative works), is filled with others' words, varying degrees of "our-own-ness," varying degrees of awareness and detachment. These words of others carry with them their own expression, their own evaluative tone, which we assimilate, re-work, and re-accentuate. (p. 89)

Hence for Bakhtin (1981, 1986) dialogue is much more than an engaged form of conversation; it is a process by which the speaker positions himself or herself *(addressivity)* in such a way as to construct context relevant meaning with others. This involves a deeper understanding of how each individual's voice—or "speaking consciousness" (Bakhtin, 1981)—engages in conversation with others *(dialogicality)*. In this fashion, a dialogue moves beyond merely understanding what is being said to understanding the reasons a speaker chooses to state what he or she chooses to say in specific historical, institutional, and sociocultural contexts. This principle is the basis for the dialogic conversation in sTc, and it is very relevant here in terms of understanding prospective teachers' resistance to teaching for diversity and understanding. In other words, through the dialogic conversation safe spaces can be created for the speaker/listener to ask the Bakhtinian question, "Who is doing the talking?" Whose voice, interests, values, and beliefs are being represented by the speaker/listener? (Bakhtin, 1986; Wertsch, 1991). So, for example, when an Anglo female, middle-class prospective teacher from the U.S. Midwest[1] states that all diverse students need to do to succeed in mathematics and science is "work hard enough," she is perhaps ventriloquating the voices of her immigrant great-grandparents who came to this country with very little financial resources, and who believed in rugged individualism. By asking the Bakhtinian question, *who is doing the talking,* in an environment of trust and respect, it is possible to better understand this prospective teacher's point of view. Consequently, the instructor is in a better position to implement effective strategies of counterresistance, strategies that would effectively assist this beginning teacher meet teacher education program requirements and better appreciate the need to learn to teach for diversity and understanding in a pluralist society.

I provide more detailed examples of how the various elements of sTc can be implemented in the classroom later, but I first continue to briefly describe the other elements of sTc.

---

[1]I would like to stress that I have also worked with some prospective teachers from diverse cultural backgrounds who also hold the same rugged individualism views.

Authentic Activity

One of the main differences between sTc and other forms of constructivism is that in addition to hands-on, minds-on activities, sTc defines authentic activities as spaces in which students explore how the subject under study is socially relevant and connected to their everyday lives. Therefore, sTc urges teachers to move away from "activity-mania" (Moscovici & Holdlund-Nelson, 1998), an approach to teaching science that "involves a collection of prepackaged, hour-long (or less), hands-on activities that are often disconnected from each other" (p. 14). Though activity-mania may provide a variety of hands-on and fun activities, teachers need to ask in what ways these activities are minds-on, and in what ways they encourage students to become aware of the roles they can play in bringing about social change.

Perhaps no other better than John Dewey (1938) has explained the importance of authentic activity in the process of learning:

> An experience may be immediately enjoyable and yet promote the formation of a slack and careless attitude; this attitude then operates to modify the quality of subsequent experiences so as to prevent a person from getting out of them what they have to give ... [E]xperience may be lively, vivid, and "interesting," yet their disconnectedness may artificially generate dispersive, disintegrated, centrifugal habits. (p. 26)

Hence, through authentic activity, learners are provided with opportunities to observe, engage in, and critique the common practices and discourses typically conducted by the community of practice (scientists) whose concepts they are studying. This should occur whether the learner is taking mathematics or science classes or enrolled in a teacher education program. For instance, instead of simply discussing the importance of preparing socially relevant and inclusive lessons in my methods courses, prospective teachers are provided with opportunities to see me model complete sTc science lessons. This is followed with a dialogic conversation on the aspects of the lessons that needed improvement or were effective. Later in the course, our roles are switched. The prospective teachers are required to team teach a complete lesson in front of the class, and then engage in a dialogic conversation with their peers about the lesson's strengths and areas in need of improvement.

Metacognition

Gunstone and Mitchell (1998) provided a detailed description of metacognition in *Teaching Science for Understanding: A Human Constructivist View*, but Baird (1990, cited in Gunstone, 1994) perhaps offers the most succinct definition yet: "[Metacognition is] the knowledge, awareness and control of one's own learning" (p. 134). Thus, in addition to requiring teachers to facilitate the learning of new content material, this process expects teachers to encourage students to also reflect on how they learn. As Gunstone indicated, through metacognition, students are encouraged to ask themselves questions such as: "What am I meant to be doing?"; "Do I know what to write/look for?"; "What is the purpose of this task?"; "Have I done everything necessary?"; "Can I explain this to someone else?" and so on (p. 135).

Sociotransformative constructivism expands on how metacognition is usually defined by adding critical and reflective aspects to the questions just mentioned. For example, learners are encouraged to ask themselves questions such as: "Why am I learning about this topic?"; "Why am I learning these concepts this way?"; "What control (voice) do I have in how to proceed?"; "By what other method(s) can I learn this subject matter best?" and so on. The goal then is to move closer to a sense of consciousness and agency in regard to one's own ways of learning.

Based on what has been presented so far, one can easily appreciate how important it is for prospective teachers to engage in metacognitive critiques of their preferred ways of learning (habits of mind). As prospective teachers become more aware of their own taken-for-granted ways of learning, they should become more conscious of how their habits of mind influence their teaching practice and of the need to assist their students to become more aware of their own learning processes.

Reflexivity

Reflexivity is a critical process by which we explore how our *social location* (e.g., ethnic and cultural backgrounds and socioeconomic status), *ideological location* (e.g., belief systems and values), and *academic location* (e.g., education level and skills) impact our perceptions of what is worth learning. Reflexivity is also tied to the individual's agency in that one has the choice to act on new knowledge and insights to bring about personal and/or collective growth (social change). Hence, in a typical sTc classroom, discussions on how knowledge is produced and reproduced, who (were) are recognized as scientists, who decides which kind of research is worth funding, and whose interests are served by that research, would be common practices.

Again it is easy to appreciate how difficult, yet important, it is for some prospective teachers to become reflexive teachers. In teacher education courses in which prospective teachers are being asked to critically reflect on their own privileged positions and taken-for-granted assumptions, it is not surprising to encounter the resistance to ideological and pedagogical change described here by the various contributing authors. Fortunately, the authors in this volume go beyond describing teacher resistance by offering promising strategies for how to counter it. This is not to imply that the proposed strategies are infallible, or that they will work for everyone in any classroom context. Rather, this book provides socially responsive and transformative pedagogical strategies that represent a better alternative to leaving teacher resistance uninterrupted.

TWO EXAMPLES: USING SOCIOTRANSFORMATIVE CONSTRUCTIVISM TO PROMOTE IDEOLOGICAL AND PEDAGOGICAL CHANGE

In this section, I described in detail two promising pedagogical strategies I have used in my methods classes to counter prospective teachers' resistance to ideological and pedagogical change. Descriptions of the sTc elements are embedded in the narrative as a way to illustrate how sTc can be used in the classroom.[2] The students' voices quoted are mainly drawn from my teaching journals and my prospective teachers' journals, as well as from samples of their reading reaction papers (which I have collected for the past 9 years). The prospective teachers cited herein were in my elementary science methods classes, which were predominantly composed of middle-class, Anglo women from the U.S. Midwest (where I taught for 4 years) or from the U.S. Southwest (where I have been teaching for more than 4 years). My bilingual science methods classes, on the other hand, are usually mainly composed of Latino/a prospective teachers from various socioeconomic backgrounds. The pedagogical strategies described herein have been implemented in both of my teaching contexts.

Controversial Issues and the Science Education Standards

The Science Education Standards (National Research Council, 1996), as well as state and local standards in the United States, require that schoolchildren be able to understand the nature of science. This involves having students become familiar with the processes associated with conducting methodologically sound experiments and presenting the results to a com-

---

[2]Those interested in seeing how sTc was used within the context of a research project with prospective teachers should see Rodriguez (1998). Those interested in an example of how sTc was used in a research project with high school students and a prospective teacher should see Rodriguez (2002). We are currently analyzing data from two longitudinal studies with cooperating and prospective teachers and their students. The results of these projects will be made available soon.

munity of peers for critical input. This is one way to expose students to how scientists construct knowledge, what is considered to be knowledge, and by whom, within scientific communities. In addition, this is also an excellent opportunity to engage students in a dialogic conversation about what research gets funded, and who benefits from that research.

Related to this topic, the National Science Education Standards (and typically state and local standards) also require that students be able to critically understand complex and controversial topics such as the theory of evolution, nuclear energy, AIDS and other sexually transmitted diseases, and so on. In all of the methods classes I have taught, I usually get a few prospective teachers who state that they will not cover controversial issues in the classroom (like evolution or AIDS) because they feel that these concepts are at odds with their own personal and religious beliefs. In addition, they are anxious about the consequences of antagonizing parents and/or students during their first year of teaching. If this type of resistance is left uninterrupted, it is safe to assume that many schoolchildren will end up not having the opportunities they deserve to learn about these important concepts (as required in the standards) because beginning teachers often feel that they need to "play it safe" (Rodriguez, 1993, 1998). Also some professors may feel that they must "play it safe" too, because they fear that they do not want to receive negative course evaluations from prospective teachers. Given this reality, what strategies can teacher educators (and prospective teachers) implement to promote ideological change? What can be done to promote the notion that engaging students with the prescribed curriculum (including controversial issues), and the exchange of one's beliefs and views, are positive aspects of how knowledge is constructed and advanced in a pluralist society? Furthermore, to function effectively in a pluralist society, it is essential to have a deeper understanding of various groups' beliefs and assumptions (including the diverse views held by members of the scientific community). Perhaps, teachers, more than anyone else, are called upon to have this kind of inclusive understanding, because they are in a position to facilitate socially relevant learning by so many students during the course of their teaching careers.

One activity I use to respond or counter resistance to ideological change using sTc is by first engaging students in a dialogic conversation after watching a videotaped program. The program is a special report on religion and politics by TV journalist, Dan Rather, that includes segments of actual parents, teachers, and school board members clashing at school board meetings. The source of the controversy documented in the video is due to the school board's decisions to: Give creationism equal instructional time as the theory of evolution, require teachers to emphasize abstinence in sex education classes, and require school personnel not to talk, or not to allow others to talk, about homosexuality at all on school grounds.

According to sTc, using this type of video is an example of an authentic activity because students are able to see how real stakeholders may engage in a debate of real issues that impact the professional lives of teachers. As the debate intensifies, conservative school board members are challenged by angry parents who do not want religious beliefs to dictate the direction of the public school curriculum. During one section, prospective teachers begin to look at each other and shake their heads in disbelief. They often commented that they could not believe these were real parents and school board members, and that this kind of controversy could really happen in this century.

After the video segment, we engage in a dialogic conversation, an honest dialogue in which we use the trust we have been building in the classroom not only to share our own ideological positions, but to really listen and understand more carefully each other's ideological positions. As Bakhtin (1986) would ask, what voices (beliefs and value positions) are being represented behind our own voices (our parents', our cultural background in general, our positive and/or negative experiences with related issues, and so on)?

For example, in one segment of the video, the topics of abstinence, homosexuality, and religion are addressed. This gives us an opportunity to talk about several related science curriculum questions such as how to manage questions about sex and sexual reproduction, how to work with groups in the classroom who are marginalized because of their sexual orientation or religious beliefs, and how to teach about AIDS and sexually transmitted diseases. The latter was an important point to emphasize because many students were still under the mistaken impression that AIDS was a "disease that affects only gay people." Most students were also unaware that they were living in an area with one of the largest teenage pregnancy rates in the country (mainly among the Latina population) and an area with a large incidence of sexually transmitted diseases (Committee on Children, Youth, and Families, 1984; Duryea, Mesrian, Semark, & West, 1997). By engaging students in a dialogic conversation about these issues, and by using an authentic activity (a videotape with real stakeholders addressing relevant topics), the prospective teachers were able to also deconstruct the activity in terms of how they learned (and felt) about these controversial issues, and how they could teach about them in their classrooms (metacognition). One student stated, "I never realized that this issue could get so ugly, but I see how important it is to talk about it [evolution] with students." Another student mentioned, "I have better ideas of how I can approach these topics [sexually transmitted diseases] in my classroom now. I have to be careful, but I can use the standards and statistics to show that I need to cover them."

Prospective teachers also find particularly useful one of the assigned readings for this seminar, Michael Reiss' chapter on how to teach controversial issues in the classroom from his book, *Science Education for a Pluralist Society* (1993). In this chapter, Reiss suggested three types of roles teachers can play when presenting controversial issues in the science classroom. These are: advocacy (stating personal support for a particular view), affirmative neutrality (exposing students to many points of views without stating one's own at first), and procedural neutrality (exposing students to many points of view without ever stating one's own). Prospective teachers often comment that they find Reiss' chapter valuable in the way it gave them "a language to label the role" they prefer to embody.

As can be expected, not all prospective teachers cheerfully embrace this activity with open minds. Some prospective teachers hold on to their conceptions and make comments like the student from the Midwest who stated, "I'm just going to teach in a private school, so this stuff does not apply to me." Another prospective teacher's comments illustrate the importance of encouraging reflexivity—another aspect of sTc that can be used to promote meaningful learning. Reflexivity is a process that allows us to examine the core of our own value positions in order to better understand what the foundations of those positions are and how they influence our course of action (or inaction).

When the issue of homosexuality came up during our discussion, one of the female students stated, "I don't know what to really do with *those people* in my classroom, how do you teach *them*?" (emphasis mine). Her honest and direct question stirred up an excellent dialogic conversation wherein her peers did not attack or ridicule her position. Instead, they asked her questions to better understand whose voice she was representing, and to encourage her to reflect more deeply about her own value position (reflexivity). For example, one student asked her, "Did you notice that you referred to gay people as 'those people'? Why do you do that?" Another asked, "How do you teach other kids, and why should you teach gay kids differently?"

I do not know if our dialogic conversations had an impact on this prospective teacher's views. This can be answered only by conducting field-based, longitudinal studies. Nevertheless, I hope that by her feeling confident to share her beliefs in the classroom, and by other prospective teachers sharing helpful responses, she may start to understand how her assumptions influence not only what she chooses to teach, but how she chooses to interact with culturally diverse children and their parents.

The class and I close this activity by deconstructing our own interactions and how the seminar was organized. This takes us back to our discussion on how sTc could be used to promote ideological change (in the university and/or school classrooms) in a way that helps to build a more inclusive and embracing society as we assist students to learn about science, about themselves, and about each other.

Building Learning Centers to Teach for Understanding

During the last 9 years of teaching methods courses at both the elementary and secondary science levels, I have noticed that some prospective teachers resist incorporating inquiry-based and constructivist teaching approaches, even when they intellectually understand these orientations. Some prospective teachers demonstrate their resistance to pedagogical change with statements such as, "It is not possible to teach that way and cover the entire curriculum you are required to teach by the state." This is a response I typically hear from secondary science methods students. Others make comments like, "I just don't believe that [elementary] students will stay focused long enough to do any of these activities . . . They are just going to start goofing off," or "You can't expect kids to do this kind of high-level thinking; the teacher has to cover the material first." Lortie's (1975) research explains why the prospective teachers' beliefs about what may or may not work in their classrooms may be so deeply entrenched— even before they try the new approaches being suggested in the methods courses. He argued that prospective teachers have been involved in an "apprenticeship of teaching" by having watched other teachers teach for 16 or more years of schooling. So, this leaves teacher education faculty with only 15 or 16 weeks to counter the prospective teachers' resistance to pedagogical change and to illustrate, in meaningful ways, teaching for understanding in the methods courses.

Furthermore, the aforementioned prospective teachers' comments and the previous discussion on how knowledge is constructed indicate that it will take a lot more than well-organized classroom activities and discussions to assist some prospective teachers to truly consider the value of using social constructivist pedagogical strategies—in short, to learn to teach for understanding.

One sTc activity that I have found useful in responding to prospective teachers' resistance to pedagogical change is the development of *learning centers*. This is a project that enables them to explore how students' prior knowledge on specific concepts can be used to teach for understanding. The prospective teachers start by interviewing at least two students (of different ethnic, gender, socioeconomic, and academic backgrounds). Their goal is to get at the core of the students' knowledge and/or beliefs about a science concept or concepts and to get know them better as individuals. For example, I share that one day when I asked elementary students what they thought were the differences between butterflies and moths, one student responded, "Well, moths are just ugly butterflies, but they are the same." In the methods class, we discuss the importance of examining the students' beliefs and ideas before instruction, and the reading assignments serve to augment our understanding of social constructivist research. In this way, prospective teachers become more aware of the key roles students' beliefs and their socioeconomic and cultural backgrounds play in how students construct new knowledge, and how they interact with each other and their teacher (Barton & Osborne, 2001; Lee, in press; Rodriguez, 2002). Hence, the prospective teachers use the information gathered from the student interviews to construct minds-on and hands-on learning centers designed to address the students' alternate (or original) conceptions on specific concepts. To this end, I model for the prospective teachers what a learning center should look like by bringing a completed center and having them engage with it. I also show video clips of other prospective teachers and/or students interacting with learning centers. In general, the learning center consists of a three-part cardboard panel (like those used for science fair displays or poster presentations) to post questions, instructions, and other kinds of information, as explained later. The learning center must also include safe materials and equipment that can be used by students without constant supervision.

I have found that most prospective teachers—even those who have had extensive teaching experience as substitute teachers and teachers' aides—are not familiar with learning centers, and they need much guidance on and examples of how to build them. For instance, one of the most important elements of a hands-on and minds-on learning center is that it should stimulate the same kind of dialogic conversation with the students as we have been carrying out in the methods class. In other words, the learning center should ask critical thinking questions, encourage students to conduct authentic activities to check and improve their understanding, reflect on how they and their peers learn (metacognition), and help students make socially relevant connections between the concept(s) and their everyday lives (reflexivity). How this is done is explained in more detail later.

Another key aspect of a learning center is that it should be self-sufficient and self-explanatory, which is one aspect prospective teachers find the most difficult. In other words, the learning center is not supposed to be just another prop for teaching (even though it can be used that way). The main objective is to have a small group of students (not more than three or four) explore their prior knowledge on the topic, engage and help one another as they conduct the suggested activities, and make socially relevant connections to their home and/or everyday lives. This implies that the teacher's role is that of a facilitator, probing and guiding only when necessary. As an example, let us consider a learning center recently constructed by one of the prospective teachers in my elementary and bilingual science methods class. In addition, I provide an analysis of how sTc is used to guide the prospective teachers with this assignment. In this example, the prospective teacher used a POE (Predict, Observe, and Explain) approach (Gunstone & Mitchell, 1998). This is one of several pedagogical strategies used to teach for understanding modeled in class. When the prospective teacher (Cesar) conducted the base student interviews, he found that his students were confused or knew very little about how magnets work. Therefore, the "Prediction" component of his POE was the following question, "How many staples can a nail [that has been wrapped with a wire] pick up after the ends of the wire are connected to a battery?" This is an excellent example of what we call in class an "attention getter" or "activator," a type of "cognitive hook" that attracts the students' attention and creates a need to know. It is important to note that an effective learning center does not start by identifying the scientific concepts under study at the onset, nor with scientific definitions copied straight out of the textbook, which are the typical ways cookbook labs are carried out. By asking probing questions first, students are encouraged to activate their prior knowledge, exchange ideas with one another, and write down their predictions and explanations *before* they conduct the activity.

The second part of the learning center is the "Observation" stage. Here is where children carry out the activity and test their predictions. When the students realize that they are essentially building a magnet, they begin to share what they know about magnets and how they work. They also begin to use the scientific discourse that allows the teacher to assess how the students are building new knowledge and where her or his guidance is needed.

In the next part of the POE, "Explain," students are encouraged to talk with one another and write down their explanations. Questions such as these are not uncommon: Were your predictions correct? If your predictions were different, what do you think is happening then? What is the scientific concept behind this activity? Draw a diagram to explain your answer. How would you modify this activity? Is there a way that you can increase the number of staples picked up by the magnet? How is this concept used in everyday life? How is it beneficial to you, your family, and others?

An effective learning center would have answers to some of these questions concealed in one way or another to allow students to answer the questions first on their own. For example, prospective teachers typically write the questions on large index cards, and put the answers on the back or in separate envelopes, which are attached with Velcro to the "Explain" section of the board.

Prospective teachers are also encouraged to make connections between school science and the students' home environment by adding a "take-home" packet or activity to their learning centers. For example, the prospective teacher doing the learning center on magnets gave each student a take-home kit that included a nail, a piece of wire, a 1.5-volt battery, and some staples in a Ziploc bag. In this way, the students were given all they needed to try the activity at home with their parents. During the preparation of the learning centers, we also discuss the political and strategic importance (reflexivity) of adding take-home components to science activities as a way of building stronger relationships with parents and to keep parents better informed about their children's growth.

After the prospective teachers have finished their learning centers and made them available to students at their school placements, we do one more closing activity that enables prospective teachers to further explore how learning centers can be used to teach for understanding. We invite three elementary school classes to come and visit with the prospective teachers and interact with their learning centers for 30 minutes each. This exhibition not only provides me with opportunities to evaluate the learning centers and the prospective teachers in action, but also enables the prospective teachers to see their peers in action, see how other students interact with different learning centers, and reflect on the pedagogical value of their own learning centers. The discussion that ensues at the end of the exhibition is rich and transformative.

Some of the prospective teachers, who have previously shown resistance to pedagogical change, typically construct a learning center that does not meet the suggested guidelines. For example, the display has too much information and requires a lot of reading by the students. In addition, the activity—although engaging—is a traditional cookbook recipe that does not allow students to explore their own questions. During our discussions, one of these prospective teachers stated, "I was able to see how the students were busy talking and having fun with Cesar's center [the POE on magnets], while they did mine in a hurry. I see now why we should include more thinking questions." Another prospective teacher also constructed a learning center that required a lot of reading and included a difficult physical-science activity. He said, "I don't think my activity was appropriate for the students' grade level [Grade 4]. I spent a lot of time explaining what they needed to do, and I'm exhausted. Esperanza only had one concept [static electricity], and the students were really getting into it."

Deconstructing the Learning Center Activity

How was this activity an example of how sTc can be used to respond to prospective teachers' resistance to pedagogical change?

- By having a dialogic conversation with students based on the assigned readings on social constructivism and sTc, theoretical frameworks are made more accessible and connected to their prior experiences.

- By modeling student-centered and inquiry-based activities (authentic activities), the prospective teachers were able to articulate their positions on the feasibility of carrying out such activities in their own classrooms (dialogic conversation).

- By modeling how learning centers can be constructed to teach for understanding and by requiring prospective teachers to present their learning centers in their own teaching contexts (authentic activities), they have multiple opportunities to explore the impact of this pedagogical strategy on students' learning and on their own preferred modes of teaching and learning (metacognition).

- By requiring prospective teachers to present the same learning centers in a different school context as part of a larger exhibition of learning centers with their peers (authentic activities), they were able to compare and deconstruct each other's learning centers (metacognition).

- Finally, by engaging in a discussion about the need to motivate all students to learn for understanding, and the importance of making stronger connections between school science and the students' everyday lives and their home environments, prospective teachers were encouraged to reflect on the multiple ways they can bring about change and make science more accessible and relevant to all students (reflexivity).

It should be obvious that not all prospective teachers reached the level of engagement with or embraced sTc as a viable theoretical framework to guide their teaching. I do not believe that any of the authors in this volume make such a claim about any of the strategies they are suggesting. However, even if a few prospective teachers were positively influenced by any of the strategies to promote ideological and pedagogical change demonstrated in my methods classes, it would mean that at least a few more teachers are now teaching children to learn science and mathematics for understanding and for diversity. What we need next is more empirical and longitudinal research on how the strategies suggested here impact beginning teachers' efforts to teach for diversity and understanding, and consequently, impact their students' academic performance and participation in science and mathematics. I am currently conducting longitudinal studies with these goals in mind, and hopefully more fellow teacher educators and researchers will be motivated to conduct similar intervention studies after reading this book.

CONCLUSION: KEEPING THE "T" IN sTc

In this chapter, I have provided a more detailed description of sTc. This framework is based on the intersection of multicultural education tenets with social constructivism, and it is the framework guiding my own teaching and research agenda. Several examples of how sTc can be used to counter prospective teachers' resistance to ideological and pedagogical change have been published elsewhere. Herein, I provided two different examples that I hoped would add to the list of promising strategies suggested by the other contributing authors.

As many readers who are also teacher educators are aware, our transformative work with teachers is very rewarding, but it can also be challenging and dangerous in terms of tenure and promotion. However, it would be more dangerous at a greater social scale, if as teacher educators and researchers, we allow new generations of teachers to graduate from our programs without interrupting their resistance to ideological and pedagogical change in positive ways, and without providing them with promising alternatives to teach for diversity and understanding. In addition, as teacher educators and researchers, we have a professional responsibility to help teachers meet the challenges associated with national policies (such as the No Child Left Behind act) and/or national and state standards. The contradictions among the calls for education reform and national policies and the multitude of factors that influence what and how teachers teach in increasingly diverse school contexts are abundant and complex. Nevertheless, teacher education programs can make a significant difference by engaging in critical dialogues with teachers, modeling effective pedagogical practices, and providing support to take the unavoidable, yet necessary, risks associated with teaching for transformative social action. Paulo Freire (1998) summed up well the importance of transformative education as follows: "As educators we are politicians; we engage in politics when we educate. And if we dream about democracy, let us fight, day and night, for a school in which we talk to and with the learners so that, hearing them, we can be heard by them as well" (p. 68).

REFERENCES

Bakhtin, M. M. (1981). *The dialogic imagination: Four essays by M. M. Bakhtin* (M. Holquist, Ed.). Austin: University of Texas Press.

Bakhtin, M. M. (1986). *Speech genres and other late essays* (C. Emerson & M. Holquist, Eds.). Austin: University of Texas Press.

Barton, A., & Osborne, M. (2001). *Marginalized discourses in science education.* New York: Teachers College Press.

Committee on Children, Youth, and Families. (1984). *Children, youth, and families in the South-west.* Hearing Before the Committee on Children, Youth, and Families, House of Repre-sentatives, 98th Congress, First Session (Santa Ana, California, December 7, 1983).

Dewey, J. (1938). *Experience and education.* New York: Macmillan.

Duryea, E. J., Mesrian, P., Semark, L., & West, C. (1997). Sexual behavior and perceptions of young women in a rural Southwest school. *Rural Educator, 19*(1), 7–12.

Freire, P. (1998). *Teachers as cultural workers: Letters to those who dare to teach.* Boulder: Westview Press.

Gunstone, R. F., & Mitchell, I. J. (1998). Metacognition and conceptual change. In J. J. Mintzes, J. H. Wandersee, & J. D. Novak (Eds.), *Teaching science for understanding: A human constructivist view* (pp. 133–163). San Diego: Academic Press.

Lee, O. (in press). Science inquiry for elementary students from diverse backgrounds. In W. G. Secada (Ed.), *Review of research in education* (Vol. 26). Washington, DC: American Educational Research Association.

Lortie, D. (1975). *School teacher.* Chicago: University of Chicago Press.

McIntosh, P. (1989, July/August). White privilege: Unpacking the invisible knapsack. *Peace & Freedom,* pp. 10–12.

Moscovici, H., & Holdlund-Nelson, T. (1998, January). Shifting from activity mania to in-quiry. *Science and Children,* pp. 14–17.

National Research Council. (1996). *National science education standards.* Washington, DC: National Academy Press.

Reiss, M. J. (1993). *Science education for a pluralist society.* Philadelphia: Open University Press.

Rodriguez, A. J. (1993). "A dose of reality": Understanding the origin of the theory/practice dichotomy in teacher education from the students' point of view. *Journal of Teacher Educa-tion, 43,* 213–222.

Rodriguez, A. J. (1998). Strategies for counterresistance: Toward sociotransformative constructivism and learning to teach science for diversity and for understanding. *Journal of Research in Science Teaching, 36*(6), 589–622.

Rodriguez, A. J. (2002). Using sociotransformative constructivism to teach for understanding in diverse classrooms: A beginning teacher's journey. *American Educational Research Jour-nal, 39*(4), 1017–1045.

Vygotsky, L. S. (1978). *Mind in society: The development of higher psychological processes.* Cam-bridge, MA: Harvard University Press.

Wertsch, J. V. (1991). *Voices of the mind: A sociocultural approach to mediated action.* Cambridge, MA: Harvard University Press.

3

Making Equity and Multiculturalism Explicit to Transform Mathematics Education

Richard S. Kitchen
University of New Mexico

[The trip to the Pueblo helped me understand] that there is more to life than math. It has given us more of an ability to relate with students thus making them more proned [sic] to desire to learn from us.

Actually, it helps me to understand how very important their culture is to them and how students from a reservation could miss a lot of school because of it [to attend religious ceremonies].

After a visit to an American Indian reservation, these two prospective mathematics teachers had developed a greater understanding of and respect for a Native-American culture. The trip to the reservation was completed during a mathematics methods course. As one of several select activities, this trip is an integral part of my strategy to support prospective teachers to become advocates for all of their students.

In this chapter, I describe my approach to prepare prospective secondary-level mathematics teachers to both implicitly and explicitly incorporate socially, culturally, and politically equitable instructional strategies in their classrooms, that is, teach for diversity. The strategies described are intended to promote achievement among culturally, linguistically, and socioeconomically diverse students. I focus on both student culture and equitable instructional strategies as a means to prepare prospective mathematics teachers to teach for diversity. Succinctly put, the goal of this work is to support prospective mathematics teachers to become advocates for all of their students, not just a select few.

Initially, I describe lessons that acknowledge and affirm the role of culture in the mathematics classroom. In these activities, prospective mathematics teachers learn about the mathematical contributions of non-Europeans and become familiar with a Native-American culture. I then summarize lessons that address equity in the mathematics classroom. I ask prospective teachers to critically examine the role of ability tracking in mathematics, use a protocol to study the opportunities diverse students have to learn mathematics, analyze data that demonstrates injustices in society, and construct a lesson that incorporates the study of highly relevant topics to students. When possible, I include the perspectives of prospective teachers as they work through these activities.

TRANSFORMING MATHEMATICS EDUCATION

Mathematics education reform documents promote the need for teachers to be prepared to teach in more culturally sensitive and responsive ways (National Council of Teachers of Mathematics [NCTM], 1989, 2000). An explicit goal of the reform movement is to improve access to challenging mathematics content and instruction to students who have historically been denied such access. In the *Principles and Standards for School Mathematics* (NCTM, 2000), students who "live in poverty," non-native English speakers, students with disabilities, women, and "many non-White students" are identified as "the [historical] victims of low expectations" (p. 13) in mathematics. Missing from documents that delineate needed reforms in mathematics education (NCTM, 1989, 2000; National Science Foundation [NSF], 1996) are references to the sociopolitical contexts in which teachers labor. Specific approaches are seldom offered to teachers to help *all* students, particularly diverse students from high-poverty communities, learn challenging mathematical content.

In addition, many prospective teachers may not have experienced standards-based mathematics instruction prior to entering the teaching profession. Prospective mathematics teachers are being asked to teach in ways that they may never have experienced, while supporting the learning of all students. In essence, mathematics teacher educators have two enormous challenges: to prepare prospective mathematics teachers to implement standards-based curriculum and instruction, and to teach diverse learners. I view these goals as complementary. Implementing challenging, standards-based curriculum and instruction that is accessible for all students requires transforming mathematics education away from functioning to legitimate a select few through selecting, sorting, and certifying students (Apple, 1985).

Transforming mathematics education to value the mathematical preparation of the majority over the achievements of a select group is a daunting challenge. Prospective secondary mathematics teachers complete a variety of mathematics courses. For the most part, prospective mathematics teachers, particularly at the secondary level, are prepared by mathematicians who maintain "an elitist and privileged position by maintaining that mathematics is abstract, objective, and independent of social, cultural and political conditions" (Burton, 1994, p. 73). Because prospective mathematics teachers primarily experience mathematics as devoid of social, cultural, and political considerations (see Hersh, 1979; Lakatos, 1976, for perspectives on how mathematics is in fact value-laden and fallible), it is highly unlikely that multiculturalism and issues related to equity are modeled or discussed in their mathematics course work. In addition, after successfully completing a series of upper-division mathematics courses, prospective secondary-level teachers are among the few who are granted legitimacy, albeit not complete, by "members of the mathematics club" (Burton, 1994, p. 73).

As teacher educators, we typically have limited opportunities to address prospective teachers' sense of entitlement. Teacher educators should consider the entitlement granted prospective secondary-level mathematics teachers as a potential reason why they may resist efforts to prepare them to teach for diversity. The ever-increasing volume of research on teachers' resistance to teaching for diversity (see, e.g., Gomez & Tabachnick, 1992; Kleinfeld, 1992; Murrell, 1992) demonstrates that this is a complex endeavor.

There are a few examples of movements that promote mathematical literacy for those who have historically been excluded in mathematics. For instance, Robert Moses' Algebra Project (Moses & Cobb, 2001) has worked to "drive a broad math literacy effort [for] the Black and poor students and the communities in which they live, the usually excluded" (p. 19). The goal of Moses' Algebra Project starkly contrasts with the traditional role of mathematics to sort people, reinforcing society's power structure that facilitates the selection of elites in society (U. D'Ambrosio, 1983; Gerdes, 1988). Research in right-wing, authoritarian nations points to how traditional mathematics curricula and instruction were not viewed as a threat by those in power, and may have actually helped to maintain and support the status quo in Brazil (B. S. D'Ambrosio, 1991) and Guatemala (Kitchen, 2001). In other words, the traditional role of mathematics to ensure the success of only a few has functioned to support and maintain a select few who brutally maintained control of power.

For progressive educators, a potential role of the mathematics education reform movement is to promote a more egalitarian and democratic society in which all students have the opportunity to develop mathematical literacy. To realize the vision of the mathematics education reform movement requires policymakers and reform advocates to pay attention to the real barriers to reform as identified by teachers, particularly in schools serving high-poverty communities (Kitchen, 2003). In particular, the mathematics education community must prioritize improving teachers' work conditions as a means to support teachers to implement reforms at schools that serve high poverty communities (Kitchen, 2003).

TEACHING FOR DIVERSITY: MULTICULTURALISM AND EQUITY FOR ALL STUDENTS

> [Multicultural education is] a field of study designed to increase educational equity for all students that incorporates, for this purpose, content, concepts, principles, theories, and paradigms from history, the social and behavioral sciences, and particularly from ethnic and women studies. (Banks & Banks, 1995, p. xii)

This definition of multiculturalism connects history, culture, and identity to educational equity. A multicultural education theoretical framework that puts educational equity in the forefront inspires my approach to teach for diversity. Specifically, to prepare prospective teachers to meet the needs of an increasingly diverse student population, my strategy is to prepare prospective teachers to understand and learn how to actively affirm their students' cultural backgrounds, while challenging prospective teachers to engage their students in learning challenging mathematical content.

By learning about, understanding, and affirming students' cultural identities, prospective teachers problematize the notion that mathematics curriculum and instruction are culturally free, neutral activities. Conceptualizing mathematics in more human ways connects students with the historical development of mathematics across cultures and promotes mathematical literacy as a means to achieve social, political, and economic justice for all (Ernest, 1991; Skovsmose, 1994). Some scholars have promoted the notion of culturally relevant instruction as a means to capitalize on student strengths—what students know instead of what they do not know (Ladson-Billings, 1994, 1995a, 1995b; Osborne, 1996). For instance, successful teachers of African American students often incorporate students' cultural strengths into their mathematics lessons (Ladson-Billings, 1994, 1995a, 1995b). In this sense, the vision of the mathematics education reform movement of "academic achievement for all students" requires integrating disciplinary knowledge with knowledge of student diversity (McLaughlin, Shepard, & O'Day, 1995). Unfortunately, the existing knowledge base for promoting academic achievement with culturally and linguistically diverse students is limited and fragmented, in part because disciplinary knowledge and student diversity have traditionally constituted separate research agendas (Lee, 1999).

Prospective teachers also need support to incorporate equitable instructional strategies in their mathematics classrooms. Research has consistently demonstrated over the past several decades that students from more affluent neighborhoods have greater access to high-quality educational opportunities than do students from high-poverty communities (Atweh, Bleicher, & Cooper, 1998; Oakes, 1990; Tate, 1997). Instead of stressing high-level thinking and the development of students' critical thinking skills, schools that serve the poor tend to focus more on rote instruction of low-level skills (Haberman, 1991; Knapp & Woolverton, 1995).

Though prospective teachers may have never confronted injustice, their students face multiple hardships that do not disappear during mathematics class. From my experiences as a teacher educator, prospective secondary mathematics teachers need help to explicitly connect the teaching and learning of mathematics with their students' socioeconomic realities. From a critical theoretical perspective, teachers play a central role in the struggle for social justice (Kincheloe & McLaren, 1994). Pragmatically put, teachers can be change agents in the lives of their students, mediating the educational inequities experienced by their students by promoting challenging mathematics curriculum and instruction in the classroom.

PREPARING MATHEMATICS TEACHERS TO WORK IN HIGH-POVERTY, DIVERSE SCHOOLS

Many prospective mathematics teachers will work in schools with racially and ethnically heterogeneous student populations that are located in high-poverty communities. These schools have unique sets of problems that distinguish them from their more affluent, suburban counterparts. For example, at high-poverty schools, students often attend classes in dilapidated facilities and have higher percentages of novice teachers, teachers without a teaching credential and teachers who are teaching subjects in which they have neither a major nor a minor (Ingersoll, 1999; National Research Council, 2001).

Among the most profound challenges faced by school districts that serve diverse student populations is the recruitment and retention of people of color into the teaching ranks. In 1996, approximately 91% of teachers in the United States were White whereas the percentage of minority teachers in schools has steadily decreased during the past three decades

(National Education Association, 1997). The decreasing numbers of teachers of color in the United States contrasts starkly with data that indicate that 50 of the largest 99 school districts in the country in 1992 had majority minority-student populations (National Center for Education Statistics, 1994). Boyer and Baptiste (1996) described some of the reasons why so few people of color pursue a career in education, such as curriculum bias toward Anglo-European culture, academic racism, and teacher education programs that do not prioritize the recruitment of racial minorities into teaching.

The huge disparities between the cultural, ethnic, and racial backgrounds of the majority of teachers and their students demonstrates why colleges of education must make preparing prospective teachers to work effectively with culturally and linguistically diverse students a priority (Nieto, 2000). The challenges inherent in preparing prospective teachers to work in high-poverty, diverse schools are well established (Jordan, 1995; Scott, 1995; Tatum, 1992). To prepare prospective teachers to work with diverse student populations, only one course in multicultural education is typically included in the course work of prospective teachers. Yet, as Gomez (1996) wrote, "efforts at multicultural education isolated in single courses or field experiences only begin to challenge prospective teachers' beliefs about diverse peoples; they seldom address the knowledge, skills, and dispositions required to increase diverse children's learning and achievement" (p. 118). Moreover, course work in multicultural teacher education has been relatively ineffective at challenging prospective teachers' beliefs about racism, White privilege (Sleeter, 1994), and their belief that through hard work, one can be successful in school and in mathematics.

Despite the difficulties associated with preparing teachers to work in multicultural settings, many scholars have identified instructional approaches to prepare prospective teachers to teach for diversity. For example, according to Zeichner (1996), continued guided reflection on the part of prospective teachers on the backgrounds and life experiences of students different from them will "result in shifts in attitudes, beliefs, dispositions, and theories that govern teachers' practices" (p. 161). Sleeter (1995) required her students to engage in research in their communities in which students "are not investigating characteristics of groups but rather comparing at least two groups' access to society's resources, such as housing or health care; or they can investigate media images that help shape our belief systems" (p. 25).

All prospective secondary-level mathematics teachers at the University of New Mexico complete a project in which they research their school's communities and interview an individual who lives or works near the school. As part of the community profile assignment (Watkins, 2000), the prospective teachers explore the unique sociocultural characteristics of the communities that their school serves. I have found that prospective teachers who complete this project may still have difficulties supporting the learning of their students, demonstrating to me that this project must be explicitly connected to classroom practice. After learning about their students' communities, prospective teachers need to develop an instructional strategy, lesson, or project based on the distinctive characteristics and needs of their students' communities. A sample lesson I have provided prospective teachers is based on a project that a teacher created for her students on a Native-American reservation. The tribe was interested in knowing how many acres on the reservation had been used for agricultural purposes. Students collected data and land use patterns on the reservation over the past 40 years and then graphically summarized these data and presented the summary to tribal leaders.

Model teacher education programs that prioritize preparing prospective teachers to work with diverse students from high-poverty communities must take into account issues of culture and context (Cole & Griffin, 1987; Delpit, 1988). Common features of these programs may include (Zeichner, 1996):

1. Support the belief that all students can succeed.
2. Help prospective teachers learn scaffolding techniques to bridge students' home cultures with the school culture.
3. Provide course work and field experiences in which prospective teachers learn about the languages, cultures, and socioeconomic circumstances of the particular students in their classrooms.
4. Learn instructional strategies that value sense making and knowledge construction.
5. Foster the involvement of parents and other community members in authentic ways in the education.

In the following section, I situate myself in this work and introduce how I prepare prospective teachers to teach for diversity.

CHALLENGING SECONDARY MATHEMATICS TEACHERS TO TEACH FOR DIVERSITY

Students in the secondary mathematics methods course are often surprised when I raise issues about multiculturalism and equity in class. After all, I am a middle-aged White man who has been successful in mathematics. Why am I raising issues that shed light on my own privilege? I try to be honest about my own successes and failures in mathematics, and communicate why I have strong beliefs about social justice as a means to build trust with prospective teachers. In particular, I want them to know that I attended public, inner-city schools and experienced firsthand the racial tensions associated with the desegregation of schools in the 1970s. My commitment to social justice is a direct response to the racism that was an integral part of my upbringing. I also want prospective teachers to know that I devote significant time and energy to working in high-poverty schools in the United States and in Latin America, not to impress them, but to demonstrate that I am putting my theoretical perspective into practice.

Of course, being honest about who I am is just an initial step in my work to prepare prospective teachers to teach for diversity. I have found prospective secondary mathematics teachers to be extremely resistant to discussions about multiculturalism and equity. Who am I to challenge their success in mathematics? They succeeded without special treatment. To them, anyone with an interest in mathematics, the self-discipline, and the aptitude can be successful in the study of mathematics. If students of color would apply themselves as they have, they can also be successful in mathematics. Generally, White teachers, for that matter, most prospective teachers "view social institutions as largely fair and open to those who try" (Sleeter, 1995, p. 18). This is especially true for prospective secondary mathematics teachers, most of whom are White and have never questioned dominant cultural norms.

To support prospective teachers in the process of learning how to teach for diversity to support the learning of all their students, not just a select few, my strategy entails incorporating multiculturalism and equity implicitly and explicitly in the methods course for secondary mathematics teachers. In the following sections, I outline first how I integrate multicultural perspectives in the methods course, and then provide some concrete strategies that I have used to promote equity in mathematics education.

EXPLICITLY AND IMPLICITLY INCORPORATING MULTICULTURALISM IN CLASS

The majority of the prospective teachers in my secondary mathematics methods courses have generally had little contact with students of diverse ethnic, racial, and socioeconomic backgrounds. For this reason, one of my goals is to introduce them to the contributions made to the development of mathematics by cultures throughout the world. A second goal is to initiate prospective teachers to the notion that understanding and actively affirming their students' knowledge and cultures is an important part of becoming an effective mathematics teacher.

Creating a Respectful and Trusting Community of Learners

Before I can even begin the process of challenging prospective mathematics teachers to teach for diversity, I know that I must first create a respectful and trusting community in which everyone feels actively supported. If we expect prospective teachers to teach for diversity, then as teacher educators, we must model what this entails. For instance, I try to demonstrate respect, affirm the teachers' cultural backgrounds, support collaborative approaches to support the learning of all, and acknowledge that every prospective teacher brings knowledge and skills to the learning process. I believe that prospective teachers need to be able to trust each other and me. For this to occur, they must feel as if they can share information about themselves in a respectful environment.

I also must show the prospective teachers that I understand and value their most immediate needs. One way to do this is by initiating classes with activities that the prospective teachers believe will benefit them in the short term. In the secondary mathematics methods course, this generally means initiating class by studying methods of teaching mathematics that the prospective teachers can try out directly with their students. Once I have gained the prospective teachers' trust by demonstrating my interest in attending to their most immediate needs, we begin to explore topics related to multiculturalism and equity.

Contributions of Diverse Cultures to Mathematics

Studying the historical contributions of distinct cultures and examining the intersection of students' cultures and mathematics is a fundamental part of my methods courses. For instance, I have asked students to read excerpts from George Joseph's book *The Crest of the Peacock: Non-European Roots of Mathematics* (1991) in which it is demonstrated that much of the mathematics taught in high school classrooms can be traced to societies other than Greece (e.g., Egypt and India). We focus on how the Chinese were the first to discover the inappropriately named Pythagorean theorem and how the Arabs should receive most of the credit for the creation of algebra. We also study "women's mathematics," such as quilting and sewing. Discussions usually follow that lead many to question why the mathematics of "men" (e.g., building bridges, highly symbolic mathematics, etc.) is more highly valued in society.

Considering Students' Cultures in the Mathematics Classroom

A culminating experience in one secondary mathematics methods course involved visiting a Native-American reservation on a feast day. There are several Indian Pueblos within a 60-mile radius of Albuquerque. On feast days, non-Indian peoples are invited to visit the Pueblo to view traditional dances and enjoy native foods and arts. Many of the Pueblos have multiple feast days during the year. Many of my prospective teachers, most of whom are native New Mexican, have never visited any of the 19 Indian Pueblos in the state.

Several weeks before the trip to the Pueblo, Dr. Joseph Suina, a colleague from the Cochiti Pueblo, gave a presentation on Pueblo cultures. He described the dances the prospective teachers would witness and their significance. He also discussed how having knowledge of Indian cultures can make them more effective teachers of Native-American children. For example, by understanding why Indian children are hesitant to divulge that they will be missing class to attend cultural ceremonies, prospective teachers may be more willing to assist Native-American children once they come back to class.

The prospective teachers returned from their visit to the Pueblo with only positive insights about how the trip would impact them as teachers. In journal entries that they completed after the visit, they wrote about their various impressions. One prospective teacher wrote: "The trip was an affirmation of differences between peoples." Another wrote: "This trip will help me as a mathematics teacher because [I now have a better] understanding of different cultures." Others discussed how the visit to the Pueblo would impact them as teachers: "I talked about my experiences on Tuesday to all of my classes [while student teaching]. These people [Native Americans] are an important part of the New Mexico Community and my students will benefit from learning about these people." Yet another wrote: "Having an understanding of these various cultures has definitely helped me with my instruction and classroom management."

Among the sampling of additional journal entries included: "[I now recognize that] people have lives outside the 'dominant' society." "I feel closer to a culture I did not understand. This new understanding will enable me to gather math knowledge of [the particular Pueblo] and share it with the classroom. Perhaps a [particular Pueblo] Day at school next year!" "The trip has opened my eyes to how culturally sensitive I should be to indigenous people."

The prospective teachers' narratives illustrated that this was a profound cultural experience that had immediate educational value for them. These teachers developed a greater appreciation for and understanding of one Pueblo's cultural traditions. Hopefully, as classroom teachers, they will have heightened awareness of Native-American children's unique cultures and greater sensitivity to their educational needs. In the section that follows, I describe an example of an assignment that confronted prospective teachers' notions about fairness and access to learn mathematics.

EXPLICITLY AND IMPLICITLY INCORPORATING EQUITY IN CLASS

Tracking and Expectations in the Mathematics Classroom

After developing a community of learners in which a certain level of respect and trust has been established, initial discussions can take place in the methods course about opportunities that diverse learners have to learn challenging mathematics. Inevitably, I bring up ability tracking in the mathematics classroom and the role that it plays to decrease access to higher level mathematics courses for students of color (Secada, 1992). Ability grouping or "tracking" has resulted in students having varying access to educational opportunities and is associated with increased dropout rates (Barro, 1984; Oakes, 1985; U.S. Department of Education, 1998). I have found that this issue generally makes most prospective teachers defensive, which may lead to resistance to discussions about their own privilege in mathematics. Nevertheless, I believe it is vital to expose the insidious role that ability tracking plays in mathematics. My goal is for prospective teachers to begin to question this taken-for-granted practice.

As a class, we also discuss the relationship between tracking and expectations. The expectations that a teacher has for students is correlated to the mathematical content covered in class and the types of interactions that take place between teacher and students (Oakes, 1990). In low-track mathematics classes, less is expected of students than in high-track classes (Johnson, 1999; Oakes, 1990). Since students from poor, minority, or non-English-speaking communities tend to populate low-track classes, mathematics teachers may hold generally lower expectations for these students (Oakes, 1990). Middle school Native-American and Hispanic students described that in addition to experiencing low expectations, they drop out of school because teachers are unfamiliar with many of their cultural traditions and even make disparaging comments about them and their cultures and communities (Kitchen, Velásquez, & Myers, 1999).

Before conversations about tracking and expectations can occur, prospective teachers must first be able to recognize and explicitly name exactly who populates low-track mathematics classes. Early in the semester, I have prospective teachers make observations about the racial and ethnic makeup of "developmental" and "honors" mathematics courses. This task challenges the beliefs held by many prospective mathematics teachers, who are highly vested in the notion that mathematical competence is innate or can be attained primarily through hard work.

Making Personal Connections With Students

I am convinced that prospective mathematics teachers need to begin to personally identify with individual students different from themselves to be able to teach for diversity. One activity that I have developed with this goal in mind is to have prospective teachers complete a classroom observation in which they use a research protocol adapted from scales to measure reform-based mathematics instruction (National Center for Research in Mathematics Education, 1992). The prospective teachers make observations and write justifications for their classroom ratings in the following three areas: (a) access to opportunities to learn, (b) mathematical analysis, and (c) mathematical discourse and communication (see Appendix for definitions and the rating scales).

The opportunity-to-learn scales include considerations such as gender equity, the use of language scaffolding to support the learning of English-language learners, and whether the teacher actively encourages a diversity of students to participate during the lesson. To score high on this scale, the teacher is clearly aware that students have different educational needs and attends to these needs in some way. Prospective teachers also consider whether students engage in mathematical analysis during the lesson. Mathematical analysis is higher order mathematical thinking that goes beyond the simple recording or reporting of mathematical facts, rules, and definitions or mechanically applying algorithms. Lastly, prospective teachers use a scale to rate how well the teacher being observed fosters mathematical discourse and communication during a lesson. In classes characterized by high levels of mathematical discourse and communication, there is considerable teacher–student and student–student interaction about the mathematical ideas of a topic; the interaction is reciprocal, and it promotes coherent shared understanding. Teacher educators could have prospective mathematics teachers focus only on specific students and rate their cooperating teacher only with respect to these students. An advantage to this approach is that it may facilitate the prospective teachers identifying more closely with individual students, particularly with students who may be quite different from them (e.g., different gender, class, race, ethnicity, etc.).

I have prospective teachers observe and rate their cooperating teachers with these three scales during the fall semester when they are primarily only observing classes while enrolled in the methods course. Their student teaching experience does not commence until the following spring semester. In one methods class, prospective mathematics teachers struggled to rate their teachers on the access-to-opportunities-to-learn scale because the majority of the teachers observed presented lecture-oriented lessons. Though many rated teachers low on the mathematical-communication-and-discourse scale, they were unsure how to assess the opportunities students had to learn mathematics because students seldom demonstrated what they understood. The fact that the prospective teachers had no idea how to rate teachers in this area motivated discussions in the methods class about the importance of assessment to understand whether a diversity of students are acquiring mathematical ideas. It also highlighted the value of alternative assessment formats that require students to communicate their thinking and elicit a range of student responses (Wiggins, 1993). In addition, several prospective teachers noticed that students rarely, if ever, engaged in mathematical analysis during the lessons observed. For the remainder of the semester, we repeatedly came back to this observation in discussions of recommended mathematics education reforms (NCTM, 1989, 2000; NSF, 1996) to promote higher order thinking in mathematics.

Though prospective teachers often rate their cooperating teachers relatively high across all areas, as the fall semester progresses they begin to re-evaluate their initial ratings. I have found that viewing video clips of mathematics lessons and continually revisiting the rating scales helps the prospective teachers become more critical about the effectiveness of their cooperating teachers to incorporate equitable opportunities for all their students to learn mathematics. This may be because prospective teachers begin to identify more with their students after spending considerable time in the classroom with them. In the process, prospective teachers begin to understand more about how particular students are treated differently based on their gender, ethnicity, sexual orientation, and/or socioeconomic background. In the section that follows, prospective mathematics teachers analyze census data as a means to motivate further reflection about the socioeconomic injustices faced by their students.

Confronting Injustices Faced by Students

During class discussions about how to meet the unique needs of all learners, I attempt to address how to affirm student diversity in the mathematics classroom without being essentializing. I believe it is vital that prospective teachers both view their students as members of distinct communities while simultaneously trying to understand their individual uniqueness. One approach to accomplish this goal is to have prospective teachers assess some students' mathematical strengths and

weaknesses while at the same time studying the socioeconomic challenges that their students face.

Though it may be difficult to know how poverty affects individual students, prospective mathematics teachers can analyze data that demonstrate inequities in opportunities available based on ethnicity, race, and
gender. Prospective teachers must first acknowledge that inequities exist
that directly impact their students' lives and their jobs as teachers before
they can begin to work to meet the individual needs of their students. I
have asked prospective teachers to read an article by Christine Sleeter
(1995) that explores the historical reasons why inequities and injustices
continue in education and in society. Prospective teachers have also reviewed and discussed census data that illustrate how almost 30% of all Latinos and one third of all African Americans live below the poverty line
(U.S. Bureau of the Census, 1993b). They have also examined how, since
1967, the mean income of the top 5% of White families has increased by
38%, to a mean of over $160,000 per year (U.S. Bureau of the Census,
1993b). Over the same period the average income for the poorest one fifth
of Black families declined by 21% to a 1992 mean family income of $4,255
per year (U.S. Bureau of the Census, 1993a). Finally, Black and Latino men
and women earn less than two thirds the income of Whites. Even those
Black and Latino men and women pursuing higher levels of formal education—all the way through master's degrees—earn only around 80% of the
income of Whites with comparable education (U.S. Bureau of the Census,
1993a; see Apple, 1996, for additional examples).

After prospective teachers read Sleeter's article (1995) and reviewed the
statistics in one secondary methods course, one prospective teacher
pointed out that the data were misleading because no figures were provided indicating the decreased earning power of middle- and lower-
middle-class Whites. I responded that the earning power of middle-
income Whites has steadily declined since the beginning of the Reagan/
Bush era in 1980 (Apple, 1996). Another woman in the class argued that
the statistics concerning the lower average earnings of people of color
with a formal education compared to Whites with comparable diplomas
were especially striking because of how these figures illustrated economic
racial bias. At this point, a woman who had left a lucrative career as an en-
gineer to become a high school mathematics teacher expressed the opin-
ion that the data were deceiving. She believed that the statistics failed to
uncover the underlying reasons why the differential earnings between
men and women were so large. Many women like her chose to pursue less
lucrative careers because of their interest in helping people. Remarkably,
many of the prospective teachers nodded their affirmation of this statement as if such gender roles were inevitable. One woman, however, in-
stantly questioned why women made such choices. She reasoned that so-

cietal expectations greatly influence how gender roles play out. Thus, many women pursue careers in nursing and teaching because these are the professions that they are expected to seek and that are available to them to obtain.

I asked what we could do about poverty, social injustice, and racial bias in the classroom. One prospective teacher responded by describing her experiences teaching a summer school course in which one particular student struggled to complete the class despite obvious economic hardships. In the end, the student earned a marginal passing grade in the course, a D minus, after she spent numerous hours with the student, providing him with the individual tutorial assistance that he needed.

Another prospective teacher who had left a lucrative position in engineering to become a licensed mathematics teacher queried why she gave him a marginal passing grade, arguing that if the student had passed the course, he deserved at least a C to reward him for his efforts and perseverance. In industry, employees were either successful or unsuccessful; there was no in between. Thus, he rationalized that those students who pass a course should not be penalized with a marginal passing grade, but rewarded with a grade that demonstrated their improvement and effort.

Many in the class responded negatively to such logic, disputing the notion that grades should be arbitrarily awarded for effort and improvement. Standards needed to be followed; besides, it was not fair to those students who merited a grade of C or better to grant a student who did not earn this grade the same mark. This discussion quickly turned into a rather spirited debate on the merits of grading, in general. Without a doubt, though, the majority of the class was adamantly opposed to the notion of "giving away" grades that students had not earned.

For my part, I took advantage of this discussion to affirm the ex-engineers' arguments, which essentially brought to light alternative conceptions of assessment such as valuing students' mathematical growth over time. I challenged the prospective teachers to consider the subjective nature of grading and to question how grading affected their ability to achieve goals such as sparking their students' interest in mathematics and increasing their students' mathematical knowledge. The controversy also provided me with an opportunity to introduce such notions as why a variety of assessment formats are worthy of exploration in the classroom. In the context of equitable instructional practices, alternative assessment formats validate students' mathematical growth in ways that traditional, norm-referenced evaluations may not. According to Kulm (1994):

> Alternative assessment approaches that include open-ended questions, presentation of solutions in both written and oral form, and other performances send very different messages to students about what is important in mathe-

matics learning. The thinking and reasoning approaches and the way mathematical thoughts are presented can receive high marks even if the answer may not be complete or correct. The shift from an emphasis on producing correct answers to the expectation that students think and communicate is a major one for many students and teachers. (p. 6)

Interestingly, when I asked this group of prospective teachers whether they believed that data that exposed socioeconomic inequities were appropriate for use in statistics lessons with high school students, many responded affirmatively. A few verbalized their belief that statistics were inherently "political" and that it would be a mistake to exclude certain data from analysis in class just because they uncover injustices. I wondered, though, how many of these prospective teachers would aspire to teach such a lesson? An intriguing research project would be to study if and how mathematics teachers use statistical data to examine social and economic injustices in society. In the section that follows, I provide an example of such a lesson that I conducted with prospective teachers that could be adapted for use in a secondary-level mathematics class.

Making Mathematics Socially and Politically Relevant

In my view, it is critically important that prospective mathematics teachers have opportunities to both review and create rigorous lessons that are socially, politically, and/or culturally relevant to their students. Too often, prospective secondary-level teachers view mathematics as a politically neutral subject (Bishop, 1991). Though science and engineering applications are prevalent in school mathematics (Roy, 2000), few resources are available that include socially oriented contexts in mathematics (for highly engaging examples, see Bohl, 1999).

I believe that teacher educators need to challenge prospective teachers to evaluate the values implicit in various mathematical contexts by selecting mathematical problems and topics that motivate critical reflection among students (Abraham & Bibby, 1988; Mellin-Olsen, 1987). For example, Kitchen and Lear (2000) created a series of lessons that inspired a group of young Mexican-American girls to reconsider their views about body image after measuring Barbie dolls. Precisely because mathematics teachers view themselves so strongly in terms of their subject area, for prospective teachers to take equity seriously, they need to engage in and create lessons that incorporate students' socioeconomic and political realities.

The lesson described here takes advantage of the variety of statistical representations found in newspapers (see Kitchen, 1999). I developed it for prospective high school mathematics teachers during a secondary-level mathematics methods class. As part of an initial assignment, prospective teachers analyzed how statistics were depicted in the newspaper over the duration of several months and were challenged to find recurring topics or themes in the actual content of the articles in which statistics were presented. For the second assignment, the prospective teachers not only constructed and made inferences from statistics, but also confronted the ramifications of the data. Throughout the semester, I maintained a journal in which I kept an ongoing record of what occurred in class.

Working in groups consisting of three or four, the prospective teachers were distributed articles collected over the course of 2 months. The only articles reviewed were those from the cover section that included a visual representation of statistics. My goals for the first part of the lesson were to engage prospective teachers in the study of statistics displayed in newspapers and to motivate examination of how the use of statistics enhanced specific stories. The prospective teachers were asked to investigate how statistics were represented over the course of 2 months in the print media. The prospective teachers' most striking finding was how few articles actually incorporated a chart, table, or graph. Surprisingly, of the 60 newspapers surveyed, only 16 editions included at least one visual statistical representation, whereas 2 newspapers included two articles in which statistics were exhibited. The prospective teachers discovered that the most common theme across the 20 articles was race or ethnicity. In six of the articles, race or ethnicity was the focal point.

The conclusions that the prospective mathematics teachers derived from the charts, tables, and graphs found in the newspaper articles led to rich discussions. Emotionally charged discussions ensued when the statistics were highly relevant to the prospective teachers. The more interesting the data, the more the prospective teachers were willing to analyze the data and draw inferences from them. We considered such divergent issues as the presentation of data in newspapers, the decision-making process involved to select the articles in which statistics are incorporated, and the relative scarcity of articles that actually included statistics in some graphic format. The assignment also inspired debate about the appropriateness of various data for inclusion in the high school mathematics curriculum.

I contend that, as mathematics teachers, we also have a responsibility to work with our students to help them clarify and deal with the conclusions that they make from statistics. With this in mind, I created a second part to the project. It was intended to serve as a sample lesson in which teachers prompt students not only to draw inferences from data, but also to deal with the potential consequences that these data have for their students' lives.

The focus of the second part of the project was on the revamped admissions policies at the University of California (UC) and the University of Texas at Austin (UT-Austin) that nullified affirmative-action policies. At the time this project was undertaken, two articles appeared in the newspaper that described how the new admissions policies at these universities benefited Asians and Whites, but were detrimental to Blacks and Latinos (Lubman, 1997). At UT-Austin, whereas the percentage of Blacks and Hispanics accepted to the university declined from 1996 to 1997 by 17% (from 54% to 37%) and by 9% (from 63% to 54%), respectively, the percentage of Whites and Asians accepted increased by 9% (from 56% to 65%) and by 8% (from 60% to 68%), respectively (Lubman, 1997; and see Fig. 3.1).

These data were especially alarming considering that fewer Blacks, Hispanics, Whites, and Asians applied to UT-Austin in 1997 than in 1996. At UC, similarly alarming trends occurred from 1995 to 1997. During this 2-year period, the number of freshman applicants decreased by 8% among Blacks and 18% among Hispanics, but increased by 11% among Asians and Pacific Islanders and 18% among Whites (Lubman, 1997).

For high school teachers, these articles provided opportunities to help students, specifically their Black and Latina/o students, to become informed about how to offset the very real repercussions that these revised admissions policies had for them. After having their students interpret the significance of these data, teachers could have their students investigate how these admissions policies would impact them. In particular, students could research the new application requirements of UC, UT-Austin, and

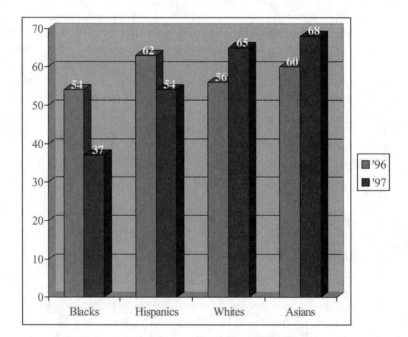

FIG. 3.1.   UT-Austin admission rates (by percentage) by race.

other universities. The purpose of the second part of the assignment was to provoke students to deal with the consequences of the new entrance policies. For instance, teachers could help their students of color understand these new admission policies and support them to overcome these changes. Teachers could also encourage their students to apply to universities that demonstrate their commitment to addressing historical injustices by actively working to recruit students of color.

I believe that we have a responsibility to K–12 students to select data that are relevant to them, and to help them resolve the inferences that they make from these data. The study of real-world statistics from the print media can also be viewed as an opportunity for teachers to demonstrate to their students that they are willing to help them resolve complex and unsettling issues. More important, teachers can offer valuable guidance and insights to students by not sidestepping the study of highly political issues in the mathematics classroom. Ultimately, this is a powerful way for mathematics teachers to show their students that they care about them.

DISCUSSION AND FINAL REMARKS

I believe the activities described are aligned with the first four of Zeichner's five characteristics (1996) of teacher education programs that prepare prospective teachers to teach for diversity. Specifically, the activities validate that all students can succeed, help prospective teachers to bridge students' home cultures with the school culture (e.g., visit to the Pueblo), and provide prospective teachers with experiences to learn about the socioeconomic and political circumstances of their students. These experiences can profoundly impact how prospective teachers view diverse students and the access that students have to learn mathematics. For some, these activities motivate the sort of critical reflection that leads to conceptual transformation.

Preparing teachers to mathematically challenge all of their students requires mathematics teacher educators to actively model the sort of respectful and trusting relationships with prospective mathematics teachers that we are asking them to pursue with their students. Without trust and respect, prospective teachers may not be open to activities that challenge them to examine their beliefs about who can be successful in mathematics. Even worse, they may even actively resist our attempts to model the value of multicultural perspectives and issues of equity. Such resistance could ultimately lead to behaviors that do little to support the learning of students who have historically been underrepresented in mathematics.

Once I have begun to establish a respectful and trusting community of learners, I initiate incorporating multiculturalism and equity implicitly and explicitly into class activities. For activities to be transformative I suggest that they must be made as explicitly connected to classroom practice as possible (see chap. 10, this volume). For example, a visit to an Indian Pueblo led to greater understanding and sensitivity about high rates of school absenteeism for children from Native-American communities. Understanding that American Indians may miss school to attend important cultural ceremonies prepares prospective mathematics teachers to meet the unique needs of Indian children. Moreover, learning about Native-American cultures is important for non-Indians who may know very little about the values of their Indian students.

Examining the insidious effects of ability tracking is directly connected with reflecting upon one's notions about who deserves to experience challenging mathematical instruction. Investigating the racial/ethnic makeup of lower-track classes can lead prospective mathematics teachers to question who has access to learn rigorous mathematical content. It also highlights injustices at the classroom level and is something that they can directly take a stand against when teaching. Using the research protocol to rate their cooperating teacher in access to opportunities to learn, mathematical analysis, and mathematical discourse and communication is related to considering ability tracking and its effects. Prospective mathematics teachers may begin to examine whether their cooperating teacher has varying expectations for students based on the level of the class that they are teaching. For instance, students in an honors algebra course typically experience higher mathematical expectations than students in low-track mathematics courses (Johnson, 1999). These activities, particularly using the research protocol to investigate the learning opportunities of specific students, are a first step toward prospective teachers making personal connections with individual students.

The lesson in which prospective teachers read Sleeter's article (1995) and reviewed statistics that revealed injustices in society should be connected to exploring how prospective teachers can support the learning of historically underrepresented peoples in mathematics. This lesson serves as a means to prompt prospective teachers to consider how poverty affects their students and to acknowledge that students from high-poverty communities may need additional support to be successful in mathematics. Once, the prospective teachers' reaction to the lesson led me to make a presentation on alternative assessment formats that are aligned with instructional approaches based on how people learn (O'Day & Smith, 1993). In my view, it is critically important to provide prospective teachers with practical tools that they can implement in the classroom that supports the learning of all of their students.

I also believe that prospective teachers need to engage in and create rigorous mathematics lessons that validate students' socioeconomic and political realities, while providing students with constructive strategies that they can pursue to improve their lives. This is very important because too often prospective mathematics teachers view multiculturalism and equity as unrelated to their specific discipline. The newspaper lesson in which students explored the revised admissions policies at the University of California and the University of Texas was undertaken with this goal in mind. Confronting an issue that has very real consequences for students makes mathematics relevant and demonstrates that we care about them. This activity also contributed to the pedagogical development of prospective teachers. When they engaged in the lesson, the prospective teachers were involved in actively making meaning of statistical data.

In the future, I want prospective mathematics teachers to read "The Victory Arc" (Froelich, 1991). In this article, it is demonstrated how to use graphing calculators to do mathematical modeling with no regard for ethical issues such as the morality of war. As an example of an applied problem-solving context devoid of consideration of larger societal issues, this article provides the impetus for critical reflection of particular values that mathematics implicitly defends and advocates. By illustrating and describing the mathematics of the firefinder radar system used during the Gulf War with no discussion of the destructive potential of this technology, the use of force is never questioned and is granted legitimacy. I suspect that reading "The Victory Arc" will provoke spirited exchanges among prospective teachers about whether they should address moral and ethical issues with their students such as how mathematics can be used to create weapons of mass destruction.

By being explicitly connected to real mathematics classrooms, these activities have the potential to profoundly influence prospective teachers' conceptions and practices. They provoke prospective teachers to construct more demanding lessons precisely because these activities motivate reflection among prospective teachers about their expectations for students while challenging them to learn more about the contexts of their students' lives. I am interested in conducting research to study how sustainable these changes in prospective teachers' conceptions are during their first few years in the teaching profession. I am especially interested in carrying out collaborative research with prospective teachers who are actively working to teach for diversity at the conclusion of the teacher education program.

I believe that our biggest challenge in doing transformative work is supporting prospective teachers to be continually reflective about their views about who can achieve and participate in mathematics in a highly diverse society. For this to be possible, mathematics educators must strive to explicitly incorporate multiculturalism and equity in all courses taken by prospective mathematics teachers. Given the ever-increasing volume of research on teachers' resistance to teaching for diversity, it is clear that this work is complex and that teachers will need ongoing professional development to build capacity to teach for diversity.

REFERENCES

Abraham, J., & Bibby, N. (1988). Mathematics and society: Ethnomathematics and the public educator curriculum. *For the Learning of Mathematics, 8*(2), 2–11.

Apple, M. W. (1985). *Education and power.* New York: Routledge, ARK Edition.

Apple, M. W. (1996). *Cultural politics and education.* New York: Teachers College Press.

Atweh, B., Bleicher, R. E., & Cooper, T. J. (1998). The construction of the social context of mathematics classrooms: A sociolinguistic analysis. *Journal for Research in Mathematics Education, 29*(1), 63–82.

Banks, J. A., & Banks, C. A. (1995). *Handbook of research on multicultural education.* New York: Macmillan.

Barro, S. (1984). *The incidence of dropping out: A descriptive analysis.* Washington, DC: Economic Research, Inc.

Bishop, A. J. (1991). *Mathematical enculturation.* Dordrecht, Netherlands: Kluwer.

Bohl, J. (1999). *Teaching mathematics for American Democracy project.* Madison: University of Wisconsin-Madison.

Boyer, J. B., & Baptiste, H. P., Jr. (1996). The crisis in teacher education in America: Issues of recruitment and retention of culturally different (minority) teachers. In J. Sikula, T. Buttery, & E. Guyton (Eds.), *Handbook of research on teacher education* (2nd ed., pp. 779–794). New York: Association of Teacher Educators.

Burton, L. (1994). Whose culture includes mathematics? In S. Lerman (Ed.), *Cultural perspectives on the mathematics classroom* (pp. 69–83). Dordrecht, Netherlands: Kluwer.

Cole, M., & Griffin, P. (1987). *Contextual factors in education.* Madison: Wisconsin Center for Education Research.

D'Ambrosio, B. S. (1991). The modern mathematics reform movement in Brazil and its consequences for Brazilian mathematics education. *Educational Studies in Mathematics, 22,* 69–85.

D'Ambrosio, U. (1983). Successes and failures of mathematics curricula in the past two decades: A developing society viewpoint in a holistic framework. In *Proceedings of the fourth international Congress of Mathematical Education* (pp. 362–364). Boston: Berkhäuser.

Delpit, L. (1988). The silenced dialogue: Power and pedagogy in educating other people's children. *Harvard Educational Review, 58*(3), 280–298.

Ernest, P. (1991). *The philosophy of mathematics education.* London: Falmer Press.

Froelich, G. (1991). The victory arc. *Consortium: The Newsletter of the Consortium for Mathematics and Its Applications, 38,* 2–5.

Gerdes, P. (1988). Culture and geometric thinking. *Educational Studies in Mathematics, 22,* 137–162.

Gomez, M. L. (1996). Prospective teachers' perspectives on teaching "other people's" children. In K. Zeichner, S. Melnick, & M. L. Gomez (Eds.), *Currents of reform in preservice teacher education* (pp. 109–132). New York: Teachers College Press.

Gomez, M. L., & Tabachnick, B. R. (1992). Telling teaching stories. *Teaching Education, 4*(2), 129–138.

Haberman, M. (1991). The pedagogy of poverty versus good teaching. *Phi Delta Kappan, 73,* 290–294.

Hersh, R. (1979). Some proposals for revising the philosophy of mathematics. *Advances in Mathematics, 31,* 31–50.

Ingersoll, R. M. (1999). The problem of underqualified teachers in American secondary schools. *Educational Researcher, 28*(2), 26–37.

Johnson, T. M. (1999). A teacher's roles and calculator tasks in two twelfth-grade mathematics courses. Columbus, OH: ERIC Clearinghouse for Science, Mathematics and Environmental Education. (ERIC Document Reproduction Service No. ED434017)

Jordan, M. L. R. (1995). Reflections on the challenges, possibilities and perplexities of preparing preservice teachers for culturally diverse classrooms. *Journal of Teacher Education, 46,* 369–374.

Joseph, G. (1991). *The crest of the peacock: Non-European roots of mathematics.* London: I. B. Tauris.

Kincheloe, J. L., & McLaren, P. L. (1994). Rethinking critical theory and qualitative research. In N. K. Denzin & Y. S. Lincoln (Eds.), *Handbook of qualitative research* (pp. 138–157). Thousand Oaks, CA: Sage.

Kitchen, R. S. (1999). Analyzing and making sense of statistics in newspapers. *The Mathematics Teacher, 92*(4), 318–322.

Kitchen, R. S. (2001). The sociopolitical context of mathematics education in Guatemala through the words and practices of two teachers. In B. Atweh, H. Forgasz, & B. Nebres (Eds.), *Sociocultural research on mathematics education: An international perspective* (pp. 151–162). Mahwah, NJ: Lawrence Erlbaum Associates.

Kitchen, R. S. (2003). Getting real about mathematics education reform in high poverty communities. *For the Learning of Mathematics, 23*(3), 16–22.

Kitchen, R. S., & Lear, J. M. (2000). Mathematizing Barbie: Using measurement as a means for girls to analyze their sense of body image. In W. G. Secada (Ed.), *Changing the faces of mathematics* (pp. 67–73). Reston, VA: National Council of Teachers of Mathematics.

Kitchen, R. S., Velásquez, D., & Myers, J. (1999). *Dropout intervention and prevention in New Mexico's schools with a special emphasis on Hispanics and Native Americans.* Albuquerque: New Mexico Research and Study Council, University of New Mexico.

Kleinfeld, J. (1992). Learning to think like a teacher: The study of cases. In J. Shulman (Ed.), *Case methods in teacher education* (pp. 33–49). New York: Teachers College Press.

Knapp, M. S., & Woolverton, S. (1995). Social class and schooling. In J. Banks & C. Banks (Eds.), *Handbook of research on multicultural education* (pp. 548–569). New York: Macmillan.

Kulm, G. (1994). *Mathematics assessment: What works in the classroom.* San Francisco: Jossey-Bass.

Ladson-Billings, G. (1994). *The dreammakers: Successful teachers of African American children.* San Francisco: Jossey-Bass.

Ladson-Billings, G. (1995a). But that's just good teaching! The case for culturally relevant pedagogy. *Theory Into Practice, 34*(3), 159–165.

Ladson-Billings, G. (1995b). Toward a theory of culturally relevant pedagogy. *American Educational Research Journal, 32,* 465–491.

Lakatos, I. (1976). *Proofs and refutations.* Cambridge, England: Cambridge University Press.

Lee, O. (1999). Equity implications based on the conceptions of science achievement in major reform documents. *Review of Educational Research, 69*(1), 83–115.

Lubman, S. (1997). UC can learn from colorblind policy at Texas. *San Jose Mercury News,* pp. 1A, March 24, 1997.

McLaughlin, M. W., Shepard, L. A., & O'Day, J. A. (1995). *Improving education through standards-based reform: A report by the National Academy of Education Panel on Standards-based Education Reform.* Stanford, CA: Stanford University, National Academy of Education.

Mellin-Olsen, S. (1987). *The politics of mathematics education.* Dordrecht, Netherlands: Reidel.

Moses, R. P., & Cobb, C. E., Jr. (2001). *Radical equations: Math literacy and civil rights.* Boston: Beacon Press.

Murrell, P., Jr. (1992, April). *Deconstructing informal knowledge of exemplary teaching in diverse urban communities: Apprenticing preservice teachers as case study researchers in cultural sites.*

Paper presented at the annual meeting of the American Educational Research Association, San Francisco.

National Center for Education Statistics. (1994). *Characteristics of the 100 largest public elementary and secondary school districts in the United States: 1991–1992.* Washington, DC: Author.

National Center for Research in Mathematics Education. (1992). Wisconsin Center for Educational Research. Madison, WI: University of Wisconsin-Madison.

National Council of Teachers of Mathematics. (1989). *Curriculum and evaluation standards for school mathematics.* Reston, VA: Author.

National Council of Teachers of Mathematics. (2000). *Principles and standards for school mathematics.* Reston, VA: Author.

National Education Association. (1997). *Status of the American public school teacher, 1995–96.* Washington, DC: Author.

National Research Council. (2001). *Educating teachers of science, mathematics and technology: New practices for the new millennium.* Washington, DC: National Academy Press.

National Science Foundation. (1996). *Indicators of science and mathematics education 1995.* Arlington, VA: Author.

Nieto, S. (2000). Placing equity front and center: Some thoughts on transforming teacher education for a new century. *Journal of Teacher Education, 51*(3), 180–187.

Oakes, J. (1985). *Keeping track: How schools structure inequality.* New Haven, CT: Yale University Press.

Oakes, J. (1990). *Lost talent: The underparticipation of women, minorities and disabled persons in science.* Santa Monica, CA: Rand.

O'Day, J. A., & Smith, M. S. (1993). Systemic school reform and educational opportunity. In S. H. Fuhrman (Ed.), *Designing coherent educational policy: Improving the system* (pp. 250–311). San Francisco: Jossey-Bass.

Osborne, A. B. (1996). Practice into theory into practice: Culturally relevant pedagogy for students we have marginalized and normalized. *Anthropology and Education Quarterly, 27*(3), 285–314.

Roy, F. M. (2000). Technology and equity: A consistent vision for school mathematics? In W. G. Secada (Ed.), *Changing the faces of mathematics* (pp. 37–46). Reston, VA: National Council of Teachers of Mathematics.

Scott, R. M. (1995). Helping teacher education students develop positive attitudes toward ethnic minorities. *Equity & Excellence in Education, 28,* 69–73.

Secada, W. G. (1992). Race, ethnicity, social class, language, and achievement in mathematics. In D. A. Grouws (Ed.), *Handbook of research on mathematics teaching and learning* (pp. 623–660). New York: Macmillan.

Skovsmose, O. (1994). *Towards a philosophy of critical mathematics education.* Dordrecht, Netherlands: Kluwer.

Sleeter, C. E. (1994). White racism. *Multicultural Education, 1*(4), 5–8, 39.

Sleeter, C. E. (1995). White preservice students and multicultural education coursework. In J. M. Larkin & C. E. Sleeter (Eds.), *Developing multicultural teacher education curricula* (pp. 17–29). Albany: State University of New York Press.

Tate, W. F. (1997). Race-ethnicity, SES, gender, and language proficiency trends in mathematics achievement: An update. *Journal for Research in Mathematics Education, 28*(6), 652–679.

Tatum, B. D. (1992). Talking about race, learning about racism: The application of racial identity development theory in the classroom. *Harvard Educational Review, 62,* 1–24.

U.S. Bureau of the Census. (1993a). *Money income of households, families, and persons in the United States: 1992* (Current Population Reports, Series P60-184, p. xviii). Washington, DC: U.S. Government Printing Office.

U.S. Bureau of the Census. (1993b). *Poverty in the United States: 1992* (Current Population Reports, Series P60-185, p. viii). Washington, DC: U.S. Government Printing Office.

U.S. Department of Education. (1998). *No more excuses: The final report of the Hispanic dropout project*. Washington, DC: Author.

Watkins, K. (2000, March). *Community inquiries: Prospective science teachers exploring the world of their students*. Paper presented at the meeting of the National Association of Research in Science Teaching, St. Louis, MO.

Wiggins, G. P. (1993). *Assessing student performance: Exploring the purpose and limits of testing*. San Francisco: Jossey-Bass.

Zeichner, K. (1996). Educating teachers for cultural diversity. In K. Zeichner, S. Melnick, & M. L. Gomez (Eds.), *Currents of reform in preservice teacher education* (pp. 133–151). New York: Teachers College Press.

APPENDIX

CLASSROOM OBSERVATION ASSIGNMENT AND PROTOCOL

The purpose of this assignment is to understand some of your cooperating teacher's practices and conceptions (beliefs and knowledge) about curriculum, instruction, and assessment. In particular, this assignment draws attention to how teachers integrate aspects of their mathematics instruction while providing diverse students opportunities to learn mathematics. For this assignment, you will rate the effectiveness of instruction of one mathematics lesson in the following areas: mathematical analysis, mathematical discourse and communication, and access to opportunities to learn. In your write-up, you will need to give a rating of the effectiveness of the teacher in each of these three areas in the lesson with a brief justification that includes examples of your rating. A brief description of each of these areas and a corresponding 3-point rating scale follow.

Access to Opportunities to Learn Mathematics

This scale assesses the extent to which students have access to opportunities to learn mathematics during the lesson. There are a variety of things to consider when assessing the teacher's effectiveness in this area. First, does the teacher allow a variety of students to speak during the listen; that is, does the teacher call on equal numbers of females and males, Hispanics and Whites? Is the classroom environment set up in such a way or does the teacher make adjustments during instruction to allow for all students to be involved in the lesson, not just the students sitting closest to the teacher? Second, students are engaged in learning mathematics during the lesson. To score high on this scale, students must be engaged in the lesson's actual content; they cannot be engaged in reading comics or in completing yesterday's homework (unless that homework assignment is the topic at hand). Third, the teacher is clearly aware that students bring different educational experiences and may not speak English as their first language. Some students may need additional assistance during a lesson or may need to be challenged further. To score high on this scale, the teacher is clearly aware that students have different educational needs and attends to these needs in some way. Also, the teacher may communicate at a level that is at or slightly above the students' level of communication to support the learning of limited English proficiency (LEP) students. Essentially, to provide equitable opportunities for students to learn mathematics, you should notice that the teacher is aware of the need to structure the learning environment and the lesson to support the mathematical learning of all students.

Mathematical Analysis

The rating scale for this area is intended to measure the extent to which students engage in mathematical analysis in the lesson that you observe. Mathematical analysis can be thought of as higher order thinking that involves mathematics, that is, thinking that goes beyond mathematically recording or reporting mathematical facts, rules, and definitions or mechanically applying algorithms. Mathematical analysis involves searching for mathematical patterns, making mathematical conjectures, and justifying those conjectures. Analysis also includes organizing, synthesizing, evaluating, speculating, arguing, hypothesizing, describing patterns, making models or simulations, and inventing original procedures. In all of these cases, the content of the thinking is mathematics. Mathematical analysis might take place almost accidentally or seemingly, as an aside to the main flow of the lesson. For example, the teacher may ask a rhetorical question whose posing, if the question were taken seriously, would provide evidence of mathematical analysis. Even if some students call out the answer before the teacher has the opportunity to proceed with the lesson, the mathematical analysis is a diversion from the lesson's real thrust.

Mathematical Discourse and Communication

This scale assesses the extent to which talking is used to learn and understand mathematics in the classroom. There are two dimensions to this construct; one involves mathematical content, and the other the nature of the dialogue. In classes characterized by high levels of mathematical discourse and communication, there is considerable teacher–student and student–student interaction about the mathematical ideas of a topic; the interaction is reciprocal, and it promotes coherent shared understanding. First, the talk is about mathematics and includes higher order thinking, such as making distinctions, applying ideas, forming generalization, and raising questions; not just reporting experiences, facts, definition, or procedures. Second, the conversation involves sharing ideas and is not completely scripted or controlled by one party (as in teacher-led recitation). Sharing is best illustrated when participants explain themselves or ask questions in complete sentences, and when they respond directly to previous speakers' comments. Third, the dialogue builds coherently on participants' ideas to promote improved, shared understandings of a mathematical theme or topic (which does not necessarily require summary statements). In short, mathematical discourse and communication resembles the kind of sustained exploration of content characteristic of a good seminar where student contributions lead to shared understandings.

Note that in classes with high numbers of LEP students, mathematical discourse and communication may be composed of very short English sentences or LEP students may speak only in their native languages. In classes where there is little or no mathematical discourse and communication, teacher–student interaction typically consists of a lecture with recitation in which the teacher deviates very little from delivering a preplanned body of information and set of questions: Students typically give very short answers. There is often little or no follow-up to student responses. Such discourse is the oral equivalent of fill-in-the-blank or short-answer study questions. In a whole-class setting, students could participate in mathematical discourse and communication by listening and being attentive to the conversations that take place. Students do *not* have to all take turns speaking; such turn taking may interfere with communication. Rather, students may selectively make comments when they have something to add. In small-group settings, mathematical communication is likely to be more broadly spread throughout the group. In both cases, the issue is one of balance; no one person should dominate the conversation.

RATING SCALES

Rating 1

- *Access to Opportunities to Learn Mathematics:* Only a few students are encouraged to participate during the lesson. Students are frequently off-task as evidenced by inattention or serious disruptions by many students (20%–50%). The teacher does not invite students to use their home language and does not communicate at or slightly above students' level.

- *Mathematical Analysis:* Students receive, recite, or perform routine procedures. In no activities during the lesson do students engage in mathematical analysis.

- *Mathematical Discourse and Communication:* Virtually no features of mathematical discourse and communication occur, or what occurs is of a fill-in-the-blank nature.

Rating 2

- *Access to Opportunities to Learn Mathematics:* The teacher appears to be aware of the need to encourage a diverse group of students to participate during the lesson. Most students (50%–90%) are engaged in class activities some of the time (10%–20%), but this engagement may be uneven and may be dependent on frequent prodding from the teacher. The teacher, some of the time (10%–20%), invites students to use their home language and encourages more-English-proficient students to assist less-proficient students, but still may not communicate at or slightly above students' level.
- *Mathematical Analysis:* There is at least one significant activity involving mathematical analysis in which some (10%–20%) students engage. Or, mathematical analysis that is primarily diversionary in nature occurs throughout the lesson.
- *Mathematical Discourse and Communication:* There is at least one sustained episode of sharing and developing collective understanding about mathematics that involves: (a) a small group of students or (b) a small group of students and the teacher. Or, brief episodes of sharing and developing collective understandings occur sporadically throughout the lesson.

Rating 3

- *Access to Opportunities to Learn Mathematics:* Most students (50%–90%) participate during the lesson. Almost all students (90% or more) are deeply involved in learning the substance of the lesson. Students are free to use their home language for clarification and learning when needed. The teacher, most of the time (50%–90%), communicates at or slightly above the students' level of communication. Most students (50%–90%), most of the time (50%–90%), understand the teacher or the lesson.
- *Mathematical Analysis:* Most students (50%–90%), for most of the time (50%–90%), are engaged in mathematical analysis.
- *Mathematical Discourse and Communication:* The creation and maintenance of collective understandings permeates the entire lesson. This could include the use of a common terminology and the careful negotiation of meanings.

4

Using Inquiry Processes to Investigate Knowledge, Skills, and Perceptions of Diverse Learners: An Approach to Working With Prospective and Current Science Teachers

Marianne B. Barnes
Lehman W. Barnes
University of North Florida

National and state science education standards are imbued with the theme of science for all learners (American Association for the Advancement of Science [AAAS], 1989); National Research Council [NRC], 1996). Science teaching strategies are incorporated into the various documents, but issues and challenges facing the goal of meeting individual learner needs are addressed in only a perfunctory fashion. Social inequalities are often made invisible in the implementation of education reform (Rodriguez, 1999) and the achievement gap separating diverse, low-income students from those who are more economically privileged remains problematic (Lynch, 2001; Warren, Ballenger, Ogonowski, Rosebery, & Hudicourt-Barnes, 2001). Even the Standards for Staff Development include equity under the heading of content and address it in a broad, general manner (National Staff Development Council, 2001).

In a recent review of research on preparing teachers for culturally diverse schools, Sleeter (2001) argued the need for more research connecting prospective teacher education with community-based learning and ongoing professional development. We are involved in a mathematics and science systemic reform initiative with the large, urban Jacksonville, Florida, school system. We engage in considerable joint planning and reflecting with school personnel on both prospective and current teacher education. Our collective goal is the development of a continuum of professional development that begins in the preservice years and is designed to equip teachers with the knowledge and skills to enhance the learning of all students.

Our efforts have led us to conclude that inquiry-focused science instruction, deemed foundational to science learning (Minstrell & van Zee, 2000; NRC, 1996), is problematic to implement, even for master teachers. Implicit in the avoidance of inquiry models is the belief that students must "prove themselves" before they can be trusted to manipulate materials toward the end of generating their own questions and hypotheses; they need structure and factual knowledge, including many special science words, first. According to Alberts (2000):

> In the worst case, a teacher of this type of science is assuming that education consists of filling a student's head with a huge set of word associations—such as mitochondria with "powerhouse of the cell," DNA with "genetic material," or motion with "kinetic energy." This would seem to make preparation for life nearly indistinguishable with the preparation for a quiz show, or the game of trivial pursuit. (p. 3)

Many teachers and prospective teachers believe that urban students learn more via "direct instruction." To them, inquiry is a level that must be earned and is not fundamental to learning and assessment processes, especially in multicultural, socioeconomically diverse, urban settings. However, evidence exists that highly structured lessons that encourage exact modeling by students are associated with less favorable attitudes toward science and lower inquiry skills achievement (Fisher & Waldrip, 1999). In addition, we and our partners have concluded that, even after years of instruction in the sciences, most prospective and current teachers have never been immersed in authentic inquiry contexts themselves. Therefore, they are not convinced of the value of inquiry, even in their own learning. Our urban initiative purports to be grounded in inquiry into both science and mathematics learning and into the needs of students and teachers. Our challenge is revealed in the following question: How are we to convince current and prospective teachers of the power of inquiry processes for themselves and all of their students, especially those from diverse, low-SES (socioeconomic status), urban settings?

To begin to answer that critical question, we have collaborated with our local, urban school system and leveraged resources from federal, state, and local funding sources. Our personal, White, middle-class backgrounds have been augmented by experiences and perceptions of other members of our ethnically diverse team and by our own reading, reflection, and relationships with prospective and current teachers and students (college and precollege) over many years. Our work with teachers supports the use of a multifaceted model that considers inquiry into science, self, the individual learner, and the learning community. In this chapter, we describe our theoretical framework, context, methods, strategies, and implications.

THEORETICAL FRAMEWORK

Our work is informed by the intersection of research, theory, and practice grounded in the following areas: how people learn; needs, prior knowledge, and behaviors of diverse learners; the processes of inquiry; teacher professional development; and coaching/mentoring.

How People Learn

In order to elucidate the complexities of human learning, multidisciplinary cognitive scientists and educators have used current research and practice to replace past models derived largely from behaviorist theories (J. R. Anderson, 1980; Gardner, 1991). The American Psychological Association (1997) offers 14 research-based, learner-centered principles, primarily internal to the learner and under the learner's control. These principles are classified into four categories that go far beyond knowledge alone: cognitive and metacognitive factors, motivational and affective factors, developmental and social factors, and individual factors.

Arguing for the importance of learning actively constructed by the learner, Novak (1998) claimed that meaningful learning underlies constructive integration of thinking, feeling, and acting and leads to empowerment for commitment and responsibility. Constructivist learning theories have been elucidated by researchers in the past few decades (Driver & Oldham, 1986; Novak, 1977; O'Loughlin, 1992; von Glaserfeld, 1992). Learners need to feel engaged in the learning process by reconciling new ideas and experiences with current conceptual frameworks. If new information does not readily integrate into learners' existing frameworks, then learners need support to accommodate the new information.

The NRC (2000) provides information on students from backgrounds that are not mainstream and middle-class. For these students, learner-centered teachers must construct bridges between subject matter and students. These supportive structures are built on a foundation of learners' prior knowledge, their past experiences, and the students' many voices. In school science settings, students express both scientific and social intentions in their discourse. Both must be valued, especially among learners who begin with stronger social and cultural rather than traditional scientific knowledge and skills.

Cognizant of the complexities associated with learning by students with varying characteristics and prior experiences, we have adopted a sociotransformative constructivist (sTc) approach to learning, focusing on science content and process in complex, diverse contexts. The sTc approach asserts that learning is constructed by individuals in social settings (O'Loughlin, 1992), mediated by multicultural considerations (Rodriguez, 1998). We fear that, in our state and others in the country, educational decisions are made on the basis of limited information emanating from selected content test scores. Schools are labeled as "failing," signaling that learning is not happening in those settings. In the words of one principal in our area: "Our school has a name and it is not 'failing.' " Our research and practice focus on nurturing the processes of learning by understanding the texture and landscape of learning and transforming erroneous, preconceived notions about diverse learners.

Needs, Prior Knowledge, and Behaviors of Diverse Learners

Learners enter classrooms with unique sets of cultural influences, life experiences, prior learnings, attitudes, and personalities. Diversity within any group must be acknowledged and includes variables such as educational levels, SES, religious and political affiliation, and occupational status (Marshall, 2002). Children's everyday ways of knowing may be considered as discontinuous or continuous with scientific ways of knowing. In this regard, evidence exists that even among learners who have been marginalized, everyday experiences and thinking patterns show rigor and generativity that may be connected to science learning (Warren et al., 2001). These connections, however, depend on a teacher's willingness to help students to negotiate border crossings between their own experiential backgrounds and the knowledge and skills that underlie science learning (Aikenhead & Jegede, 1999).

Language and culture are important dimensions in students' construction of knowledge (Lee, 2001; Lynch, 2001; Marshall, 2002; NRC, 2000). Indeed, all students need an "opportunity to learn," a civil right beyond and more fundamental than shared space in schools; student needs must encompass time, quality, and technology (Tate, 2001).

When students are not granted equitable learning opportunities, inequalities persist. National Assessment of Educational Progress (NAEP) data released in 2000 indicate an increase in the achievement gap between Black and White students for nearly every NAEP subject, reversing an apparent trend in closing that gap from the early 1970s until the early 1990s.

Commenting on these data, Sadowski (2001) acknowledged that multiple factors must be studied more deeply within the walls of individual schools if reasons behind the gap are to be comprehended. He cited efforts to design and implement research projects between schools and higher education institutions and suggested that unique school cultures and student populations argue for locally driven research. A College Board report (1999) broadens the concern with data showing academic achievement lower than White and Asian students for African American, Latino, and Native American students. Fundamental changes to many current school practices must occur if the needs of low-performing students are to be met (Goodwin, 2000). We believe that all students can learn and all must be given opportunities to inquire. Guided by inquiry into their learning needs, the teacher constructs bridges for each student between the world that the student knows and the world of science that each student has the right to know. Therefore, one of the goals of the Jacksonville Urban Systemic Initiative (JUSI) is to explore the terrain of schools and classrooms and devise strategies for transformative action leading to effective science teaching and learning for each student.

The Processes of Inquiry

Inquiry is an approach to investigation in the sciences and is essential to science learning (Bruner, 1961; Minstrell & van Zee, 2000; NRC, 1996). In the National Science Education Standards, inquiry is defined as "a set of interrelated processes by which scientists and students pose questions about the natural world and investigate phenomena; in doing so, students acquire knowledge and develop a rich understanding of concepts, principles, models, and theories" (NRC, 1996, p. 214). When students are immersed in inquiry-based learning, they engage in a number of behaviors, such as question-asking, planning, using tools and techniques to gather data, looking at relationships and explanations emerging from data, formulating and using models, recognizing and analyzing alternative explanations and models, and communicating findings (Bybee, 2000; NRC, 1996). Though many studies of inquiry have occurred with various groups of students and teachers (Rath & Brown, 1996; Roth, McGinn, & Bowen, 1998; Shapiro, 1996; Supovitz, Mayer, & Kahle, 2000), further aspects of inquiry need to be explored in diverse settings by studying multiple variables of teacher beliefs, knowledge, and inquiry practices, as well as student learning (Keys & Bryan, 2001).

Inquiry provides the organizing conceptual framework for our work. We agree with the inquiry definitions cited, but we believe that the sphere of inquiry needs to expand so that it includes ongoing investigations into science, science learning, human interactions, and teacher development.

Inquiry teaching and learning and scientific inquiry are interrelated (R. D. Anderson, 2002). We believe that when students and teachers resist learning and changing, they are defending a status quo situation because they have not experienced a better alternative. Thus, investigating the reasons that people resist change must occur. At some level, protecting the "known" is less troublesome than altering it. Only when new behaviors are regarded as more beneficial than the old ones will inertia be confronted and new directions result. Transformational work in the realm of science teaching and learning in diverse settings requires time, energy, and a perceived, worthwhile outcome.

Teacher Professional Development

The National Center for Improving Science Education (1993) identified seven principles that, when addressed, promote effective experiences in professional development. These experiences should:

1. Be driven by a well-defined image of effective classroom learning and teaching.
2. Provide opportunities for teachers to build their knowledge and skills.
3. Use or model with teachers the strategies teachers will use with their students.
4. Build a learning community.
5. Support teachers to serve in leadership roles.
6. Provide links to other parts of the educational system.
7. Continually be reassessed for improvements to ensure positive impacts on teacher effectiveness, student learning, leadership, and the school community.

Amplifying these principles, nine critical issues must be addressed in designing sound professional development experiences (Loucks-Horsley, Hewson, Love, & Stiles, 1998): ensuring equity, building a professional culture, developing leadership, building capacity for professional learning, scaling up, garnering public support, supporting standards and frameworks, evaluating experiences, and finding time for appropriate professional development. Teacher professional development research findings reinforce the importance of active teacher communities of learners who are treated as professionals and who learn through active inquiry in conducive contexts (Bell & Gilbert, 1996; Lieberman & Miller, 1999; Loucks-Horsley et al., 1998).

If teachers are to reach diverse learners with whom they interact, they must be prepared with cultural tool kits and related skills to understand and facilitate learning that builds upon experiences that may be different from their own (Seiler, 2001). Indeed, the tool kits should be introduced and embraced in teacher education programs that focus on multicultural, transformative education (Nieto, 2000). Arguing for a multicultural social reconstructionist (MCSR) approach, Martin and van Gunten (2002) advocated action research focused on positionality, a construct that has prospective teachers examine the meaning of their own lives and explore that meaning in relationship to the lives of others. Thereby, educational institutions become more democratic and humane as power relationships are transformed and historically marginalized groups are heard.

We believe in an inquiry approach to teacher professional development supported by collegial partners with multiple backgrounds and expertise. As teachers continue to build their tool kits, they need access to diverse, constructivist learning environments where change-based science teaching is wedded to reflection and support (Harcombe, 2001). Our USI has evolved into a teacher leader model dedicated to reflective practice and in-depth, long-term support of teachers within and between schools.

Coaching/Mentoring

Mentoring presupposes mutuality and an opportunity for the teacher to reveal the personhood on which good teaching rests (Palmer, 1998). Often associated with teacher induction programs, mentoring relationships require strong interpersonal skills and ongoing dialogue on the part of both parties who engage in attending and listening, reflecting and clarifying, and challenging and confronting (Brott & Kajs, 1998). A complex process that begs for a stronger literature base that goes beyond the descriptive, mentoring includes cognitive, affective, and interpersonal factors (Hawkey, 1997). Effective induction programs built on mentoring should consider orienting the teacher to setting, expectations, and curriculum; improving instruction; and changing the norms of the school culture (Illinois Staff Development Council, 1998).

Coaching employs many principles of mentoring and is used in business as well as educational settings. Using supportive interaction, coaching has enhanced emotional intelligence, nourished the ability to handle change, and increased productivity in business settings (Jay, 2001). Grounded in observation and respect, coaching uses mutual agreements to engage coach and coachee in a dialogue. Coaching requires that the coach appreciate the coachee's understanding of a situation while engaging in inquiry techniques to help the coachee to identify and solve problems. Only after inquiry does the coach use advocacy techniques, thereby strengthening the coachee's ownership of the process (Interaction Associates, 1998).

In order to better prepare ourselves for our work with school system resource teachers, we engaged in intensive professional development of our own coaching skills. We have found that the coaching paradigm supports our overall commitment to inquiry as an organizing theme undergirding constructive approaches to overcoming teacher resistance to change.

Summary of Theoretical Framework

Literature supports the pivotal role of the teacher in the process of transforming classrooms and schools into places where diverse learners thrive by engaging in science inquiry in ways that honor how each person learns. Our work is informed by sTc, with particular focus on attention to factors that are challenging to identify by means of traditional measurement approaches (for example, kinds and degree of interaction and collaboration among both students and teachers, teacher reflectivity, and flow of classroom events). We are convinced that learning is complex and multifaceted for both teachers and their students. Furthermore, we believe that the importance of inquiry and relational aspects of learning need to be acknowledged and developed in work with prospective and current teachers.

Transformation of schools cannot occur without teachers who possess the knowledge, skills, and passion to endure and even flourish in settings that continue to challenge them. If professional development programs are ongoing and relational, using principles of coaching and mentoring, then teachers can inquire well into the challenges faced by their students in science learning settings. Teachers need to model respect for diversity in learning and use strategies that meet diverse needs. We have worked with teachers who define their roles in narrow terms focused on delivery of content. They resist pedagogical change because they do not believe that their mission is to reach all students. After all, students are choosing to learn or not. Are teachers responsible for affecting that choice? Our answer is a strong affirmative in that conditions for learning affect choice. The classroom is not a neutral environment.

Needed in the collective literature of science education are examples and studies that portray and analyze the interaction of myriad elements comprising science teaching and learning, especially in large, urban settings where teacher and student resistance to change are continual challenges. This chapter tells the story of some of our collaborations that are directed at the nexus of these factors.

CONTEXT

The work we describe involves a number of players including the large, urban, Jacksonville (Duval County), Florida, school system with its National Science Foundation (NSF)–supported Urban Systemic Initiative (JUSI) and faculty and staff associated with the University of North Florida (UNF), the Crown Region Area Center for Educational Enhancement (ACEE), and the Florida Collaborative for Excellence in Teacher Preparation (FCETP). Among the 20 largest school districts in the United States, the Duval County Public School System covers more than 800 square miles and employs over 7,000 teachers and 4,000 support personnel who serve approximately 127,404 students in 163 schools. Of the teachers, 3,604 are elementary school teachers, 380 are secondary mathematics teachers, and 309 are secondary science teachers. The student ethnic population consists of 48% White, 43% African American, 4% Hispanic, 3% Asian, and 2% Multiethnic (Duval County Public Schools, 2001).

UNF is a state-supported, comprehensive university with an enrollment of about 14,000 students. UNF faculty and staff work extensively with prospective and current teachers in Northeast Florida with support from several initiatives. In addition to its partnership in JUSI, it serves as the headquarters for the postsecondary component of the Crown Region ACEE, a regional arm of the Florida Department of Education. The focus of ACEE is the professional development of teachers and administrators in 21 school districts, the largest of which is Jacksonville. ACEE focuses on the Florida reform initiatives and the concomitant statewide accountability program. As a partner with 10 other higher education institutions in the FCETP, UNF faculty members have focused on science and mathematics teacher preparation, induction, and recruitment. Our role has evolved into leveraging funding sources to develop a coordinated program for prospective and current teachers, with strong links to area schools and school staff.

METHODOLOGY

In the early 1990s, as JUSI was conceptualized in Jacksonville and focus groups met to determine priorities, partnerships, and knowledge bases, a decision was made to use an Inquiry Model as an organizing construct to guide JUSI at all levels of implementation. The model is depicted in Fig. 4.1.

In line with the spirit and substance of the scientific inquiry process, the model is iterative and grounded in observations that are affected by per-

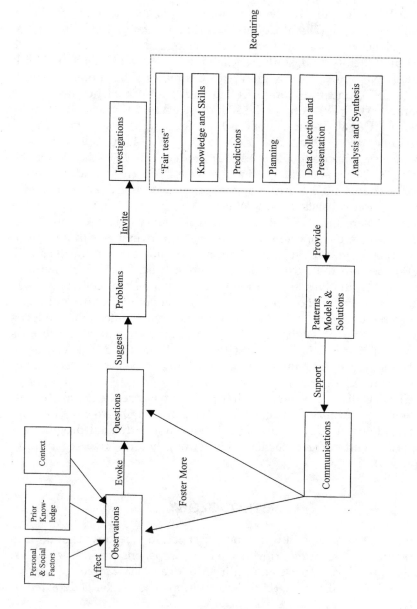

FIG. 4.1. Model for inquiry.

sonal and social factors, prior knowledge, and context. In JUSI, these observations apply to students, teachers, classrooms, schools, other learning communities, and the school system, as well as to physical phenomena. Questions emerge from multiple kinds of observations and suggest problems that need to be investigated by use of "fair tests," using both quantitative and qualitative methods. Explorations may be of physical phenomena, like the relationship between light and organism behavior, or educational situations, such as impact of group learning on achievement of culturally diverse learners. Data collection and analyses depend on relevant knowledge and skills enhanced by well-conceived and well-executed investigative processes. Investigations lead to possible explanations, models, and relationships that need to be communicated and used to inform other cycles of observations, questions, and investigations. Above all, inquiry pervades all aspects of teaching and learning.

We have been and are involved in several manifestations of this inquiry process and we describe two in this chapter. The first involves prospective and current teacher participation in an action-oriented, reflective experience in a course or workshop setting. The second is a longitudinal, action-research approach that involves two components. One component is a facilitated, teacher focus group inquiry into reluctant ninth-grade learners and the other is a teacher's ongoing account and analysis of her own classes. Our own application of the JUSI Inquiry Model allows us to expose layers of complexity that comprise resistance to teaching for diversity and understanding and test approaches to counterresistance.

Inquiry Immersion

We have used an immersion approach to teacher professional development to confront prospective and current teacher resistance by focusing on both experiential and reflective elements. On the Exploratorium Web site (http://www.exploratorium.com) under the Institute for Inquiry link are a series of inquiry activities with discussions. These activities were designed by staff of the Institute for Inquiry at the Exploratorium in San Francisco in order to engage teachers in aspects of inquiry and then consider their own experiences. We chose to use the "foam" activity as a means to introduce inquiry and to generate discussion about personal learning experiences and preferences (http://www.exploratorium.edu/IFI/activities/foam/foam1.html).

In several secondary and elementary science methods courses at our university and in school district workshops, we involved participants in the foam activity (Barnes & Foley, 1999). Students in each class were rotated through three stations, each with a different task. Each station was set up with relevant materials such as two types of detergents, electric and hand mixers, bowls, plates, meter sticks, water, and magnifying glasses. The first station was a guided activity in which students followed a worksheet with details about how to make foam and specific questions comparing the two foam preparations. At the second station, students were challenged to build a foam tower that was at least 12 inches high and was contained on an 11-inch plastic plate. At the third station, students were invited by a facilitator to share examples of foam. Then they were asked to make and observe foam, note its properties, devise questions, and plan and perform experiments with the foam. They had access to more materials at this station, such as soda, eggs, cream of tartar, and shaving cream. However, they did not receive guidelines on how to make foam. After participation in all three activities, the groups engaged in discussion of their experiences and feelings at each station. They compared and contrasted the three approaches to hands-on learning and expressed their own preferences.

Employing qualitative methodology (Guba & Lincoln, 1989), we collected data during the fall of 1998 in one elementary science methods course and one secondary science methods course of approximately 30 people per course. Both sections had a mix of undergraduate and postbaccalaureate prospective or new teachers. Data were collected via field notes, journals, photographs, videotapes, and written responses to questionnaires. We organized the data into categories reflecting the name and activity description, group identification, and whether the responses were interpreted as positive or negative by the researchers.

By rotating through stations, participants experienced three hands-on approaches to teaching science: a step-by-step, didactic method; a challenge with competition; and an open-inquiry activity in which students observe, predict, hypothesize, and engage in experimentation of their choosing. General findings for each station are summarized in Table 4.1.

In addition, sequencing of the stations had an impact on perceptions of participants. When the open-inquiry station was experienced first, more enthusiasm and initiative occurred at that station. However, when inquiry followed the other stations, learners started to explore new materials rather than to observe and examine the foam. They felt that they had already observed foam adequately, even if actual observations had not been recorded and discussed. Participants appeared to acquire knowledge and skills at the stations, either helping or inhibiting them as they progressed through the sequence. Fatigue was a factor and seemed to impact most learners as they moved through the stations. A secondary education teacher made the following comment in her class journal: "Strangely enough, although I can remember the questions my group generated from the first (free inquiry) exercise, I cannot remember the questions that we had to answer in the more directed exercise . . . (maybe these inquiry proponents have something here!)."

TABLE 4.1

Participant Responses to Three Hands-On Science Activities

Guided		Challenge		Inquiry	
Positive	Negative	Positive	Negative	Positive	Negative
• Liked structure • Easy directions • Transferable to classroom	• Boredom on completion • Little stimulation	• Problem-solving • Fully engaged • Student inventiveness • Some enjoyment of competition	• Winners and losers • Some dislike of competition • Time constraint	• Tactile elements • Use of prior knowledge • Freedom to explore • Engaged • Wonder at foam and properties • Quantified observations	• Some felt lost • Some were distracted • No guidelines • Concern with instructor expectations

Note. From Barnes and Foley (1999). Copyright 1999 by University of Nevada, Reno. Adapted by permission.

She wanted to rethink her initial assessment of the worth of the activities because she realized that memory influences learning over time. She seemed surprised at her own finding, as it was so counter to her strong belief in the need to use structured activities with her students.

Though many teachers and prospective teachers agreed that they were most engaged during the inquiry activity, they assumed that urban students need more structure and that the "cookbook" approach should be used first in their classrooms, even though many of them found it to be boring. Class discussions and journal entries indicated that their low expectations of their students or potential students and sense of themselves as classroom authority figures overshadowed their commitment to inquiry teaching. Science teaching seemed to be influenced by their collective experiences in past science courses, as evidenced by the discussions that followed the foam activity. The typical college science class is not set up to accommodate learner individual differences, even in a relatively homogeneous course population. Findings from interviews associated with the Florida Collaborative for Excellence in Teacher Preparation (FCETP), in which we are partners, indicate that faculty feel committed to transmitting the culture of the discipline and performing a gatekeeper role. Students who fail (sometimes as high as 50% of a general education class) are perceived as lazy and/or unprepared. Furthermore, these faculty are unaware of the importance of learner characteristics, including their prior knowledge. When prospective teachers are encultured into a system of winners and losers, they are apt to believe that student failure is a natural consequence of a learner's personal failure to exert the effort to learn. This belief leads to resistance to pedagogical change, as it places blame on students rather than responsibility on the teacher. Consequently, the teacher perceives no reason to delve further into strategies to enhance learning. Inquiry teaching is not even considered because students have not earned the right to inquire. How can the teacher trust underachievers to pursue scientific investigations? Indeed, many current and prospective science teachers believe that students must know and demonstrate knowledge of basic science concepts before they are afforded opportunities to inquire.

The foam activity has been a powerful tool to incorporate belief in the worth of inquiry into prospective and current teacher experiences. When our students and teachers analyze their own preferences and behaviors during this activity, they become aware of diversity even among their own peers. Indeed, many of them acknowledge that they have never engaged in this kind of science inquiry and, beyond that, in its analysis. Some are amazed at the number and quality of hypotheses they are able to generate and test. Although they have experienced and even become proficient in several processes of science, they have not had the freedom to explore and compare methodologies in their course or in-service experiences.

Inquiry into one's own learning informs discussion during which mental models of teaching and learning and beliefs about learners become explicit. We believe that teachers must know themselves and how they learn before they can begin to plan instructional strategies for other learners. Our prospective teachers and those already in classrooms need to think about learning by inquiring into their own learning via appropriate experiences in science and the teaching of science. Then they need to confront their own predictions about student behavior and probe into reasons that they would withhold the excitement of science processes from their students, especially those who are different in background from themselves and whom they feel a need to "control" in a classroom environment. In the pursuit of order in the classroom, teachers often use a form of "direct instruction" by which they tighten their control over the flow of classroom events. When the pressure of high-stakes statewide testing is added, they become even more constrained in their choice of classroom activities. These kinds of defensive tactics on the part of the teacher decrease opportunities for students to inquire and increase the likelihood that students will feel uncomfortable when they actually face inquiry experiences. The students are not "learning how to learn." Rather, they are reinforced to acquire and practice less useful learning strategies. They have less "opportunity to learn" the very strategies that make for successful science learning throughout their years of schooling.

The reflective aspect of the foam activity is critical to begin a process of cracking the resistance of teachers to ideological and pedagogical change. For example, one prospective teacher contrasted the aftermath of the structured foam activity station with the open-ended inquiry station, signaling a readiness to think about consequences of two teaching strategies: "I realized that with the structured lesson that once we were finished, that was it! Just like students do in Junior High or High School. They do what is required of them and that is it. Structured lessons may be easier to evaluate, but they seem to put limits on learning."

After personalized inquiry experiences such as the foam activity, authentic discussions of their feelings about multicultural education—often rooted in fear and defensiveness—are able to ensue and transformative work can begin. Additional in-class deliberations and personal learning experiences are needed to support inquiry teaching strategies for *all* students so that students of various backgrounds, genders, and skin colors are not limited in their learning opportunities. We have connected class discussions with models of how the mind learns and remembers, focusing first on the prospective teachers or teachers, and then on their students. Variables such as attention and perception, with their cultural, social, and emotional overtones, are identified as gatekeepers to the learning path. Sound teacher decision making and student support are required to design and pace appropriate scientific inquiries around learner needs, addressing concerns summarized in Table 4.1.

We have witnessed an increased openness in groups that have experienced and reflected on the foam activity. Working with one another on a phenomenon they have not studied in the past, they are less apt to retrieve formulas or definitions that they have learned in the past. Free to inquire around what appears to be a "childish" exercise,[1] they recapture abilities to observe, classify, infer, and predict—processes that are reinforced throughout our science methods courses and workshops. They learn about their own meaningful learning and the potential of inquiry processes and they share their insights with their peers. One of our prospective teachers affirmed the importance of being free to learn with other prospective teachers. Indeed, added self-knowledge can support reflection on knowledge acquisition by others. The inquiry model becomes useful for probing into the complexities of human learning, as well as into the world of the sciences.

ACTION RESEARCH

We view teacher education as a continuum, and inquiry persists as the prominent theme in our transition from our previous example to the following current teacher development examples. We believe that our credibility with both prospective and current teachers has increased because our own inquiries support an expansive knowledge base that includes teachers at various stages of their careers.

Ninth-Grade Teacher Learning Community

Teacher observation and data analysis in the school district underscored a problem with ninth-grade students' transition into high school and a failure and/or dropout rate of about 50%. More stringent requirements in science and mathematics have been implemented districtwide as a result of JUSI, thereby creating concern about student success in an even more rigorous system. The principal of one of the most diverse schools in the district expressed interest in sensitizing the ninth-grade teachers to the learning characteristics and needs of the ninth graders. In August 2001, ninth-grade teachers received an orientation session based on Mendler's (2000) *Motivating Students Who Don't Care*. Using a think-pair-share strategy, one of our staff members, an African American man with a rich background in working with students in inner-city, alternative schools, asked the teach-

---

[1]In actuality, the study of foam is sophisticated, interdisciplinary science. See Perkowitz, S. (2001). *Universal Foam*. London: Vintage.

ers to describe student behaviors that impede teaching and learning. To those teachers who denied they had a problem, the facilitator said: "Look at the pink elephant in the middle of the room"; that is, the low-SES, minority, nonachieving student is invisible in the system. A problem had been identified and the inquiry process continued via relevant data collection and the search for patterns.

During the ensuing months, the facilitator held monthly discussions among teachers during their planning periods. About 14 regular attendees participated in the semester-long sessions based on action planning, role playing, and recording observations and reflections in learning logs. The teachers expressed a need for tools and strategies to reach their students, especially those in the bottom 25% in achievement. The teachers had become ideologically committed to teaching for diversity, and now they wanted specific suggestions for altering their pedagogy in order to teach for understanding and related student success.

Using a group process, the teachers reflected on their own experiences with failing students and they identified four categories of learners about whom they were concerned: Immature, Disconnected, Marginal, and Defiant (L. Jackson, personal communication, January 25, 2002). Teachers developed behavioral descriptions and intervention strategies associated with those behaviors. With guidance, the teachers realized that their low-achievers were often successful in other settings in their lives, for example, community, church, sports. Their social self-concepts were intact but their academic self-concepts were very low (Kuykendall, 1992). The group members realized a need to expand their thinking toward developing and applying a caregiving model to be perfected with additional data over time. Emanating from enlightened teacher perspectives and an emerging need for stronger relationships with students, the caregiver model is not built on condescension, but, rather, uses elements of coaching as the teacher refers to student success in other areas and provides transitions to new learning opportunities. Teachers create hope by respecting the power of students to "stop" the teaching process and by sending the message that they very much want to teach the students. Individual differences among teachers and students are honored and sharing of "what works for me" occurs. The lines of communication remain open and reach even the silent, withdrawn student, perhaps the most vulnerable of all. The next phase of the project is an extension of the community of learners to include eighth-grade teacher representatives of the two feeder pattern schools.

We have learned that even if all teachers are not willing to devote time and effort toward inquiring into learner needs in a facilitated focus group, a core group of committed teachers from the various disciplines must move forward and model the inquiry process for their reluctant colleagues. With strong support from the school administration, the inquiry focus group approach has become an ongoing manifestation of a school culture rooted in the belief that "all children can learn" and the sustained actions that must accompany that belief.

Individual Teacher Action Research

One member of the ninth-grade focus group teacher team, Ms. C., has worked with us over the past 2 years. A White woman with a strong science background and previous science research experience, she came into our master's program with a desire to teach. Now as a second-year biology teacher at the school, she is involved in teaching a new curriculum. When she approached us about wanting to study her teaching, we suggested that she become involved in her own action research. She has described in detail each teaching day for the last year and she has reflected upon her successes and challenges with her diverse learners. By meeting with us periodically and enrolling in an educational research course taught by one of the authors, she has developed deeper inquiry skills, especially in the area of data analysis. Ms. C. shared two stories that reflect her skills at inquiring into sociocultural needs of her students while her students inquire into science in an experimental, inquiry-based curriculum. Her classroom decisions were based on mutual respect, sharing of power, and the realization that science teaching occurs in a social setting. The first story describes a successful negotiation involving four of her nonparticipatory, albeit nonhostile, male, minority students who sat together at the back of the classroom:

> I pulled one of the students aside and explained that I liked all of them but that I was concerned about their low achievement and lack of participation. I acknowledged that they were not disrupting the class. I told him that they had a choice and that they should talk it over. I was willing to either split them up or move them to the front of the room as a team. I wanted them to be able to learn and I could do that better in one of these arrangements. Maintaining status quo of just getting by was not an option. They discussed the options and decided to move to the front. I was not a dictator, but their concerned teacher. They had power over their choice and they knew I respected them. They moved without any difficulty. (D. Conlon, personal communication, August 7, 2001)

The second story demonstrates her sense of alternative paths to curricular engagement that arise from quick decision making on the part of the teacher. Her students were involved in a group water inquiry lab, and she noticed two minority students, one young man "kicked back in his chair" and one young woman, with "head down." Before calling them to her desk, she grabbed two clipboards and wrote down questions to ask their fellow students and places to record answers. She told them she needed their help in asking the questions as "a teacher" and recording student responses. She stated:

> My thought: in asking, answering and observing they would in essence be doing the lab. The girl grumbled a bit at first when she came up, but they both did their jobs throughout the lab. At the end, I had them summarize their results and I asked them questions in front of the class rather than have each group report. (D. Conlon, personal communication, July 31, 2002)

Indeed, she did need the help of the two students to maintain a culture of involvement in her classroom. For reasons of their own, they chose to refrain from participation until she gave them the message that she needed them. Had she not grounded her relationships with her students in mutual respect, she probably would not have succeeded in engaging them and she might have even regarded them as insubordinate. A trip to a dean's office might have followed. Instead, not only did she involve them, she expressed tacit confidence in their abilities to process and report on responses to lab-related questions to their peers so that inquiry findings could be shared. She described her teacher role as follows: "I travel with my students as we journey through our curriculum. I engender respect because I give respect. At times, not always, you can feel the electricity as connections are made" (D. Conlon, personal communication, July 31, 2002).

Ms. C. continues to search for ways to blend science inquiry with advocacy addressing the balance of individual and group needs. In this fashion, she counters students' resistance to learn in more inclusive and respectful ways.

DISCUSSION AND IMPLICATIONS FOR SCIENCE TEACHER EDUCATION

We believe an inquiry orientation is fundamental to assuring access to science educational opportunities (Kuykendall, 1992; Tate, 2001) for all students, especially the marginalized, the invisible, and the unsuccessful. The challenge is to reach these students and a primary access to them is through well-prepared, sensitized teachers. Students learn from their teachers. Hence, if inquiry processes are to be used by students, these same processes must be modeled by teachers.

Prospective science teachers learn much of their science knowledge and skills in their science classes and laboratories. However, in many cases they themselves have not been immersed in self-directed, inquiry experiences (Roth et al., 1998) and they are not convinced of the value of inquiry approaches for all of their students, especially those who are underachieving and whom they perceive to be behavior problems. Our interviews of science and mathematics faculty indicate that many are focused on their disciplines and on the transmission of knowledge to their own students. Although they want their students to learn, they are unaware of the importance of student prior knowledge and experiences and the strategies that can be used to access them. In order to provide prospective and practicing teachers with a sense of inquiry as it is described in national and state standards, teacher preparation programs must include relevant inquiry immersion experiences. Our use of the foam activity from the Exploratorium Institute for Inquiry is an example of a strategy that encourages analysis of various approaches to hands-on learning and to the teacher's own mental models of science and science learning.

Our future teachers and teachers discerned the following about inquiry (Barnes & Foley, 1999):

1. Hands-on instruction is not necessarily identical to critical thinking.
2. Hands-on instruction may not use learners' prior knowledge and ideas for shaping explorations; inquiry depends on those aspects of learning.
3. In situations in which learners generate questions, students are more likely to be active inquirers.
4. Memory of past learning experiences may be strengthened in true inquiry contexts.

Teachers need time and stimulating contexts if they are to inquire, reflect, react, and explore. We must not deny our teachers the very knowledge and skills that we deem critical to student learning (Lieberman, 1995). The critical skills of inquiry underlie science learning, but they are essential to the practices of the teacher who must determine her own learning needs and those of her students. Equally as crucial is the teacher's ability to inquire into the functioning of her classroom and school as learning communities in which students, teachers, and staff of diverse backgrounds work together in a transformative milieu of mutual respect and support. If teachers are to relinquish long-practiced resistance to change, they must acquire the knowledge and skills needed to become successful with methodologies that, initially, upset the equilibrium associated with familiar behavior patterns.

Figure 4.2 depicts the vital relationships honored and nurtured by teacher inquirers who can empower diverse learners. Some would sug-

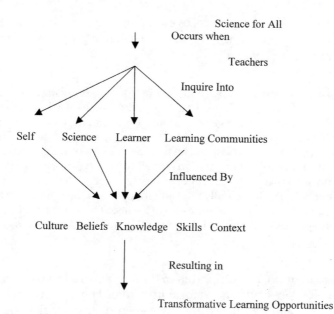

FIG. 4.2. Model for science teacher inquiry to enhance transformation of diverse learners.

gest that inquiry science learning approaches alone render strategies encouraged by the literature of multiculturalism unnecessary (Weld, 2000). Though we acknowledge that science inquiry is the overall goal, the focus of science classes must include inquiry into self, learner, and learning community, all of which are influenced by culture, beliefs, knowledge, skills, and context.

We suggest a blending of inquiry practices and multicultural research findings that becomes the teacher's tool kit to assess the unique characteristics of each individual and each learning context. Learners must feel confident and supported as they struggle with their own mental models and learn to appreciate their ways of seeing and exploring (Duckworth, 1997). Then teachers can diagnose their learning needs and use scaffolding techniques to model science inquiry and coach learners to more productive science learning (Hogan & Corey, 2001). When resistance is encountered, choices must be made. Ms. C's experiences are indicative of the teacher who deeply appreciates science but understands that a relationship between science and a student or students must grow in a conducive environment that often emanates out of the teacher–student relationship. Not all teachers want to engage in such relationships and, in their avoidance, they shortchange their students and themselves.

The adoption of inquiry as an overarching mind-set for teachers who are committed to facilitating diverse learners as inquirers was reinforced by Cochran-Smith (1995):

> We need more teachers who are moved by their own intelligence and actively involved in communities that engage in "the heresy" of systematic and critical inquiry. Teachers who are inquirers do not have to be color blind in order to be fair to all students, teach basket making in order to "do" multicultural education, or wait for the learned authorities of teacher education institutions or school administrations to tell them "*the* teaching strategies" that are not effective for "*the* culturally diverse learner." Rather, these teachers are involved in intellectually vital and independent pursuits to try to answer some of the toughest questions there are about how to work effectively in the local context with learners who are like them and not like them. (p. 520)

How can our model be supported in the context of a large, urban school system involved in a systemic reform initiative? Having worked with the JUSI since its planning phases, we have seen district curriculum reform and policy change. We have worked collegially with a committed cadre of Master teachers who provide services to teacher colleagues at school sites. However, the sheer size and diversity of the school district create issues that must be addressed by in-depth, school-based initiatives on a continuing basis. The cultures of the school and of the classroom need to be investigated continuously.

Our team's work at one high school has the strong support and endorsement of the principal, an ingredient we feel is essential to its success. The facilitator of the teacher focus groups had used inquiry skills in his own work with disenfranchised, minority youth and he possessed credibility with the teachers as he challenged them to examine their own belief systems and related classroom behaviors. Even through uncomfortable moments, the teachers' inquiry skills were honed as they analyzed student behavior patterns and suggested strategies to try in their own classrooms.

At the classroom level in the same school, Ms. C, who was a member of the school focus group, probed more deeply into her own behavior patterns as she interacted on a daily basis with diverse learners. She has created an authentic classroom learning community in which inquiry science is practiced, along with inquiry into her own and her students' individual and collective learnings about science and each other.

We, a diverse group of higher education faculty, project directors, and facilitators, have learned that we need to be viable, supportive members of inquiry-oriented learning communities if we are to participate in transformative teacher education. We must be focused, but patient, and eschew the misconception that we are "experts." Our participation in the inquiry process continues as we honor and enjoy the diversity that makes the journey worthwhile. Ms. C. has a similar message embedded in a story that, we believe, is a testimony to teachers and teaching:

> One of my minority students is rather large and imposing. He has a set of diamond studded gold teeth and likes to be noticed and recognized. I had been out ill for four days and had just returned to the classroom. The last day I was in class I had prodded him, making him look into my eyes and acknowledge that he was not on task and that he needed to choose a more constructive path. He knew I was right but couldn't help putting in a little dig . . . Ms. C, I don't know . . . maybe I won't come anymore. My response was "You and I both know your capability. You need to fight settling for mediocrity. How come I'm the only one in the room who knows how smart you are! Think about that . . . But I respect your choice . . . I trust you will do what you know in your heart is right. I hope you continue to come because quite frankly I would miss you if you choose not to."
>
> Upon my return, I looked at the attendance roster and saw that he had been absent 3 out of the 4 days I was ill. I rehashed our last encounter and started to worry. The last period in the day, I was starting to feel really physically drained. Into my class came this large guy. He stopped in the doorway and at the top of his lungs with a huge smile on his face he proclaimed: "Oh yeah, Oh yeah. My teacher is back! My teacher is back!" My heart nearly exploded and I put my hand on his arm, looked deep into his eyes and said, "I am glad you are here." (D. Conlon, personal communication, July 31, 2002)

ACKNOWLEDGMENTS

The authors acknowledge the dedication and work of current and past colleagues on their research team: Diane Conlon, Kathy Foley, and Leo Jackson, as well as team members on the Jacksonville initiatives cited earlier.

In addition, the authors acknowledge the support of the NSF Jacksonville Urban Systemic Initiative for Mathematics and Science (Contract Grant ESR-9727647), the Crown Region Area Center for Educational Enhancement (supported by Florida Department of Education with Postsecondary Eisenhower funds, Contract Grant 161-22521-2CE01 [CFD 84.281X]), and the NSF Florida Collaborative for Excellence in Teacher Preparation (Contract Grant DUE-9753546). Opinions, findings, conclusions, or recommendations are those of the authors and do not necessarily reflect the views of the supporting agencies.

REFERENCES

Aikenhead, G. S., & Jegede, O. J. (1999). Cross-cultural science education: A cognitive explanation of a cultural phenomenon. *Journal of Research in Science Teaching, 36*(3), 269–287.

Alberts, B. (2000). Some thoughts on science as inquiry. In J. Minstrell & E. H. van Zee (Eds.), *Inquiring into inquiry learning and teaching in science* (pp. 3–13). Washington, DC: American Association for the Advancement of Science.

American Association for the Advancement of Science. (1989). *Science for all Americans.* New York: Oxford University Press.

American Psychological Association. (1997). *Learner-centered psychological principles.* Washington, DC: Author.

Anderson, J. R. (1980). *Cognitive psychology and its implications.* San Francisco: Freeman.

Anderson, R. D. (2002). Reforming science teaching: What research says about inquiry. *Journal of Science Teacher Education, 13*(1), 1–12.

Barnes, M., & Foley, K. (1999). Inquiring into three approaches to hands-on learning in elementary and secondary science methods courses. *Electronic Journal of Science Education, 4*(2). http://unr.edu/homepage/crowther/ejse/barnesfoley.html

Bell, B., & Gilbert, J. (1996). *Teacher development: A model from science education.* Washington, DC: Falmer Press.

Brott, P. E., & Kajs, L. T. (1998). Developing a professional identity of first-year teachers through a "working alliance." *NAAC Journal Online.* Retrieved August 1, 2001, from http://www.alt-teachercert.org/Working%20Alliance.html

Bruner, J. (1961). The act of discovery. *Harvard Educational Review, 31*(1), 21.

Bybee, R. W. (2000). Teaching science as inquiry. In J. Minstrell & E. H. van Zee (Eds.), *Inquiring into inquiry learning and teaching in science* (pp. 20–46). Washington, DC: American Association for the Advancement of Science.

Cochran-Smith, M. (1995). Color blindness and basket making are not the answers: Confronting the dilemmas of race, culture, and language diversity in teacher education. *American Educational Research Journal, 32*(3), 493–522.

College Board. (1999). *Reaching the top: A report on the national task force on minority high achievement.* New York: Author. http://www.collegeboard.com/research/html/991017r.html

Driver, R., & Oldham, V. (1986). A constructivist approach to curriculum development in science. *Studies in Science Education, 13,* 105–122.

Duckworth, E. (1997). *Teacher to teacher: Learning from each other.* New York: Teachers College Press.

Duval County Public Schools. (2001). *Jacksonville Urban Systemic Initiative Year 3 Annual Report to the National Science Foundation.* Jacksonville, FL: Author.

Fisher, D. L., & Waldrip, B. G. (1999). Cultural factors of science classroom learning environments, teacher–student interactions and student outcomes. *Research in Science and Technologial Education, 17*(1), 83–96.

Gardner, H. (1991). *The unschooled mind: How children think and how schools should teach.* New York: Basic Books.

Goodwin, B. (2000). *Raising the achievement of low performing students* (Mid-Continent Research for Education and Learning Policy Brief, May). Aurora, CO: McREL.

Guba, E. G., & Lincoln, Y. S. (1989). *Fourth generation evaluation.* Newbury Park, CA: Sage.

Harcombe, E. S. (2001). *Science teaching, science learning: Constructivist learning in urban classrooms.* New York: Teachers College Press.

Hawkey, K. (1997). Roles, responsibilities, and relationships in mentoring: A literature review and agenda for research. *Journal of Teacher Education, 48*(5), 325–335.

Hogan, K., & Corey, C. (2001). Viewing classrooms as cultural contexts for fostering scientific literacy. *Anthropology and Education Quarterly, 32*(2), 214–243.

Illinois Staff Development Council. (1998). *Characteristics of successful mentoring programs.* Retrieved July 12, 2001, from http://www.mentors.net/3M.PurposeGrid.html

Interaction Associates. (1998). *The coaching edge: A breakthrough approach to enhancing performance.* Cambridge, MA: Author.

Jay, M. R. (2001). *The business case for coaching.* Retrieved July 31, 2001, from http://www.b-coach.com/papers/businesscase.htm

Keys, C. W., & Bryan, L. A. (2001). Co-constructing inquiry-based science with teachers: Essential research for lasting reform. *Journal of Research in Science Teaching, 38*(6), 631–645.

Kuykendall, C. (1992). *From rage to hope: Strategies for reclaiming Black and Hispanic students.* Bloomington, IN: National Education Service.

Lee, O. (2001). Culture and language in science education: What do we know and what do we need to know. *Journal of Research in Science Teaching, 38*(5), 499–501.

Lieberman, A. (1995). Practices that support teacher development. *Phi Delta Kappan, 76*(8), 591–596.

Lieberman, A., & Miller, L. (1999). *Teachers transforming their world and their work.* New York: Teachers College Press.

Loucks-Horsley, S., Hewson, P., Love, N., & Stiles, K. (1998). *Designing professional development for teachers of science and mathematics.* Thousand Oaks, CA: Corwin Press.

Lynch, S. (2001). Science for all is not equal to "one size fits all": Linguistic and cultural diversity and science education reform. *Journal of Research in Science Teaching, 38*(5), 622–627.

Marshall, P. L. (2002). *Cultural diversity in our schools.* Belmont, CA: Wadsworth/Thomson Learning.

Martin, R. J., & van Gunten, D. M. (2002). Applying positionality and multicultural social reconstructionism in teacher education. *Journal of Teacher Education, 53*(1), 44–54.

Mendler, A. (2000). *Motivating students who don't care.* Bloomington, IN: National Education Service.

Minstrell, J., & van Zee, E. H. (Eds.). (2000). *Inquiring into inquiry learning and teaching in science.* Washington, DC: American Association for the Advancement of Science.

National Center for Improving Science Education. (1993). *Profiling teacher development programs: An approach to formative evaluation.* Washington, DC: Author.

National Research Council. (1996). *National science education standards.* Washington, DC: National Academy Press.

National Research Council. (2000). *How people learn: Brain, mind, experience, and school.* Washington, DC: National Academy Press.

National Staff Development Council. (2001). *Standards for staff development—revised.* Oxford, OH: Author.

Nieto, S. (2000). Placing equity front and center: Some thoughts on transforming teacher education for a new century. *Journal of Teacher Education, 51*(3), 180–187.

Novak, J. (1977). *A theory of education.* Ithaca, NY: Cornell University Press.

Novak, J. (1998). The pursuit of a dream: Education can be improved. In J. J. Mintzes, J. Wandersee, & J. Novak (Eds.), *Teaching science for understanding: A human constructivist view* (pp. 3–28). Orlando, FL: Academic Press.

O'Loughlin, M. (1992). Rethinking science education: Beyond Piagetian constructivism toward a sociocultural model of teaching and learning. *Journal of Research in Science Teaching, 29*, 791–820.

Palmer, P. J. (1998). *The courage to teach: Exploring the inner landscape of a teacher's life*. San Francisco: Jossey-Bass.

Rath, A., & Brown, D. E. (1996). Modes of engagement in science inquiry: A microanalysis of elementary students' orientations toward phenomena in a summer science camp. *Journal of Research in Science Teaching, 33*(10), 1083–1097.

Rodriguez, A. J. (1998). Strategies for counter-resistance: Toward sociotransformative constructivism and learning to teach science for diversity and understanding. *Journal of Research in Science Teaching, 35*(6), 589–622.

Rodriguez, A. J. (1999). Making ethnicity invisible in the name of equity: Standard contradictions in the National Science Education Standards. *Multicultural Perspectives, 1*(2), 3–7.

Roth, W. M., McGinn, M., & Bowen, G. M. (1998). How prepared are preservice teachers to teach scientific inquiry? Levels of performance in scientific representation practices. *Journal of Science Teacher Education, 19*(1), 25–48.

Sadowski, M. (2001). Closing the gap one school at a time. *Harvard Education Letter Research Online*. Retrieved October 3, 2001, from http://edletter.org/past/issues/2001-mj/gap.shtml

Seiler, G. (2001). Reversing the "standard" direction: Science emerging from the lives of African American students. *Journal of Research in Science Teaching, 38*(9), 1000–1014.

Shapiro, B. L. (1996). A case study of change in elementary student teacher thinking during an independent investigation in science: Learning about the "face of science that does not yet know." *Science Education, 80*(5), 535–560.

Sleeter, C. E. (2001). Preparing teachers for culturally diverse schools: Research and the overwhelming presence of whiteness. *Journal of Teacher Education, 52*(2), 94–106.

Supovitz, J. A., Mayer, D. P., & Kahle, J. B. (2000). Promoting inquiry-based instructional practice: The longitudinal impact of professional development in the context of systemic reform. *Educational Policy, 14*(3), 331–356.

Tate, W. (2001). Science education as a civil right: Urban schools and opportunity-to-learn considerations. *Journal of Research in Science Teaching, 38*(9), 1015–1028.

von Glaserfeld, E. (1992). Questions and answers about radical constructivism. In M. Pearsall (Ed.), *Scope, sequence and coordination of secondary science: Vol. 2. Relevant research* (pp. 169–182). Washington, DC: National Science Teachers Association.

Warren, B., Ballenger, C., Ogonowski, M., Rosebery, A. S., & Hudicourt-Barnes, J. (2001). Rethinking diversity in learning science: The logic of everyday sense-making. *Journal of Research in Science Teaching, 38*(5), 529–552.

Weld, J. (2000). *Less talk, more action, for multicultural science* (Report No. SE 063 602). Cedar Falls: University of Iowa. (ERIC Document Reproduction Service No. ED 442 637)

5

Breaking Through the Ice: Dealing With Issues of Diversity in Mathematics and Science Education Courses

Jacqueline Leonard
Temple University

Scott Jackson Dantley
Bowie State University

> *Progress lies in gradually narrowing real gaps that continue to exist among people of different races . . . bringing people together—at the very best, by educating them together.*
> —Neil L. Rudenstine (former president of Harvard University)

After teaching mathematics and science education courses at Temple University, helping prospective teachers to realize the importance of diversity remains a daunting task. Although these teachers in our classes are diverse in terms of race, ethnicity, religion, gender, sexual orientation, and economic status, a conversation about diversity is usually met with apathy. Thus, a discussion of pedagogical and ideological change is often met with resistance. One White female prospective teacher stated: "Our professors are idealistic and disconnected from the real world of teaching. We cannot teach [inquiry-based instruction] in the way that you are telling us because we cannot change the way things are. It isn't fair that there are inequities in education, but that's the way it is, and we cannot do anything about it."

However, after the events of September 11, 2001, it has been our experience that prospective teachers are more receptive to discussing issues of diversity and equity in teacher education courses. Prior to this event, the impetus for improvement in mathematics and science education in the United States has been linked to our competition with other nations. One of the objectives of Goals 2000 was that America would be first in mathematics and science by the year 2000 (Vinovskis, 1996). Rather than a spirit of competition, future goals should now focus on a spirit of understanding that embraces the differences and uniqueness of people living in a global society. By the year 2010, projections are that people of color will be in the majority in more than 50 cities in the United States (Tran, Young, & Di Lella, 1994). Furthermore, ethnic minorities are now the largest student population in 23 out of 25 of the nation's largest urban school districts (Phuntsog, 1995). However, teachers are becoming increasingly White and female, particularly at the elementary school level (Banks, 2001; Cochran-Smith, 1995; Wade, 1998). Therefore, it is imperative that White prospective teachers learn to effectively teach urban students, who are more likely to be poor, minority, and outside of the teacher's cultural experience (Diller, 1999; Martin & Lock, 1997; Wade, 1998), if we are to leave no child behind (No Child Left Behind, 2001).

The purposes of this chapter are to explain both how issues of diversity fit into a larger framework within teacher education to include methods courses and how teacher educators can empower prospective teachers to become change agents by using "reconstructionist pedagogy" (Cochran-Smith, 1995) and "culturally relevant teaching" (Ladson-Billings, 1994). Both reconstructionist pedagogy and culturally relevant teaching provide the theoretical framework for our work. The sociocultural context and our strategies for counterresistance follow these theories, placing diversity issues in mathematics and science education courses within the context of teacher research.

THEORETICAL FRAMEWORK

The theoretical framework of this chapter is based on three related but distinct concepts: multiculturalism, reconstructionist pedagogy, and culturally relevant teaching. Multiculturalism focuses on the activities of specific subgroups within a dominant culture. Reconstructionist pedagogy is not specific to any particular group; it is a way of teaching that brings social issues to the forefront and encourages students to take action against social injustice. Culturally relevant teaching is specific to a particular group, such as African Americans, Asians, Latinos, and Native Americans; it is a way of teaching that not only addresses social injustice as reconstructionist pedagogy does but also celebrates the diversity and cultural gifts that students of color bring into the classroom. Each of these concepts is explained in more detail in the following subsections.

What Is Multiculturalism?

Phelan, Davidson, and Cao (1991) defined culture as the norms, values, expectations, and conventional actions of a group. Multiculturalism, then, is the norms, values, expectations, and actions that are specific to diverse groups. Yet, teachers must develop thoughtful cultural, national, and global identifications for themselves, if students are to become compassionate and reflective individuals in a multicultural world (Banks, 2001). In other words, "Whiteness" is not necessarily monoculturalism. Within the race classification of White, there are differences in gender, religion, ethnicity, socioeconomic status, and sexual orientation. The concept of multicultural citizenship should be embraced by teachers and students alike (Banks, 2001). Teachers should think more broadly about how they may fit into multiple categories.

In order for prospective teachers to become change agents, they must see teacher educators actively engaged in efforts to change the status quo in teacher education programs (Price & Valli, 1998). Teacher educators should help prospective teachers realize that teaching is a political activity and that social change is necessary for the job (Cochran-Smith, 1995). Teachers can begin the process of social change by realizing that the cultural capital students bring to the classroom (Delpit, 1988; Hollins, Smiler, & Spencer, 1994), whether it is urban or suburban, public or private, religious or nonsectarian, should be recognized and valued. Cultural capital is the cultural knowledge that children have about the world. A culturally responsive pedagogy recognizes that all children bring some knowledge into the classroom and makes links to the everyday lives of diverse students, their family and friends, and the subculture of science and mathematics (Aikenhead, 1999).

Reconstructionist Pedagogy

Reconstructionist pedagogy is "pedagogy intended to help children understand and then prepare to take action against the social and institutional inequities that are embedded in our society" (Cochran-Smith, 1995, p. 494). It focuses on action aimed at altering the social values and behavior of the mainstream or dominant group in society, attempting to promote a sense of social justice or a disposition toward opposing inequity in education (Nieto, 2000; Wade, 1998). Concern for social justice means that teachers must be willing to look critically at our schools and analyze school policies and practices that value the identities of some students and devalue others (Nieto, 2000). Teacher educators can help prospective teachers to develop critical inquiry by providing opportunities to develop the following perspectives: "(1) reconsidering personal knowledge and experience, (2) locating teaching within the culture of the school and the community, (3) analyzing children's learning opportunities, (4) understanding children's understanding, and (5) constructing reconstructionist pedagogy" (Cochran-Smith, 1995, p. 500); in short, promoting teaching as a lifelong journey of transformation where teachers learn about students and learn from students affirms diversity (Nieto, 2000). After affirming students' identities by recognizing that everyone brings uniqueness to the classroom, culturally relevant teaching is the next step in creating more equitable classrooms.

Culturally Relevant Teaching

Culturally relevant teaching is described as "a pedagogy that empowers students intellectually, socially, emotionally, and politically by using cultural referents to impart knowledge skills, and attitudes" (Ladson-Billings, 1994, pp. 17–18). Culturally relevant teaching embeds student culture into the curriculum in order to maintain that culture and transcend the negative effects of the dominant culture. It draws on the history of students' lives as well as unique ways of communicating, behaving, and knowing while preparing students to effect change in society, not merely fit into it (Ladson-Billings, 1994).

Ladson-Billings (1994) believed that the low achievement of minority children in mathematics is the result of poor teaching practices that are disconnected from students' cultural experiences. The National Council of Teachers of Mathematics (NCTM) has stated that mathematics instruction should be connected to the lives of students (NCTM, 2000). Though many textbook companies are attempting to address diversity, their attempt to be inclusive is shallow. Many texts are diverse only in terms of using multicultural names, images of children from different races and backgrounds, and holidays (Irvine & Armento, 2001). The experiences of children of color are often overlooked, and mathematics problems that deal with culturally relevant ideas other than food and customs are practically nonexistent (Irvine & Armento, 2001; Leonard & Guha, 2002). Teachers can learn to become cultural brokers (Aikenhead, 1996) by helping their students to build new knowledge and scaffolding on the "personal/cultural" knowledge that students bring to school (Banks, 2001). Ladson-Billings (2000) suggested the following strategies for improving teacher education: (a) autobiography, which allows individuals to speak as subjects in their own voices, (b) restructured field experiences in urban classrooms to confront stereotypes and racist attitudes, (c) situated pedagogies to make the school and home experiences of diverse learners more congruent, and (d) returning to the classrooms of experts who use a culturally relevant pedagogy and set high standards for all students.

These two perspectives—reconstructionist pedagogy and culturally relevant teaching—have informed our thinking about teacher education. Preparing teachers who are sensitive to diversity requires much more than taking a single course (Bollin & Finkel, 1995; Phuntsog, 1995; Price & Valli, 1998). "All courses need to be infused with content related to diversity" (Nieto, 2000, p. 183). One way to do this is to include readings from authors of diverse backgrounds. It is important for prospective teachers to see the world through the eyes of those who may have different experiences.

We consider our first task, as professors of color, to be helping our prospective teachers realize the importance of multicultural education and teaching diverse children differently from mainstream children. These are complex issues that are difficult to get teachers to buy into. However, White prospective teachers must begin with their own racial identity, understand how that identity has created privilege for them and disadvantage for others, and internalize a multicultural identity that actively seeks to learn from other cultural groups (Bollin & Finkel, 1995). Teaching in a diverse classroom means seeing African American and Hispanic children as "equal" learners and not culturally deficient (Tran et al., 1994).

SOCIOCULTURAL CONTEXT

Discussions about race and racism are absent from the discourse in teacher education classrooms primarily because the instructors themselves are "overwhelmingly White, monocultural, and culturally insular" (Price & Valli, 1998, p. 115). Thus, the culture of the institution itself can be a barrier to or a catalyst for social change. Institutions have the power to legitimize the restructuring of teacher education curriculum and to attract more faculty and students of color (Price & Valli, 1998). Colleges and universities must better define themselves, their mission, and their commitment to diversity because they have the potential to profoundly impact those who have access to economic goods and will become teachers of the next generation (Haugabrook, 1998).

Temple University's main campus is located in North Philadelphia and, thus, is an urban university. In 2000, Temple restructured its teacher education program. All undergraduate education majors must take a course called "Inclusive Education for a Diverse Society" (ED 155). This course focuses on different aspects of diversity including race, gender, class, sexual orientation, and persons with disabilities. Such courses add to prospective teachers' knowledge of multiculturalism by helping them to see how they fit into multiple categories.

As professors of color at Temple University, we are committed to diversity and social justice. However, as faculty at a predominantly White institution, we are also cognizant that we have limited power to make change. First, professors of color may be perceived negatively by White college students because of racial stereotypes. Second, White college students are more apt to believe that faculty of color will use their power in the classroom to influence change, which will often result in resistance to change (McElroy, 1998). Moreover, teacher educators who attempt to bring issues of race and racism to the forefront have been subject to harsh criticism and negative course evaluations that may impact tenure decisions (Ladson-Billings, 2000; McElroy, 1998). Third, White college students are more likely to see diversity as an issue that does not involve them and may not see the need to discuss race and racism (Wade, 1998).

We are two African American associate professors, one female and one male, with a strong religious faith. Because of our faith, we feel more freedom to push the envelopes of equity and justice in mathematics and science education. Even if we lose our current positions, we know that we will find a niche in higher education where our ideas and philosophies are valued, regardless of race or gender. With the support of our dean, we choose to embed issues of culture and diversity into our methods courses. Our experiences may be cast in the genre of teacher research.

Teacher Research and Teacher Preparation

Teacher research has become a common practice for looking at the dynamics that occur in single classrooms (Cochran-Smith & Lytle, 1990). Data sources, which are usually qualitative, may include journal writing, interviews, surveys, audio and/or videotaping of classroom discussions, and/or focus group sessions. However, this kind of research has been most prominent in K–12 schools as teacher-researchers from universities collect data on research projects taking place in elementary and secondary classrooms. Teacher research in higher education has been scarce, perhaps due to its low status, heavy teaching loads, too many committee assignments, and pressure to publish (Gregory, 1998). Yet, teacher research is critically needed in teacher education courses to examine how well prospective teachers are being prepared to teach mathematics and science content to diverse students in urban classrooms.

METHODOLOGY

Participants

The participants who provided the qualitative data for this chapter include all of the prospective teachers who were enrolled in the mathematics methods course (MTH ED 141) during the 2001–2002 academic year (n = 107) and the science methods courses (SCI ED 150) during the 2000–2001 academic year ($n = 110$). The objective of the courses was to teach the pedagogy needed to deliver high-quality instruction in mathematics and science to all children. The prospective teachers in these classes were seeking elementary certification.

The undergraduate population in the College of Education on the main campus is 87% female. The racial demographics were as follows in 2001: African American 17.9%, Asian 3.7%, Hispanic 3.4%, Native American 0.4%, White 67.7%, and Other 6.4%. However, teacher education courses are taught at both the main campus and the suburban Ambler campus, which is less diverse. The demographics of the Ambler campus is 3.9% African American, 3.2% Asian, 4.8% Hispanic, 0.2% Native American, 77.1 White, and 6.5% Other.

Measures

The data sources that were used to examine our strategies for effective counterresistance included our syllabi, reflection papers, exams, informal interviews, and course evaluations. The reflection papers were written on current literature in the field. Some of the literature was on mathematics and science content. However, there was also literature on equity and culture in the teaching of mathematics and science. Open-ended exam questions also provided a rich source of data as the prospective teachers tried to tie what they learned in class with what they experienced in the field. We also had informal conversations with prospective teachers one-on-one to gauge how they were thinking about the course materials, lectures, and activities. Finally, written comments on the course evaluations provided us with confidential feedback about specific aspects of our courses.

Procedures

We reviewed the literature and discovered that Banks (2001), Ladson-Billings (2000), and Nieto (2000) addressed diversity issues in teacher education courses. Banks used the concept of citizenship to engage prospective teachers in thoughtful discussions and to clarify their identification. Banks said "to develop clarified cultural and national identifications, teacher education students must be helped to critically analyze and rethink their notions of race, culture, and ethnicity and view themselves as cultural and racial beings" (pp. 11–12). In order to do this, he incorporates readings, activities, lectures, and discussions designed to help prospective teachers construct new concepts of race, culture, and ethnicity. The activities include historical readings, discussions, and role-playing events dealing with ethnic and racial groups in the United States. Thus, perspectives of insiders and outsiders provide comprehension of the experiences of others within an historical and cultural context. Nieto addressed social justice by helping prospective teachers critically examine school policies and practices, which include examination of curriculum, textbooks and materials, instructional strategies, tracking, recruitment and hiring of staff, and parent involvement. Ladson-Billings believed that autobiography, restructured field experiences, situated pedagogies, and examining the classrooms of experts were critical in providing the kinds of experiences needed to help prospective teachers to be successful with African American students.

We then examined our own syllabi and pedagogy to determine what strategies of counterresistance were just as effective in bringing about teacher change. We also looked at our texts, readings, videos, and assignments to learn from our teaching what worked and what could be improved upon. During the teaching of our respective courses, we read and evaluated the teachers' work, both written and oral, paying careful attention to how they were feeling and reacting to the assignments, videos, and texts. Data were analyzed to group strong opinions either positively or negatively into like categories. Moreover, we analyzed the teachers' written responses by race and gender to determine if the kinds of statements they made were similar or different. Lastly, we kept journals of our own feelings about confronting issues of racism, classism, and sexism in our courses and how we believed the prospective teachers were reacting to us.

Research Questions

The following questions guided our inquiry about diversity issues and counterresistance:

1. What activities were most effective to influence prospective teacher's attitudes and beliefs about teaching diverse students?
2. How can a changed consciousness be sustained after prospective teachers leave our classes at the university?

JACQUELINE'S MATHEMATICS METHODS COURSE

Jacqueline taught the mathematics methods course 12 times to undergraduate and graduate students on the main campus of Temple University from 1997 to 2002. Over these 5 years, she used a variety of strategies to improve prospective teachers' exposure to diverse students and culturally relevant teaching. These strategies included the following: (a) selecting a text that attended to culturally relevant teaching, (b) watching videotapes of excellent teaching in an urban setting, (c) visiting urban classrooms to observe high-level thinking and reasoning skills in mathematics, (d) reading, writing, and discussing reflection papers on diversity and equity in mathematics education, (e) use of multicultural children's literature that deals with mathematical themes, (f) telling stories about personal experiences in teaching, and (g) student-centered teaching demonstrations that incorporate strategies that are known to benefit diverse learners, such as cooperative learning, use of manipulatives, and inquiry-based instruction.

Choosing a Mathematics Education Text

Jacqueline had the benefit of being a summer fellow at Virginia Tech prior to her appointment as a full-time faculty member at Temple University. She cotaught a summer course with Dr. Jeff Frykholm. There she was introduced to *Mathematics Methods for Elementary and Middle School Teachers* (Hatfield, Edwards, Bitter, & Morrow, 1997). The text not only addressed issues of cultural relevance but also mentioned examples of diverse students' learning styles. For example, chapter 2 of the text is titled "Culturally Relevant Mathematics." African contributions to mathematics as well as those of Hispanic, Asian, and Native Americans are discussed. Examples of Egyptian, Mayan, and Hindu numerals are modeled as well as other types of numeration systems. The fourth edition of the text (Hatfield, Edwards, Bitter, & Morrow, 2000) also includes a CD-ROM, which allows prospective teachers to watch video vignettes of effective mathematics teaching. One of the video vignettes shows a Latina teacher reading the story *Sweet Clara and the Freedom Quilt* (Hopkinson, 1993) to her bilingual class. Then the students used pattern blocks to make their own patterns and created designs for a classroom quilt. Thus, the students learned about shapes, symmetry, and patterns within the cultural context of the Underground Railroad. The text also provides prospective teachers with an overview of the *Standards* (NCTM, 2000) and a review of mathematical content within the context of culturally relevant teaching.

"The Kay Toliver Files"

While working with Dr. Frykholm, Jacqueline was also exposed to "The Kay Toliver Files," which is a four-part videotaped series (Toliver, 1993). Each tape focuses on a specific mathematics lesson taught by Kay Toliver, who was a middle school mathematics teacher in Harlem, New York. The lessons are on estimation, fractions, geometry, and problem solving. Kay Toliver dressed up as different characters to demonstrate each of the lessons. For example, Ms. Toliver dressed up as an African queen in the estimation video. She dressed as a chef in the fraction video and as a witch in another video. She explains that the dressing up is her attempt to motivate her students to learn mathematics. However, the dressing up is also a means of setting the mathematics within a cultural context. She says that "Lombardini brought the first pizza to America" in the fraction video. Thus, her dress as a chef set the stage for the students to make pizzas in order to learn about fractions. In the lesson on estimation, Ms. Toliver made a replica of the pyramids in Africa. She posed a problem that challenged the students to estimate how many cat biscuits were in a large container hidden under the pyramid. The answer was written on the board in Egyptian numerals. Students counted the cat biscuits in smaller containers to make a better estimate. Finally, they discovered the Egyptian numbers and decoded them to learn how many cat biscuits were in the large container.

By watching the videos, the prospective teachers were able to see how middle school students in Harlem, New York, work and learn in a mathematics class. According to one student on the videotape, "The work is never boring." The students used complete sentences and correct mathematical terms in the videos. It was evident from the videos that these urban students of color were excited about mathematics and were eager to learn. Thus, assumptions that African American and Hispanic children do not want to learn are challenged, and the videotapes leave a lasting impression, which is captured by excerpts of the prospective teachers' written work.

Examples of prospective teachers' comments that deal with each of the strategies Jacqueline tried to use in her methods class follow. The excerpts that are presented from Jacqueline's class reveal a sharp contrast among African American and White prospective teachers' responses. White prospective teachers mentioned the importance of multicultural education and using a variety of methods to teach students with different learning styles. However, their responses were general and theoretical in nature. By contrast, the African American prospective teachers' responses were more detailed. They internalized what was said in class and tried it out in their practicum courses, describing the enthusiasm with which the students responded to their teaching or how they might use the information they learned in their own classrooms. The following set of excerpts provides comments about the Kay Toliver video series:

Excerpt 1 (data source: exam): In one of the videos in the series with Kay Toliver, Ms. Toliver taught fractions to her class. She taught them about fractions using a hands-on activity with pizzas. I feel that the students learned about fractions much quicker, being able to see the concept firsthand. (White woman)

Excerpt 2 (data source: exam): During my educational experience in Dr. Leonard's class, I had the opportunity to observe a video of a well-known educator by the name of Kay Toliver. She used several methods of teaching her students a short history lesson or a language arts lesson while teaching mathematics. The lessons were innovative, and the students were interested in learning more about the subjects she introduced. Ms. Toliver's methods are recognized throughout the country as a unique way of teaching, and if I can motivate my students to crave more information as the students in the video, then I believe that my methods will exceed the recommended way of teaching. (African American woman)

Visiting Urban Classrooms

Having been exposed to Project SEED in Dallas, Texas, Jacqueline learned that some schools in the School District of Philadelphia had Project SEED. Project SEED is a program that uses a Socratic method of questioning to help students learn algebraic rules and concepts (Phillips & Ebrahimi, 1993). A Socratic style is one where the instructor teaches primarily by asking questions. The answers students give lead the instructor in what to ask next. Thus, this approach is driven by student understanding or lack thereof.

Seeing predominantly African American students explain their thinking and articulate their ideas about abstract concepts that she herself did not have until ninth grade, intrigued Jacqueline when she was an elementary teacher in 1986. It changed her mind about who could and could not learn mathematics. She wanted to become a Project SEED instructor and mathematics teacher. Jacqueline went back to school at night to obtain secondary mathematics certification, and she hoped that her prospective teachers would have a similar experience. Thus having learned that Project SEED was offered in Philadelphia, Jacqueline arranged for one of her classes to visit a Project SEED class at a nearby middle school.

In one of the lessons the prospective teachers had the opportunity to observe, middle school students learn that "E" is the operation of exponentiation. The notion that is used to help students understand the operation of exponentiation is 2E3 instead of 2^3. Before long students are able to generalize (2E3) * (2E4) = 2E7 because 2E3 is $2 \times 2 \times 2$ and 2E4 is $2 \times 2 \times 2 \times 2$, which is a total of seven twos. Once the students understand the system then power notation such as 3^5 is introduced.

Although Project SEED is no longer offered in Philadelphia, the experience is worth noting because research concurs that field experiences do more to challenge White teachers' misconceptions about students of color than simply taking a course (Banks, 2001; Cochran-Smith, 1995; Ladson-Billings, 2000). This is an area for further study because Project SEED is now being offered in Camden, New Jersey.

Reflection Papers

During the course, prospective teachers were required to read two articles and write reflection papers on current issues in mathematics education. Although the prospective teachers were free to select any article, many of the articles raised issues related to teaching "all" children mathematics more effectively. These articles challenge teacher education students' views about diversity and different learning styles. Two excerpts high-lighting prospective teachers' reflections are presented next:

> *Excerpt 3* (data source: position paper): I believe that the research that was done to support this article [Malloy & Jones, 1998] is sound, and the findings of this study appear to have merit. It is only natural that children with different backgrounds will have different learning styles, and these differences should be investigated and documented. I find it particularly interesting that while high confidence levels correlated with the problem solving success of the mainstream population, the same correlation was not true of this sample of African American students. It would be interesting to further study the phenomenon to understand why this may be the case. (White woman)

> *Excerpt 4* (data source: position paper): This article [Stiff & Harvey, 1988] is about inequity in school in math education. As described in this article [some] cultural factors are not likely to be those of Black students. Here we are playing the race card again. I have to seriously disagree with this article. Math is math period! How can a link be made between culture and math? (White man)

Needless to say, Jacqueline was surprised with the blatant resistance she experienced from the White man who wrote the preceding excerpt in her course. White women, for the most part, were much more willing to have an open mind or a broader perspective on racial differences and learning styles. Some White men, on the other hand, were very entrenched in their views and often more critical of the literature written by African American mathematics educators than were White women and persons of color. Regardless of race, men represent about 13% of the undergraduate students enrolled in Temple's elementary education program. Thus, it is difficult to get a representative sample of White men to study. Nevertheless, additional research is needed to understand how gender and race interact to impact prospective teachers' racial consciousness and resistance to multiculturalism.

Multicultural Books Related to Mathematics

Another strategy that Jacqueline used to help her prospective teachers understand the importance of cultural relevance and ways to motivate diverse students to learn mathematics was to read several literature books that focused on different cultures. She read culturally relevant stories to emphasize that students at all levels enjoy being read to and to ensure that prospective teachers understood the impact these stories had on mathematics and culture. Prospective teachers commented not only on the books but also on how they used them to motivate students in urban classrooms during their teaching practicum, as in the following excerpts:

> *Excerpt 5* (data source: exam): Dr. Leonard would read us stories during class. She would then show us the strong connection math has to other subject areas. A perfect example of this would be the time Dr. Leonard read us a story called *One Grain of Rice* [Demi, 1997]. In this story a young Indian girl is granted one wish from the raja. Her wish is to receive a grain of rice and then that amount doubled each day for thirty days. While Dr. Leonard read this story, everyone in the class feverishly tried to figure out the end result of the story, once again proving that math can cut across all content areas. (White woman)

> *Excerpt 6* (data source: exam): I had a chance last semester to make a difference with a classroom of children who had low reading and math scores. Using a book suggested by Dr. Leonard, I began to have the children relate to real life, learn about math, and practice on their reading skills all in one. We read *Alexander Who Used to be Rich Last Sunday* by Judith Viorst [1978]. In the book, Viorst uses the main character, Alexander, to explain the importance of money and the encouragement of careful spending through Alexander's calamities. While reading, I gave the children coins for a worksheet, which added up to 7 dimes, 4 nickels, and 10 pennies. Together, the class and I counted the coins together and established the amount as being 100 cents or one dollar. We then reread the story, asking children to remove the corresponding coins as Alexander spends or loses them. In the end, the children were able to show how much money Alexander had left at the end of the story, which was zero. I can't tell you how enthusiastic the children were and how eager they were to read, participate in the activity, and learn about money. (African-American man)

> *Excerpt 7* (data source: exam): Mathematics is a subject that can be easily integrated into language arts. For that reason, I have read various works of literature during math lessons. I read a book titled *The Doorbell*

Rang by Pat Hutchins [1986]. The book is about two children, Sam and Victoria. Their mother, who is called Ma in the story, bakes 12 cookies. Ma invites them to share the cookies. Before they begin to eat, the door-bell rang again and again until there were many hungry children in the house. As the children enter, the story invites listeners (which are my students) to divide the amount of cookies according to the number of children. During that part of the story, my students were intensely di-viding the numbers with great excitement and enthusiasm. Why? The book presented a stimulating, culturally relevant and age-appropriate problem solving activity for my students. (African American woman)

The Art of Telling Real-Life Stories

Telling real-life stories or sharing one's experiences as a teacher is another way to put a human face on the information that teacher educators give to prospective teachers. Stories from the trenches, discussing real problems and inequities in education, and how one might respond are empowering for new teachers who are primarily concerned about getting tenure and/or keeping their jobs.

Jacqueline told her teacher education students about Barbara Ann (pseudonym), an angry African American fourth-grade student that she had taught in Dallas, Texas. She explained how she was able to penetrate her anger by visiting her home and taking Barbara Ann roller skating with her own family. As a result, Barbara Ann became an advocate for Jacque-line in the classroom, calling on other students to listen and learn. Barbara Ann volunteered to pass out papers and began to show improvement in mathematics. At the end of the school year, Barbara went from the 4th per-centile in math on the Iowa Test of Basic Skills to the 38th percentile. Though she still remained below grade level, significant progress had been made. These and other stories are told to help teachers realize that they can make a difference, even if it is with only one child.

Comments from the course evaluations included the following: "She added humor and personal experience to the curriculum presented." "She has something interesting to say. She had many years of teaching in ele-mentary schools and can easily convey this wisdom . . . sometimes she could wander a bit in her storytelling, but that just made her more ap-proachable." "One weakness is that she goes off on a tangent." These com-ments imply that Jacqueline may need to clarify why she tells the stories in order to help prospective teachers to see that the stories are her way of re-lating the content.

Teaching Demonstrations

In order to provide prospective teachers with opportunities to present the ideas that they learned in the course, they were required to present a lesson to the class. The prospective teachers were allowed to work in teams of two or three. One teacher may be the main spokesperson, another may demonstrate the activity, and a third may explain the rationale of the lesson and field any questions that arise. These lessons were meant to be examples of best practice, including hands-on activities, cooperative learning, or other features that were known to benefit diverse learners. These lessons were presented not only in our class but also out in the field where prospective teachers tried their ideas out. The following prospective teacher reveals how her philosophy and teaching style were impacted by the course:

> *Excerpt 8* (data source: exam): For many years, teachers have used the direct style of teaching. However, I have learned that direct teaching is most effective when conveying basic step-by-step directions. As a teacher in the 21st century, my goal is to stretch student's knowledge beyond basic skills. Therefore, I use the constructivist approach to enhance and strengthen students' learning in math. The components of constructivism include hands-on materials, minds-on discovery and open inquiry. In my classroom, I've created a learning environment where students are encouraged to think critically while problem solving. The thinking process of my students is the focus and center of attention instead of the right or wrong answer. Along with creating an environment of inquiry, I provide hands-on materials as well so that students can visually see that two halves make a whole, 10 dimes equal a dollar, and so forth. (African American woman)

These foregoing strategies were employed in varying degrees each semester and helped Jacqueline to shape and reshape her pedagogy as she engaged prospective teachers in the difficult conversation about race and diversity.

Data Analysis

At the outset, it was difficult for Jacqueline to break the ice and talk about diversity and equity in mathematics education in her classroom. Some White teachers are resistant to the idea that "Whiteness" and cultural differences contribute to the achievement gap between majority and minority students in mathematics. Some White teachers are quick to blame the students' parents, drugs, or crime for students' lack of motivation. However, using a cultural text and reading materials that dealt with issues of diversity made broaching the subject less difficult. In one class, Jacqueline broke the ice to discuss issues of diversity by having prospective teachers in her class read "Identity Matters: An Asian-Caribbean-American's Perspective" (Softky, 2000). The discussion, as well as the course evaluations, helped Jacqueline learn what was most effective in helping prospective teachers to understand and possibly attend to diversity in their own classrooms.

The materials, activities, and strategies that were most effective in transforming prospective teachers' opinions about students of color and culturally relevant teaching in mathematics were the Kay Toliver tapes and the multicultural literature books, respectively. Even the White male prospective teacher who stated "Math is math period!" admitted that integrating literature and mathematics created an easy link to the students' culture. However, a few evaluations of the course showed that some prospective teachers did not like the textbook, and one was critical of Jacqueline's stories. In future courses, Jacqueline plans to make the goals and purposes of the course more explicit. Prospective teachers need to know that teaching is political and that teachers can change the status quo by empowering their students with the mathematics knowledge they need to gain access to higher education and better jobs and living conditions.

SCOTT'S SCIENCE EDUCATION COURSE

Scott is a new teacher educator. He taught the science methods course at Temple University for the first time during the 2000–2001 academic year. Two of the courses were taught at the main urban campus whereas the other two courses were taught at the suburban campus, which had markedly less diversity than the main campus. Out of an average of 55 undergraduate students in the two courses, approximately 3 were African American men, which accounts for the disproportion in the excerpts mentioned later. Nevertheless, as an assistant professor in his first year on the tenure track at Temple, he wanted the prospective teachers to have good science content knowledge and to be prepared to teach students in the School District of Philadelphia and surrounding suburbs.

The Culture of Science: Misalignment With Diversity

The culture of science has always been described as an elitist subject. It has never been thought of as a subject for those who have less than the above-average aptitude for mathematics and strong critical thinking skills.

Tobias' book, *They're Not Dumb, They're Different* (1990), found that science instruction was not user friendly in three categories: student–teacher interactions, physical environment, and content delivery.

Prospective teachers in university science classes often have little to no contact with other college students and often experience didactic lectures and study from textbooks that are heavily factual without supporting narrative. The current preservice model continues to build upon the notion that prospective teachers take their science courses in science departments where they not only acquire very structured scientific skills but also obtain the narrow scientific view of who should be permitted to study and participate in science. Generally, it is left to the novice teacher to make the transition from a myopic view of science inclusion to promoting equity for all students in science.

Sleeter and Grant (1987) wrote about the cultural deficit model that assumes that the university or educational institution can "fix" students who are not considered to be mainstream because they lack the mental capacity or skills to align with the culture of science. Two worldviews can be formulated based on their work: One views students as challenged or at risk and therefore rehabilitates them to assimilate into the established culture of science. The other worldview sees students' misalignment with the culture of science as a sign of diversity and not a deficiency, specifically, "a multicultural approach to education promotes cultural pluralism and social equality by reforming the school program for all students to make it reflect diversity" (Sleeter & Grant, 1987, p. 139). Furthermore, equity in science means that all students regardless of their background will be given the same opportunity to learn quality and meaningful science. The outcome of this experience should prepare scientifically literate people to make informed decisions and secure science or science-related careers (Atwater, Crockett, & Kilpatrick, 1996). Thus, it becomes important to choose a science education text that addresses these issues.

Choosing a Science Education Text

There were several strategies Scott used to develop the course and aid in the textbook selection that allowed him to address the needs on both campuses. The strategies to develop the course included topics that would (a) allow prospective teachers to examine their own thinking about diversity and what it means to support science literacy for all students, (b) discuss the nature of science with a multicultural context, (c) examine sociocultural aspects of group learning and diversity, and (d) examine issues that are unique to urban settings. The textbook *Science in the Multicultural Classroom: A Guide to Teaching and Learning* (Barba, 1998) captures these strategies, which are outlined later, along with corresponding science activities that are designed for all students.

Content Integration

Efforts to integrate science with other subjects, such as mathematics, have a long history but are not widespread (Lehman, 1994). Reasons for integration include: "the close relationship of science and mathematics to the physical world; science provides students with concrete examples of abstract mathematical ideas; mathematics can help students achieve deeper understanding of science concepts; and science activities illustrating mathematics concepts can provide relevancy and motivation for learning mathematics" (Lehman, 1994, pp. 286–287). Furthermore, content integration can be a means of addressing diversity.

Banks (1994) and Atwater (1996) suggested that content integration should include illustrations from a variety of cultures to explain content, principles, and theories. The degree to which each of these areas is addressed strengthens the multicultural connections to science and broadens students' worldview on culture. Yet others (Baptiste & Key, 1996) suggest that content integration involves three levels: awareness, integrating the contributions of many cultures, and making cultural and social issues the focus of the curriculum. For culturally diverse students to be successful, the culture of science must be familiar or culturally harmonious. Barba's text, *Science in the Multicultural Classroom* (1998), coined the term culturally harmonious and suggested that "harmonious variables are those culture-of-origin beliefs, attitudes, and practices which influences either positively or negatively the teaching and learning process" (p. 14). Scott used several science activities that allowed prospective teachers' to understand the impact that teachers and society in general have on one's perceptions and images of science and scientists.

SCIENCE ACTIVITIES

Draw-A-Scientist

Prospective teachers were asked to create a free-hand drawing of their image of a scientist. Each person was asked to explain the factors that influenced the ways that they perceived science and scientists by using their drawings as examples. This line of questioning helped Scott to discuss how personal images of scientists are developed and what sociocultural factors influenced their image development. This idea was based on the Draw-A-Scientist Test (Mason, Kahle, & Gardner, 1991), which developed as an instrument to test elementary students' attitudes and stereotypes. The test is scored on the number of standard stereotypical items drawn as indicated from a checklist. The higher the score, the more the student harbors negative stereotypes of scientists. Mason et al. (1991) provided a list of indicators such as a laboratory coat, eyeglasses, symbols of research (i.e., flasks, test tubes, microscope, Bunsen burner, etc.), symbols of knowledge (i.e., books, chalkboards, etc.), symbols of technology, captions (e.g., "he's a nerd"), gender, pocket protector, and unkempt appearance. Additional conversations were held about how their preconceived images of scientists influence the career choices of underrepresented groups.

Typical Scenario. The first scenario captured the majority of the class who drew images of scientists with the following indicators: lab coat, glasses, pocket protector (i.e., pencils and pens), symbols of research (i.e., flasks, test tubes and Bunsen burner), and male gender.

Prospective teachers chose many of the same indicators regardless of their gender and ethnic background. This scenario was labeled typical because the indicators chosen by this group align nicely with what previous research predicts. Such a model is reinforced by the science courses prospective teachers have taken, universities they have attended, and visual representations provided by the media. Men ($n = 14$) were more likely to draw images of men and not women, although some did acknowledge knowing female scientists. Women ($n = 96$) were also likely to draw pictures of male scientists. Both White ($n = 90$) and African American ($n = 20$) prospective teachers drew scientists that were White, yet the opposite never occurred. It was not surprising that prospective African American teachers chose to draw White scientists and not persons of color. Many prospective teachers felt that nondominant images are emerging but that the scientific community is still not very diverse.

New Science Culture Scenario. A subset of prospective teachers produced drawings that did not align with the traditional models of a scientist as purported in the literature. These teachers, many of them White and female, provided identifying characteristics of a scientist as the following: female or male gender, White or aligned with their own ethnicity, trendier in appearance, and symbols of research (flask, test tube, etc.). Prospective teachers who provided information in this scenario all suggested that their parents and friends, educational experiences through formal and informal exposure of diverse people, and diverse experiences in science courses heavily influenced their images of scientists. This exercise allowed prospective teachers to examine their individual mental framework and what they believed constitutes a scientist. It also allowed them to examine the external influences that can shape one's thinking and a help to create perceived worldviews in science. The objects of the exercise attempted to reveal and challenge things that shape their worldview and have students to engage metacognitively on issues of aligning their thinking with what their future students might think and believe. The further the misalignment of what these prospective teachers truly believed the culture of science represents, what the acceptable constructs of the nature of science should look like, and who should participate in science, the more challenged they felt about teaching science in an urban setting.

Inferring and Predicting

This activity was designed to allow prospective teachers to identify metacognitive strategies one might use to explore familiar objects concealed by a closed box.

Prospective teachers were required to either infer what objects were in each box or try to make a prediction, which was the purpose of the activity. The scientific processes involved in inferring include observations, interpretation, and knowledge and experience where they repeat this cyclical process until the object(s) are clearly identified. Similar scientific skills such as generating possible outcomes, making forecasts, and possessing knowledge of patterns and trends are required to make predictions. Several mystery boxes were labeled from one to seven, and each contained a different object. For example, Box 1 contained pieces of cut paper, whereas Box 2 contained paper clips and other pieces of metal objects.

Given that predictions are future forecasts based on solid evidence whereas inferring is based on one's conjectures or conclusions, Scott was able to generate discussions about cognitive differences and prior knowledge in relation to cultural diversity. The excerpts that follow represent prospective teachers' responses to the discussion on cognitive differences and things that influenced their prior knowledge:

> *Excerpt 1* (data source: classroom discussion): I was able to distinguish between some of the objects because of past experiences and recognition. I mainly relied on sounds of the objects hitting the sides of the box. Also the weight of the objects inside the box served as a clue as well as helping me to gauge the size. I was able to identify most of the objects except for those that were not commonly experienced during my everyday life. (White man)
>
> *Excerpt 2* (data source: classroom discussion): I liked the activities, especially the mystery boxes. It really made you think about objects that you encounter in everyday life but take for granted. It makes you wonder about students who have had less experiences and imagination,

how would they answer this question. I think that as a new teacher entering an urban school system; it will be a challenge to bring as many diverse experiences into the classroom so that they will have a broader view. My basic strategy was to shake the box, listen, and compare sounds. (White woman)

It was clear that the more experiences, exposure, and prior knowledge prospective teachers had, the better they were able to guess the items in each box. One of the prospective teachers suggested that exposure to experiences beyond a regular classroom encounter aided in his or her inferences. Another prospective teacher felt that working in an urban environment would present some added challenges of ensuring that all students are given a broader scientific worldview beyond regular classroom experiences. Scott observed that in both cases, each teacher used observations, knowledge, and prior experiences to infer what each mystery box contained. Some teachers were more apt to use prior knowledge and experience whereas others focused more on less scientific processes. As Scott began to reflect on these scenarios, it was clear that the degree of successfully inferring was related directly to prospective teachers' past experiences. Additional research questions that could be addressed related to this activity are how does one come to know what they know? And what is proof of that evidence?

Ball and Ramp

Another activity was an investigation of the position and motion of an object down a ramp. A marble was placed on a ruler that was set at a specific height and rolled toward a cup that was cut in half at the base of the ruler. The object of the activity was to place a marble at a determined beginning position and predict how far the cup would be moved after the marble was released. Additional beginning positions were tried and predictions were made related to those as well. Prospective teachers were required to make predictions on each of the beginning positions and measure the end position of the cup, as in the following excerpts:

> *Excerpt 3* (data source: written assignment): I know that different sized marbles would move the cup at different lengths, but it was hard to predict in any case how far each marble would move the cup. I also noticed the height of the ladder did matter. It seems that as the height of the ladder increased the faster and farther the cup will move. (White man)
>
> *Excerpt 4* (data source: written assignment): My group decided to do something different; we noticed that carpeted floor added a factor that

we didn't initially think about. So we moved to the hall outside of the classroom and conducted our trials. The same relationship was found with the exception of the marble moving the cup farther. (White woman)

Both of the aforementioned teachers felt that they had to use scientific skills, such as predicting, observing, measuring, and some calculating, in order to produce the final answer. Furthermore, they felt that these skills were important parts of producing scientifically based results, especially in the case that required multiple trials. After this task, each group was asked how did they "act like scientists" to conduct this experiment. Although many of the prospective teachers felt that ethnic diversity was not a factor in acting like a scientist, most felt that the culture (i.e., the way they think and act) and scientific processes (i.e., skillful measurements, etc.) that scientists use are important. Scott then posed this question: In an urban setting where some students might not view themselves as scientists, what support structures can be used to aid students in developing this view? Following are excerpts from two teachers' answers:

Excerpt 5 (data source: journal): Well, they need to know that regardless of race, scientists use skills that all of us can learn to use, such as measuring, observing, and predicting. I try to demonstrate some of these skills through my activities. I think it would be helpful to bring in ethnically diverse scientists for them to mingle with. It might help them to relate better and allow them to ask questions about why they do what they do. (Latina woman)

Excerpt 6 (data source: journal): My students always seem impressed when I tell them that the skills they just used were what scientists do on a regular basis. Sometimes they are amused at their ability to mimic scientists. Getting them to understand the culture of scientists is tough. I don't think I understand it myself. I realized that after polling my students about possible careers, none of them mentioned they wanted to become a scientist. Well, some said they might become a medical doctor. I believe it is a tough sell, since most of us don't understand what it truly means. (African American woman)

Public Speaker

An invited speaker presented a lecture about what it means to belong to various group memberships. He approached the subject from a cultural perspective that challenged the prospective teachers to cross-examine their membership status. For example, he explained what it means to be male, African American, and studying science or being perceived as an

African American scientist. He asked these teachers to reflect on their images of a scientist. Did they view them as only being White, male, and wearing glasses? He further explained how characteristics are shared across different group memberships and how each characteristic projected differs with perceived levels of power and influence. Each characteristic can be categorized as belonging to a dominant group or subgroup. If a person is White, male, and tall, these characteristics project a certain image, whereas a different image can occur with being African American and female. The speaker urged Scott's prospective teachers to be aware of the groups or subgroups they belong to and how this might affect the images their future students hold about them. The speaker mentioned that one cannot change group memberships, but one can become sensitive to the images projected. Other discussions explored how one group membership might be perceived as an inherited subordinate group whereas another group might perceive themselves as being superior. For example, male group membership as compared to female group membership might pose different rules on what are appropriate career choices and responsible social behaviors. Prospective teachers were challenged to differentiate between meanings of cultural diversity and group memberships and were admonished to reexamine their scientific worldview. See the following teacher responses:

> *Excerpt 7* (data source: class discussion): As a white male, I never considered myself in a dominant group both in ethnicity and gender. Yet, I am working in a field (i.e. teaching) that is perceived by many as a subordinate career chosen by White females. I do get questions about my career choices, but because I am in this dominant group, most feel that I am trying to give back rather than having limited options. (White man)
>
> *Excerpt 8* (data source: class discussion): As an African American female, I see can how these images of dominant verses subdominant groups play out in a classroom. It might take me longer to gain students' trust and confidence while my classmate might immediately get their attention just based on their perceived images of dominant memberships. I am not sure if this will happen with an all-white classroom where I am the teacher. (African American woman)

Position Paper

Prospective teachers were asked to write a three-page paper supporting ways to include all students in the practice and learning of science. Prospective teachers were asked to provide meaningful activities that coincided with the local and national standards while carefully explaining ways to incorporate diversity issues that are common in an urban school

setting. As a precursor to this assignment, a discussion was held with prospective teachers regarding the meaning of diversity. The papers also provided Scott with the feedback he needed to improve the objectives of the
course in future years, as in the following excerpts:

> *Excerpt 9* (data source: position paper): I believe that you have to pic-
> ture diversity differently when most of the classes in the city are ethni-
> cally diverse. I mean I always look at diversity from a race perspective,
> but when most of my students are African American or Hispanic
> American then I guess that diversity should have a broader meaning.
> Most of my students needed support in science content, yet they all had
> possible responses and only a few knew the right answer. I found that I
> needed to focus less on there being a homogeneous group but more on
> their skills and abilities. (White woman)
>
> *Excerpt 10* (data source: position paper): Based on my experiences, I
> have worked in very diverse settings. My challenge was with issues of
> diversity around gender. How do I as a female teacher, make sure that
> girls are engaged as much as boys during science activities. I thought
> about our discussion about female teachers who gravitated more to-
> wards boys than girls during open discussion and science activities. I
> also thought about the ways that I grouped students in terms of various
> abilities levels particularly reading levels and gender. I wanted to cre-
> ate a balance in these areas. (African American woman)

The reflection papers allowed Scott's prospective teachers to think
about their own instructional practices within the context of diversity.
They were encouraged to speak openly about their issues so that each issue could be addressed. Both of the preceding excerpts show that each
had a different experience with diversity and focused on different facets
of diversity.

DATA ANALYSIS

Scott used the foregoing strategies, activities, and materials to engage his
class in a conversation about the culture of science and the images of who
does science. The conversations enlightened prospective teachers about
their own perceptions and showed that the science community has a long
way to go to change these images. Prospective teachers' consciousness
about diversity was raised most by the Draw-A-Scientist activity, the public speaker, and the reflection papers. The public speaker was particularly
powerful because of the status the individual held. Moreover, he added

credibility and value to what Scott was teaching because, as a member of the scientific community, he validated Scott's work. Prospective teachers struggled to see how experiences limited or enhanced students' ability to infer and use other scientific processes. Yet, they believed that student experiences were important in the learning process. However, the challenge was how to relate the culture of science to an urban setting. Moreover, teacher self-efficacy in science was low. Self-efficacy is "the perceived judgment that an individual conceptualizes regarding his or her capacity to perform in a particular setting or situation" (Wilson, 1996, p. 53). Therefore, a two-sided dilemma existed in Scott's classroom. On the one hand, you have prospective teachers who are trying to understand what science is. On the other hand, you have these same teachers trying to impart what science they know to students, who may already have strong preconceptions about who scientists are.

Addressing the issue of diversity, then, is multifaceted and dependent on the level of teacher content knowledge in science, the challenges of the urban setting, and the alignment of the culture of science and the culture of the community. Culturally relevant teaching in science classrooms requires teachers to meet the cultural, social, personal, and academic needs of all students. Teachers must learn how to become cultural brokers (Aikenhead, 1996) who can fuse the concepts of science and urban culture together. Scott intends to address these issues succinctly in future courses as he studies teacher content knowledge in advanced-level science courses, which will impact his ability to learn what is needed at the elementary level.

SUMMARY

White teachers often have strong preconceptions about teaching urban children (Ladson-Billings, 2000). In order to challenge that view and help them to realize the importance of teaching all children, we engaged in the activities described earlier in our teacher education classes. These data imply that our activities are promising, but we must continue to explore ways to help prospective teachers to critically reflect on their positions of privilege and to take transformative action.

Bollin and Finkel (1995) explained that the first step in the process of developing a positive racial identity and engaging in antiracist work is to move prospective teachers from the stage of naiveté and to help them realize their own racial identity and that race does make a difference. Aaronsohn, Carter, and Howell (1995), Cochran-Smith (1995), and Ladson-Billings (2000) suggested writing autobiographies or personal narratives. Such narratives can be written anonymously at the beginning and the end of the course, allowing teacher education students the free-dom to write whatever they want. Then near the end of the course, discus-sions about how perspectives have changed or have been informed by the course activities will help to document that change did or did not occur and what activities were most effective in bringing the change about. As junior faculty in mathematics and science education, we were unaware of many of these strategies. In future courses, we intend to use strategies such as these to help our prospective teachers realize their own identities and reflect upon their personal goals in teaching.

Because our nation's children are becoming more diverse, it is impor-tant that all prospective teachers learn what strategies they can use to help students of color to become mathematically and scientifically literate. The focus of mathematics and science reform has been on increasing student understanding. As a result of reform, a dominant view in mathematics and science education is that individuals must construct their own mean-ing of new experiences (Campbell & Johnson, 1995; Warren & Rosebery, 1995). In the constructivist paradigm, teachers are encouraged to facilitate learning in a student-centered environment that promotes inquiry. Rather than being receivers of information, students are able to make choices about what and how much they will learn. The subjects of mathematics and science lend themselves to inquiry-based learning as students and teachers engage in classroom discourse (Leonard, 2000), explaining their thinking and reasoning about why a certain solution strategy in mathe-matics works or a certain concept in science has certain characteristics or properties.

Preparing prospective elementary teachers to teach mathematics and science to children involves the use of similar pedagogical tools. These tools are constructivist methods, use of manipulatives or hands-on activi-ties, and culture. Connecting science to the culture of the community al-lows students to develop deeper scientific understanding from a cultural perspective. For example, Conant, Rosebery, Warren, and Hudicourt-Barnes (2001) found that connecting the concept of sound to drum beats helped Haitian students to distinguish features of sound in a more pro-found way by focusing on data and inscriptions. Students learned that waveforms for a sound stroke made by a stick stroke differed from a waveform made by a hand stroke. Thus, students began to recognize how differences in sound produced different sound waves, which enriched their understanding of sound, pitch, and volume with firsthand experi-ences. Not only did this activity motivate students, it encouraged students to do additional research on their own, enriching the discourse in science classrooms.

On the contrary, there is a negative relationship that exists between Afri-can American children and the mathematics process (Stiff & Harvey, 1988).

Black students often have different ways of knowing, talking, and interacting from their White peers, and this background is not often acknowledged or supported by teachers from mainstream culture (Boykin & Toms, 1985; Delpit, 1988; Remillard, 2000; Warren & Rosebery, 1995). Poor performance is the result of inappropriate instructional practices that are insensitive to the social and cultural needs of the African American students (Ladson-Billings, 1994). Lakoff and Nuñez (1997) contended that "mathematics has not been properly understood as a product of inspired human imagination, and has been taught—generation after generation—as if it were . . . a mere grasping of transcendental truth" (p. 29). Rather than "teaching by telling" and asking students to regurgitate facts, mathematics should be taught in a manner that values student thinking and classroom discourse (Campbell & Johnson, 1995; Leonard, 2000; Schifter & Fosnot, 1993).

Allowing children opportunities to construct their own algorithms and solution strategies to solve mathematics problems is motivating and encourages children to value multiple perspectives. From a cognitive-science perspective, students can articulate how they think and process strategies to solve different kinds of problems (Carpenter, Fennema, Franke, Levi, & Empson, 1999). For example, one child might solve the problem 53 + 28 by adding 50 + 20 + 11. Another child might solve the same problem by counting 53, 63, 73, 74, 75, 76, . . . , 81. The variety of children's thinking is restricted only by their background knowledge (Leonard, 1997). Therefore, mathematics curriculum should change with the needs, interests, and cultures of students (Banks, 1994; Vinovskis, 1996; Wlodkowski & Ginsberg, 1995). Moreover, problems can be placed in a context that is meaningful and purposeful for students. Thus, mathematics education courses are important because they can help prospective teachers to see the cultural relevance of mathematics and develop an appreciation for the variety of children's thinking.

Clearly, additional research is needed to determine which strategies work best and which ones prospective teachers continue to use once they enter the field. Ladson-Billings (1994) explained that teachers must find ways to support the learning of all students with culturally responsive teaching. Cochran-Smith (1995) encouraged prospective teachers to learn about the school and the community in which the children live. One way of breaking down the barriers is to take the initiative to learn who they are and where they come from. A community visit is one of the means to accomplish this goal. The school counselor, administrator, or another teacher may be willing to collaborate on a community visit. Visiting the neighborhood church is another opportunity for teachers to see the children and their parents from a different perspective. Such experiences may be long lasting and encourage novice teachers to construct a reconstructionist pedagogy (Cochran-Smith, 1995).

Finally, we realize that there is a delicate balance between teaching about cultural diversity and teaching the content prospective teachers need to be effective with students. After teaching our courses in the manner described herein, we realize our dilemma is twofold as African American faculty on a tenure track. On one hand, cultural diversity is important in our teaching of mathematics and science content, which are the gatekeepers to student access to higher education. On the other hand, we are responsible to teach the content that prospective teachers in elementary programs are so desperately lacking. Without sufficient content knowledge, however well meaning, prospective teachers will be ineffective with students of any race or culture. Leaning too much in one direction or the other creates tension in the classroom that may be detrimental to our quest for tenure. Prospective teachers evaluate our courses and will make comments that will have an impact upon tenure decisions. Nevertheless, mathematics and science literacy begins in the classroom with teachers realizing their own racial identity and ends with transculturalism (Bollin & Finkel, 1995), which is the recognition that we are all citizens of a multicultural identity. Thus, a balance must be struck between passion and wisdom as teacher educators attempt to break the ice and deal with issues of cultural diversity in teacher education programs.

ACKNOWLEDGMENT

We acknowledge Ms. Cara M. Moore, M.S.Ed., for her work in editing this paper.

REFERENCES

Aaronsohn, E., Carter, C. J., & Howell, M. (1995). Preparing monocultural teachers for a multicultural world: Attitudes toward inner-city schools. *Equity & Excellence in Education, 28*(1), 5–9.

Aikenhead, G. S. (1996). Towards a first nations cross-cultural science and technology curriculum. *Science Education, 81,* 217–238.

Aikenhead, G. S. (1999, June). *Barriers to accommodating culture in science classrooms.* Paper presented at the 9th Symposium of the International Organization for Science and Technology Education, Durban, South Africa.

Atwater, M. M., Crockett, D., & Kilpatrick, W. J. (1996). Constructing multicultural science classrooms: Quality science for all students. In J. Rhoton & P. Bowers (Eds.), *Issues in science education* (pp. 167–176). Washington, DC: National Science Teachers Association.

Banks, J. A. (1994). *Multiethnic education: Theory and practice.* Boston: Allyn & Bacon.

Banks, J. A. (2001, January/February). Citizenship education and diversity: Implications for teacher education. *Journal of Teacher Education, 52*(1), 5–6.

Baptiste, H. P., & Key, S. G. (1996). Cultural inclusion: Where does your program stand? *The Science Teacher, 63*(2), 32–35.

Barba, R. H. (1998). *Science in the multicultural classroom: A guide to teaching and learning.* Boston: Allyn & Bacon.

Bollin, G. G., & Finkel, J. (1995). White racial identity as a barrier to understanding diversity: A study of prospective teachers. *Equity & Excellence in Education, 28*(1), 25–30.

Boykin, A. W., & Toms, F. D. (1985). Black child socialization: A conceptual framework. In H. McAdoo & J. McAdoo (Eds.), *Black children: Social, educational, and parental environments* (pp. 33–51). Beverly Hills, CA: Sage.

Campbell, P. F., & Johnson, M. L. (1995). How primary children think and learn. In I. Carl (Ed.), *Prospects for school mathematics: 75 years of progress* (pp. 21–42). Reston, VA: National Council of Teachers of Mathematics.

Carpenter, T. P., Fennema, E., Franke, M. L., Levi, L., & Empson, S. B. (1999). *Children's mathematics: Cognitively guided instruction.* Portsmouth, NH: Heinemann.

Cochran-Smith, M. (1995). Confronting race, culture, and language diversity. *American Educational Research Journal, 32*(3), 493–522.

Cochran-Smith, M., & Lytle, S. L. (1990, March). Research on teaching and teacher research: The issues that divide. *Educational Researcher, 19*(2), 2–11.

Conant, F. R., Rosebery, A., Warren, B., & Hudicourt-Barnes, J. (2001). The sound of drums. In E. McIntyre, A. Rosebery, & N. Gonzalez (Ed.), *Classroom diversity: Connecting curriculum to students' lives* (pp. 51–59). Portsmouth, NH: Heinemann.

Delpit, L. (1988). The silenced dialogue: Power and pedagogy in educating other people's children. *Harvard Educational Review, 58*(3), 280–290.

Demi. (1997). *One grain of rice: A mathematical folktale.* New York: Scholastic Press.

Diller, D. (1999, May). Opening the dialogue: Using culture as a tool in teaching young African American children. *Reading Teacher, 52,* 820–827.

Gregory, S. T. (1998). Faculty diversity: Effective strategies for the recruitment and retention of faculty of color. *Trotter Review,* pp. 5–7.

Hatfield, M. M., Edwards, N. T., Bitter, G. G., & Morrow, J. (1997). *Mathematics methods for elementary and middle school teachers* (3rd ed.). Boston: Allyn & Bacon.

Hatfield, M. M., Edwards, N. T., Bitter, G. G., & Morrow, J. (2000). *Mathematics methods for elementary and middle school teachers* (4th ed.). New York: Wiley.

Haugabrook, A. K. (1998). Leadership for diversity: Effectively managing for a transformation. *Trotter Review,* pp. 17–19.

Hollins, E. R., Smiler, H., & Spencer, K. (1994). Benchmark's in meeting the challenges of effective schooling for African American youngsters." In E. R. Hollins, J. E. King, & W. C. Hayman (Eds.), *Teaching diverse populations: Formulating a knowledge base* (pp. 163–174). Albany: State University of New York Press.

Hopkinson, D. (1993). *Sweet Clara and the freedom quilt.* New York: Knopf.

Hutchins, P. (1986). *The doorbell rang.* New York: Mulberry Books.

Irvine, J. J., & Armento, B. J. (2001). *Culturally responsive teaching: Lesson planning for elementary and middle grades.* New York: McGraw-Hill.

Ladson-Billings, G. (1994). *The dreamkeepers: Successful teachers of African American children.* San Francisco: Jossey-Bass.

Ladson-Billings, G. (2000, May/June). Fighting for our lives: Preparing teachers to teach African American students. *Journal of Teacher Education, 51*(3), 206–214.

Lakoff, G., & Núñez, R. E. (1997). The metaphorical structure of mathematics: Sketching out cognitive foundations for a mind-based mathematics. In L. English (Ed.), *Mathematical reasoning: Analogies, metaphors, and images* (pp. 21–69). Mahwah, NJ: Lawrence Erlbaum Associates.

Lehman, J. R. (1994, February). Integrating science and mathematics: Perceptions of preservice and practicing elementary teachers. *School Science and Mathematics, 94*(2), 58–64.

Leonard, J. (1997). *Characterizing student discourse in a sixth-grade mathematics classroom.*

Leonard, J. (2000, April). Let's talk about the weather: Lessons learned in facilitating mathematical discourse. *Teaching Mathematics in the Middle School, 5*(8), 518–523.

Leonard, J., & Guha, S. (2002, October). Creating cultural relevance in teaching and learning mathematics. *Teaching Children Mathematics, 9*(2), 114–118.

Malloy, C., & Jones, G. (1998). An investigation of African American students mathematical problem solving. *Journal for Research in Mathematics Education, 29*(2), 143–163.

Martin, R. J., & Lock, R. S. (1997, Spring). Assessing the attitudes of student teachers toward issues of diversity: A dilemma for teacher educators. *The Journal of Intergroup Relations, 24*(1), 34–44.

Mason, C. L., Kahle, J. B., & Gardner, A. L. (1991). Draw-a-scientist test: Future implications. *School Science and Mathematics, 91*(5), 193–198.

McElroy, K. (1998). Obstacles facing new African American faculty in predominantly White colleges and universities. *Trotter Review,* pp. 14–16.

National Council of Teachers of Mathematics. (2000). *Principles and standards for school mathematics.* Reston, VA: Author.

Nieto, S. (2000). Placing equity front and center: Some thoughts on transforming teacher education for a new century. *Journal of Teacher Education, 51*(3), 180–187.

No child left behind: Reauthorization of the Elementary and Secondary Education Act of 2001. (2001). A report to the nation and the Secretary of Education, U.S. Department of Education, President Bush Initiative.

Phelan, P., Davidson, A., & Cao, H. (1991). Students' multiple worlds: Negotiating the boundaries of family, peer, and school cultures. *Anthropology and Education Quarterly, 22,* 224–250.

Phillips, S., & Ebrahimi, H. (1993). Equation for success: Project SEED. In National Council of Teachers of Mathematics (Ed.), *Reaching all students with mathematics* (pp. 59–74). Reston, VA: National Council of Teachers of Mathematics.

Phuntsog, N. (1995). Teacher educators' perceptions of the importance of multicultural education in the preparation of elementary teachers. *Equity & Excellence in Education, 28*(1), 10–14.

Price, J., & Valli, L. (1998, Spring). Institutional support for diversity in prospective teacher education. *Theory into Practice, 37*(2), 114–120.

Remillard, J. T. (2000). Prerequisites for learning to teach mathematics to all students. In W. Secada (Ed.), *Changing the faces of mathematics: Perspectives on multiculturalism and gender equity* (pp. 125–136). Reston, VA: National Council of Teachers of Mathematics.

Schifter, D., & Fosnot, C. T. (1993). *Reconstructing mathematics education.* New York: Teachers College Press.

Sleeter, C. E., & Grant, C. A. (1987). An analysis of multicultural education in the United States. *Harvard Educational Review, 57*(4), 421–444.

Softky, E. (2000, February). Identity matters: An Asian-Caribbean-American's perspective. *Black Issues in Higher Education, 16*(25), 27.

Stiff, L. V., & Harvey, W. B. (1988). On the education of Black children in mathematics. *Journal of Black Studies, 19*(2), 190–203.

Tobias, S. (1990). *They're not dumb, they're different: Stalking the second tier.* Tucson, AZ: Research Corporation—A foundation for the Advancement of Science.

Toliver, K. (1993). The Kay Toliver Mathematics Program. *The Journal of Negro Education, 62,* 35–45.

Tran, M. T., Young, R. L., & Di Lella, J. D. (1994, May/June). Multicultural education courses and the student teacher: Eliminating stereotypical attitudes in our ethnically diverse classroom. *Journal of Teacher Education, 45*(3), 183–188.

Vinovskis, M. A. (1996, Spring). An analysis of the concept and uses of systematic educational reform. *American Educational Research Journal, 33*(1), 53–85.

Viorst, J. (1978). *Alexander, who used to be rich last Sunday.* New York: Aladdin Paperbacks.

Wade, R. (1998). Brick walls and breakthroughs: Talking about diversity with White teacher education students. *Social Education, 62*(2), 84–87.

Warren, B., & Rosebery, A. (1995). Equity in the future tense: Redefining relationships among teachers, students, and science in linguistic minority classrooms. In W. Secada, E. Fennema, & L. Adajian (Eds.), *New directions for equity in mathematics education* (pp. 289–328). New York: Cambridge University Press.

Wilson, J. D. (1996). An evaluation of the field experiences of the innovative model for the preparation of elementary teachers for science, mathematics, and technology. *Journal of Teacher Education, 47*(1), 53–59.

Wlodkowski, R. J., & Ginsberg, M. B. (1995, September). A framework for culturally responsive teaching. *Educational Leadership, 53*(1), 17–21.

6

Unpacking Teachers' "Resistance" to Integrating Students' Language and Culture Into Elementary Science Instruction

Aurolyn Luykx
Peggy Cuevas
Julie Lambert
Okhee Lee
University of Miami

The increasing diversity of the nation's student population has created a growing interest in issues of culture and language in education, and a compelling need for effective instruction for all students (Lee & Fradd, 1998). As four women (three native-born Anglo-Americans and one foreign-born Asian American) with combined expertise in cultural and linguistic anthropology, science education, literacy, and teacher education, we offer our insights on leading teachers toward a better understanding of students' cultural and linguistic diversity. We have gained these insights from our participation in, and analysis of, the professional-development component of an elementary school science intervention. We believe that teachers who are able to view the world from students' perspectives and learn about their cultures can empower those students in the educational process. Multidisciplinary research can provide crucial information and guidance in this endeavor. Nevertheless, researchers' recommendations for improving instructional practice will not be achieved unless obstacles to their implementation are recognized and addressed. As Sykes (1999) argued, research-based "best practices" have an effect only to the extent that teachers adopt them. The challenge is greater with schoolwide intervention efforts involving teachers who may lack interest in—or even resist—participating, as opposed to those involving volunteer teachers actively seeking opportunities for professional growth (Elmore, 1996).

Our purpose in this chapter is to examine the evolution of our efforts at professional development and their impact on teacher beliefs. The chapter begins by explaining why it is important for teachers to articulate content knowledge with students' linguistic and cultural experiences. The subsequent sections describe the research context, teacher professional-development activities, the intervention's impact on teachers' beliefs about incorporating students' home language and culture in science instruction, and possible reasons behind some teachers' continued resistance to doing so. The chapter concludes with suggestions for future professional-development efforts.

TEACHING FOR DIVERSITY: PERSPECTIVES AND CHALLENGES

"Teaching for diversity" comprises a broad and complex realm of both theoretical and practical concerns. Below, we present a conceptual framework—*instructional congruence*—that aims to identify and delimit some of the instructional issues involved in making academic achievement accessible to all. We then examine some of the challenges that teachers face as they try to respond to these issues.

Instructional Congruence: Articulating Academic Disciplines With Student Diversity

From a sociocultural perspective, both the content and the process of instruction are important to student achievement. It is not enough for practitioners to be knowledgeable in the content area in which they teach. They must also have knowledge of how students learn and of factors influencing students' learning styles. Cultural congruence is a well-established construct addressing the variability in students' culturally based learning styles and how these mesh—or fail to—with the cultural expectations operating in mainstream classrooms. When teachers engage in communication and interactional patterns that are familiar and intelligible to students, the burden for students of navigating the tacit rules of the classroom is eased, and learning is facilitated (Au & Kawakami, 1994; Gay, 2002; Ladson-Billings, 1994, 1995; Osborne, 1996; Trueba & Wright, 1992; Villegas & Lucas, 2002).

Most of the cultural congruence literature has focused on the style and organization of teaching and learning, rather than the nature and content of academic disciplines. More recently, educational researchers have characterized science disciplines themselves as being shaped by cultural forces (Cobern, 1998; Eisenhart, 1996; Lemke, 2001; Milne & Taylor, 1998). Students from groups traditionally marginalized from school science must, in essence, become "cultural border-crossers" in order to participate successfully in science learning communities (Aikenhead, 2001; Aikenhead & Jegede, 1999). Teachers, to the degree that they become aware of students' cultural diversity and its implications for learning, can give crucial support to this process.

In an effort to further promote teachers' efforts to teach for diversity, Lee and Fradd (1998) proposed the notion of instructional congruence: "the process of mediating the nature of academic content with students' language and cultural experiences to make such content (e.g., science) accessible, meaningful, and relevant for diverse students" (p. 12). This suggests that effective subject area instruction must consider the ways in which students' cultural and linguistic experiences articulate with the knowledge and practices characteristic of specific academic disciplines. The notion of instructional congruence highlights the role of teachers in establishing congruence between academic content and practice, on the one hand, and students' linguistic and cultural patterns, on the other.

The goal of establishing instructional congruence in science classrooms is not easy to achieve. Academic disciplines have ways of producing and evaluating knowledge that have been defined by the Western tradition. Although all cultures have points of contact and overlap with this tradition, a substantial body of literature in multicultural science education indicates that some students' home cultures include practices, forms of talk, and interactional norms that are discontinuous with modern Western science. According to science education standards documents (American Association for the Advancement of Science, 1989, 1993; National Research Council, 1996; for summary, see Lee & Paik, 2000, and Raizen, 1998), science learning involves gradual mastery of three distinct areas. "Knowing" science implies an understanding of science concepts and "big ideas" (patterns of change, systems, models, and relationships) to explain natural phenomena. "Doing" science is linked to the practice of scientific inquiry: asking appropriate questions, designing and implementing investigations, and drawing valid conclusions. "Talking" science means learning the rules of scientific discourse, such as making arguments based on evidence, communicating scientific information through oral, written, and graphic forms of representation, and using scientific terminology appropriately.

Recent research indicates that diverse student groups may bring to the classroom a variety of ways of knowing, investigating, and talking about the natural world, as well as distinct values and attitudes concerning the content and format of instruction (Lee, Fradd, & Sutman, 1995; Rodriguez, 1997; Rosebery, Warren, & Conant, 1992). For many students, learning science means not only learning scientific ideas and content, but also learning how to participate in inquiry activities, how to talk about science, and how to act as part of a science learning community. Acquiring these tacit skills can often be more difficult than simply acquiring explicitly taught content knowledge (Delpit, 1988; Sleeter, 1992). Many teachers are unaware of different ways of knowing, doing, and talking about science, and may fail to discuss these implicit requirements for academic success with nonmainstream students.

Lave and Wenger (1991) viewed learning as coming to participate in a particular discourse, first in a peripheral and later in a more active way. Thus, teaching in general, and science teaching in particular, is partly a matter of socializing students from diverse languages and cultures into new ways of talking and interacting in the classroom. Some teachers may share the language and culture of their students and thus be able to establish cultural congruence in the classroom, either consciously or unconsciously. But they may still fail to establish instructional congruence if their science knowledge is insufficient to lead students toward scientific understandings and practices. Other teachers, of whatever cultural background, may have difficulty establishing instructional congruence if they identify with the scientific community but fail to recognize the value of students' own linguistic and cultural practices. Still others may fail to establish instructional congruence because they lack knowledge of both science disciplines and students' language and culture.

Obstacles to Teaching for Diversity

Although some teachers' difficulties in teaching for diversity might be interpreted as "resistance," such an interpretation may divert researchers' attention from other factors that hinder teachers from incorporating diverse learning styles and cultural patterns into instruction. Teacher behaviors that many educational researchers and commentators attribute to opposition or resistance may be due to a lack of knowledge or feelings of inadequacy on the part of teachers who have not been prepared to integrate nonmainstream students' language and culture into instruction. Is it really resistance when a teacher feels that she or he simply can't cope with trying to figure out all of the cultural patterns represented by the students in her/his class?

Most teacher education programs devote minimal attention to the multitude of learning styles and cultural patterns that teachers will likely face in the classroom. When a new teacher enters the classroom for the first time, she or he is inundated by a barrage of new experiences, not to mention an enormous amount of paperwork, pressure from parents, and often lack of support from school administrators. Delving into academic publications to find out what current educational research has to say about teaching for diversity is likely to be low on the list of teachers' day-to-day priorities. As the new teacher gains more experience in the classroom and is no longer operating in "survival" mode, her/his interest in improving instruction by learning about the particular instructional needs of individual students or specific student groups may manifest itself. Unfortunately, in the real world of teaching today, years of experience are no guarantee that a teacher will be assured, in control, and continually seeking to improve and refine the quality of instruction. Teachers' responsibilities seem to become more complex with each passing year, with high-stakes testing, reform efforts, and classroom management issues representing only a few of the challenges that divert teachers' energies from improving classroom instruction for students of diverse languages and cultures.

Many teachers undoubtedly prefer to teach according to the model of instruction with which they were taught, and assume that this traditional pedagogy will work equally well for nonmainstream students (Lortie, 1975). Their reaction to professional development focused on student diversity may be: "What do you expect me to do with all the other responsibilities I have?" There are also many others who recognize the need to incorporate different learning styles and cultural patterns into their lessons, yet lack the knowledge to accomplish this goal. We believe that most teachers sincerely want to be knowledgeable and caring professionals, but are simply inundated with more academic and emotional responsibilities for students than many, even the highly dedicated, can realistically handle. Even for teachers who have both the knowledge and the desire to take student diversity into account, external factors such as working conditions, district or state policies, or the institutional culture of the individual school may work against their efforts.

This is not to label as futile efforts to empower teachers to integrate the language and culture of their students into informal classroom interactions as well as formal instruction. Rather, it is our hope that the educational research community will concentrate its efforts on providing a solid, comprehensible, accessible research base to assist teachers in integrating, as fully as possible, the languages and cultures represented by their students. Sarroub (2002) argued that "in order for researchers and educators to support diversity in public schools they must be aware of its existence" (p. 146). She contended that an awareness of different ways of learning is a first step toward developing teaching practices that take students' cultural diversity into account. In order for this to happen, teachers must listen to students and learn about their students' home culture and community life. Teachers may feel overwhelmed as they attempt to establish congruence between academic disciplines and students' linguistic and cultural experiences. It is at this point that they need well-thought-out, effective professional development. Sykes (1999) pointed to the weak effects of attempts to promote teacher change that are unsupported by adequate professional development. Developing an understanding of how cultural patterns affect learning may imply modifications in content and presentation of curriculum—changes many teachers may resist, or simply not understand how to accomplish. Effective professional-development programs are essential components of efforts to assist teachers as they face the challenge of teaching diverse students to know, do, and talk science.

"SCIENCE FOR ALL": PROMOTING ACHIEVEMENT AND EQUITY IN SCIENCE AND LITERACY

The research project described herein is an instructional intervention to promote achievement and equity in science and literacy, focusing particularly on scientific inquiry, for linguistically and culturally diverse elementary students. Scientific inquiry occurs when students generate questions, design and carry out investigations, analyze and draw conclusions, and report findings. Inquiry also involves higher order thinking about science that includes searching for scientific patterns, making and justifying conjectures, organizing, synthesizing, evaluating, hypothesizing, making models or simulations, and inventing original procedures. The project's curriculum materials, observation protocols, and professional development are all oriented, though not exclusively, around the notion of scientific inquiry.

Merging subject-specific and diversity-oriented pedagogies, the intervention is based on two conceptual notions of effective instruction (Lee, 2002, 2003; Lee & Fradd, 1998). The first, instructional congruence, involves teachers' ability to mediate academic content and practice (in this case, science) with students' linguistic and cultural experiences, thus making it accessible and relevant for diverse groups of students. The second involves providing instructional scaffolding to promote scientific inquiry among students with limited science experience, or those from cultures where scientific inquiry is not encouraged. The *teacher-explicit to student-exploratory continuum* is used to conceptualize the goal of promoting student initiative in doing science inquiry as teachers gradually move away from more explicit instruction. These two notions have guided the development of instructional materials, teacher professional development, observations of classroom instruction, and assessment of students within the project.

The project has developed a standards-based, inquiry-based science curriculum for third, fourth, and fifth grade that is being implemented in six schools of varying demographic makeup in a large urban school district. All 52 third- and fourth-grade teachers in the six schools currently participate in the project (fifth-grade teachers will be added the following academic year)—teaching the curriculum units, administering pre- and posttests to students, participating in individual and focus group interviews, and attending professional-development workshops. Of the participating teachers, 49% described themselves as Hispanic, 24% as African American, 19% as White non-Hispanic, and 4% (two teachers) are from the Caribbean. One teacher identified herself as "Asian/Multiracial," and two declined to answer the question. Forty-one percent reported English as their native language, 34% Spanish, and 11% both English and Spanish. The majority (72%) are certified in teaching English to Speakers of Other Languages (ESOL; through either college course work or district professional development), and 50% have master's degrees.

We would like to point out that "White non-Hispanic" is the term used by the school district, and thus was chosen for the questionnaire. Throughout the remainder of the chapter, we use the term "Anglo" to refer to fair-skinned, native-born citizens of European descent (most of whom are monolingual in English), because this is the term most commonly used in the city where the study took place. For similar reasons, we also use the term "Hispanic" to refer to the region's Spanish-speaking population (mostly first- and second-generation immigrants), despite its rather dubious status as a bureaucratic "catchall" term for people from a wide range of nationalities and ethnic backgrounds.

The fact that the teachers were not selected for their interest in "teaching for diversity" means that their opinions on cultural and linguistic diversity, as well as their ways of (and reasons for) resisting change in their instructional practice, are more representative of teachers in general than a self-selected group of volunteer teachers would be. Professional development must therefore speak to a broad range of positions on the issue, and include strategies for overcoming many differently motivated forms of teacher resistance.

PROFESSIONAL DEVELOPMENT ON THE ROLE OF LANGUAGE AND CULTURE IN SCIENCE INSTRUCTION

This section describes professional-development activities designed to increase teachers' awareness of the importance of establishing instructional congruence within their elementary school classrooms, as a means of improving science instruction for culturally and linguistically diverse students. Though the project has included other professional-development activities as well, the present discussion is limited to the teacher work-shops. All teachers received four full-day workshops over the course of the 2001–2002 school year, with separate workshops for third- and fourth-grade teachers. Workshop activities were structured to encourage active involvement of all teachers, sharing of experiences in small groups, and collective reflection on their own beliefs and practices. At the first work-shop, several teachers from our previous research projects guided new teachers as they worked through specific science content and explored how to structure science instruction around inquiry activities. The second workshop focused on incorporating strategies for English-language and literacy development into specific science lessons, particularly for ESOL students. The third workshop, which is described in greater detail later, focused on the role of language and culture in science instruction. The fourth workshop was largely for purposes of teacher feedback, as well as discussion of district-level issues such as the effects of high-stakes stan-dardized testing on the implementation of the project.

Students' Home Language and Science Instruction

The first part of the third workshop was mostly expository, focusing on theoretical issues related to the role of students' home language in science instruction. These included the difference between informal and academic speech registers, the importance of students' home language for building concepts, potential semantic confusions around particular science terms, and how lack of English proficiency can masquerade as lack of science knowledge. In order to impress upon teachers the relevance of these is-sues for their own classrooms, we shared with them written test responses from their students (presented on transparencies), as well as anecdotes from our classroom observations, that illustrated some of these points.

In order to demonstrate the importance of linguistic scaffolding using key terms from students' home language, we asked teachers to read an untitled passage describing a series of procedures whose objective was purposefully vague. Before revealing the title of the passage, we asked teachers to explain what they thought the passage meant, and how well they thought they would be able to remember or reproduce its content. Understandably, most felt unable to do so. We then revealed the title ("Washing Clothes") and, after the expected "Aha!" reaction from teach-ers, explained how the lack of just a few key English terms could lead ESOL students to miss the entire meaning of a lesson.

From this discussion of more strictly language-related issues, we moved to the topic of communication and interactional patterns in the classroom, and how different students may be more or less familiar with the types of participation teachers expect of them. Because scientific inquiry is characterized by types of communication and interaction that differ from more traditional forms of instruction, teachers as well as students may find inquiry-based school science difficult if they are more accustomed to the IRE *(initiation - reply - evaluation)* pattern of classroom discourse. Drawing upon Lave and Wenger's (1991) view of learning as increasingly active participation in a particular discourse, we discussed how teaching scientific inquiry involves not only content knowledge, but also new ways of speaking and interacting in the classroom. Project personnel and teachers also shared their knowledge of the interaction patterns of Hispanic, Haitian, and Anglo children, and how these patterns might foster or limit students' participation in science classrooms, as well as shaping teachers' perceptions of different groups of students. For instance, in Haiti, elementary students are generally not encouraged to question information provided by their teachers or textbooks; Haitian immigrant students thus may be perceived by U.S. teachers as shy or passive. Conversely, U.S. classrooms in which students freely question and even interrupt the teacher may initially appear to Haitian students as if there were no rules at all governing teacher–student interaction.

In the workshop, it was emphasized that learning the forms of verbal participation necessary to engage in scientific inquiry can be even more difficult for students than learning science content. On the one hand, teachers are often unaware of the communication patterns and interactional styles characteristic of different cultures, and therefore do not talk to students about these implicit requirements for academic success (Delpit, 1988; Gay, 2002; Osborne, 1996; Villegas & Lucas, 2002). On the other hand, talking to students about these requirements—for example, the norms of inquiry-based discourse—may not be enough for students to change the ways they habitually approach content. Students from nonmainstream cultures often consider it rude or combative to address points made in the previous person's contribution, defend one's arguments with logic and evidence, or look for anomalies in another person's statement (Atwater, 1994; Deyhle & Swisher, 1997; Nelson-Barber & Estrin, 1995; Solano-Flores & Nelson-Barber, 2001).

Students' Home Culture and Science Instruction

The second part of the workshop focused on integrating elements of students' home cultures into science instruction. We began by reviewing teachers' responses to a brainstorming exercise on the meaning of the term "culture" and discussing how different definitions of the term were more or less useful for thinking about the role of culture in science instruction. After discussing how shared experiences and group identity contribute to defining a person's culture, teachers were also encouraged to think about cultural differences *within* ethnic groups, related to gender, age, socioeconomic status, and so on. We then linked this discussion to the previous discussion of interactional patterns by pointing out how people of different cultural backgrounds may have different perceptions, expectations, and interpretations of what sorts of behavior are polite, disrespectful, intelligent, childish, and so forth. Culturally patterned reactions to different topics were also discussed, using the example of people's weight (which was not only the topic of a science activity in one of the instructional units, but also a topic of friendly banter among teachers).

This discussion was followed by an activity designed to illustrate the importance of existing cultural frameworks for the interpretation of new experiences. Teachers were asked to read another purposefully ambiguous passage, and then were shown a picture (of a man serenading a woman) that made the meaning of the passage clear. Together, teachers and project personnel tried to identify the cultural knowledge that was necessary to correctly interpret the scene portrayed in the picture. We then related this to the types of cultural knowledge that students need in order to recognize scientific procedures, interpret new information, and interact appropriately in science classrooms.

Throughout these discussions, teachers found it easier to apply the culture concept to cultural "others" than to themselves. This was only natural, inasmuch as people's own cultural patterns are largely invisible to them, or are interpreted as simply what "normal" people do. In order to combat teachers' tendency to think of culture as something that non-mainstream students had to overcome in order to succeed academically, we asked them to discuss cultural influences on their own teaching. Teachers were organized into small groups and presented with the following questions:

1. How does your culture influence:
   - Your teaching style?
   - The sorts of classroom activities you feel comfortable or uncomfortable doing?
   - Your tolerance toward different types of student behavior?
2. Where does your own teaching style come from?
3. What experiences were your biggest influences in developing your personal teaching style?

The subsequent general discussion revealed this exercise to be only partially successful. Teachers reported some insights, such as the fact that each school has its own institutional culture that constrains teacher practice, and a few referred to their own upbringing or early schooling, but there was a marked tendency for the discussion to drift back to the cultural peculiarities of nonmainstream students. One teacher admitted to continued uncertainty as to "what [project personnel] were looking for." A few other teachers mentioned how people from different cultures might interpret concepts such as disrespect, copying, and shyness. The discussion then turned back to language, as teachers reflected on how ESOL students might be confused by English metaphors and idioms or teachers' common habit of phrasing commands as questions.

During the next phase of the workshop, we presented the teachers with examples of cultural influence in students' written test responses. Some examples also revealed details of students' home life, such as one Hispanic student who wrote that one would need a sweater to go out and play even in 90°F weather, because "you always take a sweater when you go outside." After sharing these examples, we asked teachers to go back into small groups to discuss the following questions about cultural influences on students' learning, though we realized that the teachers had already broached this topic in the previous discussion:

1. What differences have you observed among your students with regard to:

   • How they interact in class (with you and with each other)?
   • Their preferences for certain activities or topics?

2. How well do you know your students' culture(s), home life, or personal backgrounds?
3. What knowledge do you feel you would need to tailor instruction to your students' cultural background?
4. How do/could you get this information?

These questions were designed not only to move teachers away from a simplistic conception of culture as "food, fairs, and festivals," but also to lead them to consider the differences they had already observed among their students as possibly having a cultural basis. The final two questions were aimed at orienting the teachers to think more concretely about the kinds of information and instructional adaptations they would need in order to teach more effectively in situations of cultural diversity.

To avoid the discussion becoming a litany of nonmainstream students' supposed deficits, we began it by mentioning skills common among Haitian children, such as handling money and constructing toy kites, that could be academically beneficial. One teacher said that her students preferred to work in groups, and that she met informally with parents to find out about students' home life. Another pointed out that her school, one of the predominantly Anglo schools, had more diversity than people realize, and that its preponderance of "gifted" students had as much to do with parental pressure to place students in gifted programs as with their actual academic ability. There was agreement that getting children to write about their lives outside of school was a good way to find out more about their culture, though several teachers from the lower-income schools remarked that their students often see them as substitute mothers and "tell us more than we want to know" (e.g., anecdotes involving substance abuse or violence in the home). A teacher who, during an earlier discussion, had dismissed the influence of culture in learning mentioned another issue: the political view that science is Western propaganda intended to showcase the United States as a superior culture. Although this provocative comment could have launched another interesting conversation, the advancing hour obliged us to close the discussion and move on to the planning and presentation of individual lessons by small groups of teachers.

Teachers' Strategies for Incorporating Students' Language and Culture Into Science Lessons

As teachers worked in teams of four on specific lessons from the matter unit (third grade) and the weather unit (fourth grade), we asked them to devise activities relating the science content of the lessons to their students' home languages and cultures. After a period of planning and preparation, each team came forward to share their efforts with the entire group. Some of the teams' suggestions for mediating science content with students' cultural experiences were the following:

- Demonstrate air pressure using examples of a pressure cooker (*olla de presión*) and changes in air pressure in one's ears while downhill skiing.
- Have students give "TV" weather reports in the classroom, in both English and their home language.
- Have students discuss the climate in different countries, using a world map.
- Discuss synonyms for the term *hurricane* (such as *cyclone* and *typhoon*) and what countries/cultures use them.
- Show pictures of the different types of houses on the island nations that are vulnerable to hurricanes.

As encouraging and valuable as some of these suggestions are, two things were notable during this part of the workshop. First, several of the groups simply failed to mention any strategies for incorporating students' language and culture into the science lessons. In these cases, project personnel offered suggestions on how to do so (such as asking students if they know any folk sayings or beliefs concerning the weather, and if they think these might have some scientific validity). Second, all of the strategies offered by the teams involved the insertion of cultural *content,* rather than adaptations in the organization of classroom activity or discourse. This is not surprising, given that the latter sort of adaptations often require more subtle knowledge (and more in-depth planning) than was available to the teachers in the limited context of a 1-day workshop. But it also suggests that such a workshop may not be sufficient to expand teachers' conceptions of "culture" beyond its more concrete material manifestations, to include the patterns of interaction and interpretation that are fundamental to everyday classroom processes.

CHANGE IN TEACHERS' BELIEFS ABOUT STUDENTS' LANGUAGE AND CULTURE

Teachers' beliefs about incorporating students' language and culture into science instruction were examined through questionnaires administered at the beginning (fall 2001) and end (spring 2002) of the school year. Teachers responded using 5-point Likert scales. In addition, the spring questionnaire contained several open-ended questions, including: "How has your participation in Science for All affected how you incorporate students' home language and culture into science instruction?"

Teachers' Quantitative Responses Regarding Students' Language and Culture

The questionnaires obtained teachers' self-reports of their *knowledge* of how to incorporate students' home language and culture into science instruction, and also their opinions of the *importance* of doing so. The set of questions about culture referred to: (a) the ways students' cultural experiences may influence science instruction, (b) culturally based ways students communicate and interact in their home and community, (c) students' lives at home and in the community, and (d) students' cultural artifacts, culturally relevant examples, and community resources. The set of questions about students' home language referred to: (a) using key science terms in students' home language to enhance understanding, (b) supporting use of the home language among students to construct meaning, and (c) encouraging more English-proficient students to assist less-proficient students through their home language.

TABLE 6.1
Means and Standard Deviations for Students' Home Language
and Culture: Teachers' Self-Reports of Knowledge and Importance
in Fall 2001 and Spring 2002 (N = 52)

Construct	Teachers' Self-Reports of:	Time	M	SD
Culture	Importance	Fall	4.29	.62
		Spring	4.37	.66
	Knowledge	Fall	3.74	.85
		Spring	3.73	.79
Home Language	Importance	Fall	4.25	.73
		Spring	4.25	.63
	Knowledge	Fall	3.58	.95
		Spring	3.72	.93

At the beginning of the school year, on a 5-point Likert scale (1 = very low, 5 = very high), teachers emphasized the importance of incorporating students' culture (M [mean] = 4.29, SD [standard deviation] = .62) and home language (M = 4.25, SD = .73) in science instruction (see Table 6.1). In contrast, teachers gave lower scores to their own knowledge of how to incorporate students' culture (M = 3.74, SD = .85) and home language (M = 3.58, SD = .95) in science instruction. At the year-end workshop, teachers again emphasized the importance of incorporating students' culture (M = 4.37, SD = .66) and home language (M = 4.25, SD = .63) in science instruction, but again gave relatively lower scores to their knowledge of how to do so (culture: M = 3.73, SD = .79; language: M = 3.72, SD = .93).

Significance tests of mean scores between fall and spring indicate that teachers' self-reported knowledge level and the importance they assigned to incorporating students' languages and cultures into science instruction did not show statistically significant change. The effect size (d magnitude) was less than small (see Table 6.2). Teachers apparently remained convinced of the importance of this goal, though they remained less certain of how to achieve it.

TABLE 6.2
Significance Test Results for Students' Home Language and Culture:
Mean Differences Between Fall 2001 and Spring 2002

Construct	Teachers' Self-Reports of:	t	p	Cohen's d (effect size)	d magnitude
Culture	Importance	.78	.44	.11	less than small
	Knowledge	−.05	.96	.01	less than small
Home Language	Importance	1.44	.16	.20	less than small
	Knowledge	.85	.40	.12	less than small

Increased Acceptance of Students' Home Language and Culture

Written responses of almost half of the teachers (24/52) on the open-ended items included in the postquestionnaire indicated an awareness of the importance of providing instructionally congruent instruction. Three major patterns emerged from postquestionnaire responses.

First, teachers' incorporation of students' cultural diversity was most often reported as allowing students to share relevant stories and experiences from their home or community within the context of the planned science lesson. One fifth (2/10) of the teachers from the predominantly Anglo schools, one fourth (6/24) of the teachers from the Hispanic schools, and almost one third (5/18) of the teachers from schools with many Haitian students used this strategy. Some of these responses, though not directly manifesting resistance, seemed to indicate only minimal commitment to instructional congruence, with teachers leaving it to students to seek links between science content and their home culture. One teacher wrote, "Sometimes when we have an oral discussion the kids may relate things that have occurred in their native country or things that they have noticed that transpired when they were with their parents." Recognition of the relevance of students' language and culture to the success of the lesson was illustrated by the response of one teacher from a predominantly Hispanic school: "Student's language and culture is a strength not only in science instruction but all subject areas. Allowing the students to provide anecdotes from their own backgrounds makes instruction real for the students and places instruction at their own level."

Second, in contrast to those teachers who simply reported "allowing" students to offer their own cultural examples and experiences, other teachers reported actively seeking to include nonmainstream students' language and culture in their science instruction. One fourth (6/24) of the teachers in the predominantly Hispanic schools, one sixth (3/18) of the teachers in the predominantly Haitian-American schools, and one tenth (1/10) of the teachers in the predominantly Anglo schools fell into this category. According to their self-reports, teachers' efforts in this regard included preparing assignments that encouraged students to share aspects of their culture (though they did not mention specific assignments), helping students become more sensitive to diverse backgrounds and cultures, and using teachers' own knowledge of students' home language to develop deeper science understandings. One teacher in a predominantly Haitian-American school wrote: "I now realize I need to incorporate students' language and culture. I use the language as needed to help my students make connections to what they have already experienced at home. I take the culture into consideration and carefully explain to my students that questioning the teacher is acceptable and not a sign of disrespect." This teacher's effort to encourage inquiry and questioning on the part of students whose home culture prohibits such expression in the classroom is a clear indication of cultural scaffolding. In addition, although she herself does not speak Haitian Creole, she reported asking bilingual children in the classroom to translate phrases or words into Creole for their classmates whose English proficiency was more limited. The teachers' guides to the curriculum units also provide translations of key science terms, for use by teachers who do not speak their students' home language.

Finally, some teachers mentioned efforts to incorporate students' home language, but not their culture, into science lessons. One fourth (6/24) of the teachers in the predominantly Hispanic schools, slightly over one third (7/18) of the teachers in the predominantly Haitian-American schools, and almost half (4/10) of the teachers in the predominantly Anglo schools were in this category. Teachers' reported strategies for incorporating students' home language included (a) encouraging peer tutoring among students and (b) using words from students' home language when explaining science vocabulary or class procedures. Five of the six teachers who used peer tutoring extensively did not speak the home language of some of their students. Consequently, they encouraged students who were more fully bilingual to help those children who were less so. Of the 10 teachers whose efforts focused primarily on the use of translated terms and phrases, only 3 actually spoke the students' home language. The rest relied on the translated science vocabulary provided in the units, on other teachers and paraprofessionals who spoke the students' language, and on impromptu translation assistance from students themselves. Typical of this approach was the comment of a teacher from one of the predominantly Hispanic schools: "Occasionally I need to have a word in Spanish but the students figure it out for me." A teacher from one of the predominantly Haitian-American schools responded, "By using the 'bank' of bilingual teachers we have at the school."

Teachers' Continued Resistance to Embracing Cultural Diversity in the Classroom

Although almost half of the teachers appeared to make an effort to establish instructional congruence, especially with regard to students' home language, slightly more than half (28/52) of the respondents indicated a negative or, at best, neutral attitude toward integrating students' cultures into science instruction.

Teachers' resistance to embracing cultural diversity in the classroom was manifested on the questionnaire in two forms. The first involved simply declining to answer the part of the question referring to culture. This occurred with more than one fifth (5/24) of the teachers at predominantly Hispanic schools, one third (6/18) of the teachers at predominantly Haitian-American schools, and almost one third (3/10) of the teachers at predominantly Anglo schools. Five other teachers (three from predominantly Anglo schools and two from a predominantly Hispanic school) indicated simply that they did not incorporate students' culture. Three teachers at a predominantly Anglo school and one teacher at a predominantly Hispanic school referred to their classes' lack of ESOL students or students from other cultures as their reason for not incorporating culture into instruction. Examples included: "I don't need to very often. My students are ESOL level 5"; and "The workshop on culture identified different ways to 'reach' other cultural differences. However, I found that most was not applicable at my school. Most of the students speak English [as a] first/primary language."

Two teachers gave clearly negative statements regarding the incorporation of students' culture. Both were Hispanic teachers in predominantly Hispanic schools. One wrote: "I incorporate the students' language into the science instruction but not their culture. I believe that in the real world no one is going to ask me or adapt to my culture to be able to function in society." The other teacher wrote: "We teach the language. However, even though we discuss the cultures of other countries, I believe that culture of other countries should not be incorporated into our science instruction. We learn and understand, but it is not or should not be considered in our lesson plan!" Although these responses seem to express resistance to teaching for diversity, it is also possible that they represent, not an unwillingness to provide culturally congruent instruction, but the misconception that doing so means incorporating "food, fairs, and festivals" of other cultures into science instruction—or perhaps a more general lack of knowledge as to what "incorporating students' culture" might mean.

Though most teachers had little difficulty recognizing the importance of students' home language, this attitude did not always extend to students' culture, perhaps because the culture concept itself and the relation of culture to learning are more subtle and harder for the nonspecialist to grasp. Teachers who are not knowledgeable regarding culturally congruent teaching practices are likely to assume that "incorporating students' culture" means learning about the folklore of other countries.

Teachers' resistance to the notion that culture is an important factor in students' science learning and thus should be taken into account in science instruction was not based on a single, unified perspective. Rather, in the discussions that arose around this question at professional-development workshops, teachers expressed a variety of viewpoints about the relationship between science learning and students' culture. Following are listed some of the different arguments presented by teachers on the subject of students' culture and their own instruction.

Culture Is Irrelevant to Science.   This was perhaps the most common view held by teachers, reflecting the widespread assumption that science knowledge is universal and therefore "culture-free." In fact, many of the teachers who later became convinced that it was important to take students' culture into account in science instruction probably did not abandon the assumption of science's universality. Rather, they came to feel that whereas science itself may be culture-free, styles of teaching and learning are not, and thus may productively be adjusted if diverse groups of students are to get the most out of science instruction. A teacher of Haitian-American students wrote: "I now realize I need to incorporate students' language and culture. I use the language as needed to help my students make connections to what they have already experienced at home. I take the culture into consideration and carefully explain to my students that it's OK to disagree with me as long as they do it with respect." Others also came to feel that by incorporating cultural examples familiar to students into instruction, science could be made more accessible to students whose cultural backgrounds did not predispose them to an affinity for the subject; for example, "I allow the students to provide anecdotes from their own backgrounds which makes the instruction real for the students." Either of these perspectives is compatible with the assumption that science knowledge itself is culture-free; thus, in many cases teacher change may be achieved without challenging that assumption (itself a much more difficult task).

Culture Is Irrelevant to Learning.   This represents a less common, more extreme position, but one that was argued forcefully by at least one teacher on the project. At the workshop described previously, this teacher argued that "neuroscientists have proven" that all human behavior is innate and genetically determined, and therefore culture does not affect children's learning. Though numerous arguments, both intuitive and research-based, can be marshaled against this position, demonstrating the logical fallacies in others' positions is not necessarily the most effective way to promote teacher change, nor is it always feasible within the context of a professional-development workshop. On the other hand, it is notable that several teachers assumed that students' culture was not a relevant factor once students became reasonably fluent in English. Additionally, the fact that few teachers at predominantly Anglo schools mentioned incorporating students' culture into instruction attests to the ever-present and (to its practitioners) "invisible" nature of mainstream culture in most schools. Apparently, the frequent references to mainstream culture that occur in most classroom settings are not perceived by most teachers as "cultural."

It's Not Our Job to Teach Them Their Culture. This position reflects a misconception around the goals of the project and perhaps of culturally congruent instruction in general. The main goal of such instruction is usually not "to teach students their own culture" (though honoring or maintaining that culture may be among a program's goals), but rather to use elements of students' home culture so that students may more effectively acquire the knowledge that the dominant culture considers important. Clarifying program goals may thus be effective in overcoming this type of resistance. On the other hand, this argument may also be indicative of a deeper, often unspoken feeling that cultural diversity is threatening to the maintenance or integrity of the dominant culture, and therefore should not be granted a foothold in important social institutions such as the school. If so, clarification of goals may be ineffective in convincing teachers to make accommodations to other cultures in their science instruction.

They're Becoming More Americanized Anyway. In other words, ongoing cultural assimilation of nonmainstream students means that cultural diversity, whatever relation it may have to students' learning, will not be a problem much longer. According to this argument, making adjustments for students' cultures may only delay the process of assimilation, which is best completed as quickly as possible. In reality, Deyhle and Swisher (1997) indicated that diverse students do better academically when they maintain strong ties to their ancestral communities, traditions, and cultural identities. Still, the power of the assimilationist position lies in the fact that it is usually rooted in teachers' commonsense experience and firsthand knowledge of their students; and on such rhetorical terrain, those attempting to promote teacher change are at an obvious disadvantage relative to teachers themselves. This perspective, by minimizing the importance of cultural differences, also implicitly challenges those who advocate "teaching for diversity" to concretely assess the magnitude and educational significance of cultural differences for specific student populations, which is no easy task.

Upon reflection, it is clear that each of these arguments arises from particular notions about science, learning, culture, the role of schooling in students' socialization, and the place of cultural minorities in the larger society. Such notions are themselves rooted in deeper political or epistemological assumptions that are not easily engaged in the process of large-scale professional development—though they may be engaged quite productively with small groups of highly motivated teachers, if the group has developed the level of trust necessary to broach such thorny questions (cf. McIntyre, 1997; Spindler & Spindler, 1994). Though entrenched, such assumptions are not necessarily immovable; many deeply held beliefs evolve or are discarded over the course of an individual's lifetime. More commonly, significant changes in teacher practice may be achieved without challenging such assumptions directly, either by appealing to other values that teachers hold dear or by showing how the desired change may articulate with teachers' perspectives in ways they had not foreseen. For example, teachers who are not receptive to political or humanistic arguments for incorporating students' culture into classroom instruction may nonetheless be persuaded that it is worth doing if it can be shown to have positive effects on students' academic achievement.

CONCLUSIONS

Some teachers in the project gradually moved away from their prior viewpoints on the relation between science instruction and students' culture, as their participation in the project evolved and deepened. Others maintained their original viewpoints, or perhaps even deepened their conviction that science instruction need not be adjusted in response to students' cultural backgrounds. Notably, teachers who did change their perspective seldom cited those arguments or examples presented to them by project personnel at workshops as the reason why. Instead, they often cited specific experiences with their students that had led them to believe that taking students' culture into account did, in fact, lead to more effective instruction. This would seem to support the notion that "arguments from the outside" are a much less effective catalyst for change than personal experience, especially if teachers have the opportunity to reflect on that experience, either individually or collectively. Of course, the types of experiences leading to teacher change are more likely to arise when teachers are willing to suspend the assumptions underlying their current instructional practices and experiment with different teaching strategies, even though they may not initially be convinced of the effectiveness of such strategies. Just bringing teachers to the point where they are willing to invest effort in experimenting with new, unproven techniques may be the first essential task of many professional-development initiatives.

The lesson to be learned for those who would engage in professional development is that teachers' resistance to teaching for diversity has different sources, and should not be treated as a single, unified phenomenon. In fact, the term *resistance* may often be misapplied to teachers who lack not the will, but the knowledge or the power to tailor their instruction to their students' backgrounds. Researchers and teacher educators should not assume that resistance accounts for every discrepancy between professional-development goals and teachers' classroom practice. Is teachers' failure to embrace their students' cultural and linguistic diversity based on prejudice, lack of knowledge, lack of time, competing demands (such as helping other students with special needs), or the pressure of accountability measures imposed by the education system? Do all of these stances represent true resistance? Many teachers would undoubtedly argue that they do not.

For these and other reasons, not all strategies for overcoming resistance will be effective with all teachers (and of course, some teachers may not respond to any of them). Teacher educators thus must be equipped with a variety of strategies for fostering teacher change. They must also listen closely to individual teachers in order to determine what sort of change is needed and what strategies are most likely to promote it in each particular case. Just as we would encourage teachers to listen to students, so we encourage teacher educators, researchers, and those engaged in professional development to listen to teachers. If linking instruction to students' prior knowledge is essential to building scientific understandings, linking professional-development strategies to teachers' own concerns and institutional constraints is just as essential to producing profound and lasting teacher change.

ACKNOWLEDGMENTS

This work is supported by the National Science Foundation, U.S. Department of Education, and National Institutes of Health (Grant REC-0089231). Any opinions, findings, conclusions, or recommendations expressed in this publication are those of the authors and do not necessarily reflect the position, policy, or endorsement of the funding agencies.

REFERENCES

Aikenhead, G. (2001). Students' ease in crossing cultural borders into school science. *Science Education, 85*(2), 180–188.

Aikenhead, G., & Jegede, O. J. (1999). Cross-cultural science education: A cognitive explanation of a cultural phenomenon. *Journal of Research in Science Teaching, 36*(3), 269–288.

American Association for the Advancement of Science. (1989). *Science for all Americans.* New York: Oxford University Press.

American Association for the Advancement of Science. (1993). *Benchmarks for science literacy.* New York: Oxford University Press.

Atwater, M. M. (1994). Research on cultural diversity in the classroom. In D. L. Gabel (Ed.), *Handbook of research on science teaching and learning* (pp. 558–576). New York: Macmillan.

Au, K. H., & Kawakami, A. J. (1994). Cultural congruence in instruction. In E. R. Hollins, J. E. King, & W. C. Hayman (Eds.), *Teaching diverse populations: Formulating a knowledge base* (pp. 5–24). Albany: State University of New York Press.

Cobern, W. W. (1998). Science and a social constructivist view of science education. In W. W. Cobern (Ed.), *Socio-cultural perspectives on science education* (pp. 7–24).Boston: Kluwer Academic.

Delpit, L. (1988). The silenced dialogue: Power and pedagogy in educating other people's children. *Harvard Educational Review, 58*(3), 280–298.

Deyhle, D., & Swisher, K. (1997). Research in American Indian and Alaska Native education: From assimilation to self-determination. In M. W. Apple (Ed.), *Review of research in education* (Vol. 22, pp. 113–194). Washington, DC: American Educational Research Association.

Eisenhart, M. (1996). The production of biologists at school and work: Making scientists, conservationists, or flowery bone-heads? In B. Levinson, D. Foley, & D. Holland (Eds.), *The cultural production of the educated person: Critical ethnographies of schooling and local practice* (pp. 169–186). Albany: State University of New York Press.

Elmore, R. (1996). Getting to scale with good educational practice. *Harvard Educational Review, 66*(1), 1–26.

Gay, G. (2002). Preparing for culturally responsive teaching. *Journal of Teacher Education, 53*(2), 106–116.

Ladson-Billings, G. (1994). *The dreammakers: Successful teachers of African American children.* San Francisco: Jossey-Bass.

Ladson-Billings, G. (1995). Toward a theory of culturally relevant pedagogy. *American Educational Research Journal, 32,* 465–491.

Lave, J., & Wenger, E. (1991). *Situated learning: Legitimate peripheral participation.* New York: Cambridge University Press.

Lee, O. (2002). Science inquiry for elementary students from diverse backgrounds. In W. G. Secada (Ed.), *Review of research in education* (Vol. 26, pp. 23–29). Washington, DC: American Educational Research Association.

Lee, O. (2003). Equity for culturally and linguistically diverse students in science education. *Teachers College Record, 105*(3), 465–489.

Lee, O., & Fradd, S. H. (1998). Science for all, including students from non-English language backgrounds. *Educational Researcher, 27*(3), 12–21.

Lee, O., Fradd, S. H., & Sutman, F. X. (1995). Science knowledge and cognitive strategy use among culturally and linguistically diverse students. *Journal of Research in Science Teaching, 32,* 797–816.

Lee, O., & Paik, S. (2000). Conceptions of science achievement in major reform documents. *School Science and Mathematics, 100*(1), 16–26.

Lemke, J. L. (2001). Articulating communities: Sociocultural perspectives on science education. *Journal of Research in Science Teaching, 38*(3), 296–316.

Lortie, D. C. (1975). *Schoolteacher: A sociological study.* Chicago: University of Chicago Press.

McIntyre, A. (1997). *Making meaning of whiteness: Exploring racial identity with White teachers.* Albany: State University of New York Press.

Milne, C. E., & Taylor, P. C. (1998). Between a myth and a hard place: Situating school science in a climate of critical cultural reform. In W. W. Cobern (Ed.), *Sociocultural perspectives on science education* (pp. 7–24). Boston: Kluwer Academic.

National Research Council. (1996). *National science education standards.* Washington, DC: National Academy Press.

Nelson-Barber, S., & Estrin, E. T. (1995). Bringing Native American perspectives to mathematics and science teaching. *Theory Into Practice, 34*(3), 174–185.

Osborne, A. B. (1996). Practice into theory into practice: Culturally relevant pedagogy for students we have marginalized and normalized. *Anthropology and Education Quarterly, 27*(3), 285–314.

Raizen, S. (1998). Standards for science education. *Teachers College Record, 100,* 66–121.

Rodriguez, A. J. (1997). The dangerous discourse of invisibility: A critique of the NRC's National Science Education Standards. *Journal of Research in Science Teaching, 34,* 19–37.

Rosebery, A. S., Warren, B., & Conant, F. R. (1992). Appropriating scientific discourse: Findings from language minority classrooms. *The Journal of the Learning Sciences, 21,* 61–94.

Sarroub, L. K. (2002). In-betweenness: Religion and conflicting visions of literacy. *Reading Research Quarterly, 37,* 130–148.

Sleeter, C. E. (1992). *Keepers of the American dream.* London: Falmer Press.

Solano-Flores, G., & Nelson-Barber, S. (2001). On the cultural validity of science assessments. *Journal of Research in Science Teaching, 38*(5), 553–573.

Spindler, G., & Spindler, L. (Eds.). (1994). *Pathways to cultural awareness: Cultural therapy with teachers and students.* Thousand Oaks, CA: Corwin Press.

Sykes, G. (1999). Teacher and student learning: Strengthening their connection. In L. Darling-Hammond & G. Sykes (Eds.), *Teaching as the learning profession: Handbook of policy and practice* (pp. 151–180). San Francisco: Jossey-Bass.

Trueba, H. T., & Wright, P. G. (1992). On ethnographic studies and multicultural education. In M. Saravia-Shore & S. Arvizu (Eds.), *Cross-cultural literacy: Ethnographies of communication in multiethnic classrooms* (pp. 299–338). New York: Garland.

Villegas, A. M., & Lucas, T. (2002). Preparing culturally responsive teachers: Rethinking the curriculum. *Journal of Teacher Education, 53*(1), 20–32.

7

Engaging Prospective Teachers in Critical Reflection: Facilitating a Disposition to Teach Mathematics for Diversity

Thea K. Dunn
University of Wisconsin-River Falls

> *Reflection is action-oriented, social and political. Its product is praxis (informed, committed action) the most eloquent and socially significant form of human action.*
>
> —Kemmis (1985, p. 141)

As the student population continues to diversify (Jordan, 1995), the prospective-teacher population is becoming increasingly homogeneous (Nieto, 1998). Facilitating a disposition to teach mathematics for diversity requires that teachers embrace the notion that teaching should promote the learning of mathematics with understanding by all students, regardless of demographic characteristics. Because teachers play a pivotal role in achieving equity in the mathematics classroom (Tate, 1996), this discussion examines a multiyear initiative designed to facilitate prospective elementary teachers' ability to create learning environments that engage all learners in constructing mathematical understandings, refining their thinking, and developing confidence in their ability to do mathematics. Embedded in this progressively evolving initiative is the goal of addressing the mathematics education of diverse student populations by eliminating the long-standing disparities in mathematics achievement.

Instructional practices embody teachers' beliefs, which are a reflection of their own experiences and background (Cabello & Burstein, 1995). Teachers' expectations, experiences, and personal theories about learners from diverse ethnic, linguistic, socioeconomic, and educational and family backgrounds provide a lens through which they view teaching. These prior beliefs and knowledge act as filters (Kagan, 1992), making it difficult to influence prospective teachers' beliefs (Zeichner & Gore, 1990) about teaching mathematics for diversity. This discussion illustrates how engaging prospective teachers in critical reflection can begin to reverse the cycle of underachievement and educational disadvantage for diverse learners by facilitating a disposition to teach mathematics for diversity. The design of the elementary mathematics methods courses that comprise the initiative examined here is structured to reflect the vision that all access and equity in mathematics education must be a major goal of mathematics teaching and learning. The implications highlighted by this study continue to inform the design and structure of elementary mathematics methods courses. This chapter concludes with a discussion of the challenges and potential of this project to move mathematics teaching away from the exclusionary practices of the past to enhance mathematics teaching and learning for all learners.

THEORETICAL FRAMEWORK

A goal of many teacher education programs is to develop the prospective teacher into a reflective practitioner, a "lifelong learner who perceives every experience as an opportunity for growth, change, and development of understanding" (Hutchinson & Allen, 1997, p. 226). Critical reflection is distinguished from technical reflection in that it goes beyond the procedural to consider whether equity, justice, caring, and compassion inform educational goals (Gore & Zeichner, 1991). It involves examining the moral and ethical implications and consequences of teaching (Zehm & Kottler, 1993). As such, it transcends practical reasoning to "consider how the forms and contents of our thoughts are shaped by the historical situations in which we find ourselves" (Kemmis, 1985, p. 141). The process of facilitating critical reflection in teachers draws upon the notion that teachers are expected to become more self-consciously reflective about their actions (Schon, 1983). Reflective practice, as defined by Dewey (1933), may be viewed as a dynamic process that requires an action outcome:

> Reflective thinking, in distinction to other operations to which we apply the name of thought, involves (1) a state of doubt, hesitation, perplexity, mental difficulty, in which thinking originates, and (2) an act of searching, hunting, inquiring, to find material that will resolve the doubt, settle and dispose of the perplexity and demand for the solution of a perplexity, is the steadying and guiding factor in the entire process of reflection. (Dewey, 1933, p. 14)

The foundation of working toward learning to teach mathematics for diversity is to provide prospective teachers with opportunities for critically reflecting on new information and experiences. This is especially crucial during experiences in settings with diverse student populations because, whereas teacher behavior may be influenced by prior educational experiences, experience is educative only with time for reflection (Richardson, 1990). During the course of teacher preparation programs, myths and stereotypes regarding diverse student populations may be woven and reinforced time and time again (Flores, Tefft Cousin, & Díaz, 1991). Without structured reflection, prospective teachers' misconceptions of diverse learners may be reinforced rather than challenged (O'Grady, 1998). As Risko, Roskos, and Vukelich (1999) insisted, "prospective teachers need explicit guidance in reflection so as to advance their natural tendencies beyond mindless ritual towards a critical stance on the pedagogic understandings and actions" (p. 7). In an effort to address the mathematics education of diverse student populations, the current study draws inspiration from these earlier studies. The initiative examined within this study seeks to draw together the findings from these works to inform practice by moving prospective teachers away from unreflective practice and engaging them in critical reflection that incorporates moral and ethical criteria.

SOCIOCULTURAL CONTEXT

An overarching goal of the ongoing, multiyear initiative examined here is to respond to the disparities that exist in the mathematics teaching, learning, and performance of diverse learners and their White peers. Arguing that teachers must be both critical and transformative, this study examines the experiences of White prospective elementary teachers enrolled in elementary mathematics methods courses designed to prepare teachers to teach mathematics for diversity by engaging them in critical reflection. The prospective elementary teachers who enroll in the methods courses typically have low mathematics self-concepts (McLeod, 1992; Reyes, 1984) and come from educational systems dominated by traditional teaching practices (Zeichner & Gore, 1990). In contrast, the methods courses examined here are structured to emphasize a social reconstructionist orientation to teaching and learning mathematics that highlights the relationship between the social conditions of schooling and practices that take place in the classroom (Liston & Zeichner, 1991). Consistent with the social reconstructionist orientation of the methods course, the prospective teachers are encouraged to examine the social and political implications of instructional practices and the contexts in which these occur to work for their contribution to greater equity and justice in schooling and society. Embracing a social reconstructionist orientation entails a deliberate commitment by teacher educators to work for social change (Zeichner, 1994). Therefore, as the instructor of the methods course, I engage prospective teachers in critical conversations about equitable and socially just teaching. This process often reveals conceptualizations about mathematics teaching and diverse learners held by prospective elementary teachers.

The learning environment of the methods courses models constructivist mathematics teaching and learning and attention to diversity. Throughout the semester, I model inquiry-based, student-centered, collaborative learning and, by modeling the process of critical reflection, illustrate for the prospective teachers how to encourage and foster reflective thinking in their own learners. Reflecting a vision of mathematics teaching and learning as described in the National Council of Teacher of Mathematics [NCTM] *Principles and Standards for School Mathematics* (NCTM, 2000), the methods courses strive to enhance prospective elementary teachers' ability to teach mathematics in such a way that all of their students develop "mathematical power" (NCTM, 2000). Mathematical power includes both ability (to conjecture, reason logically, solve nonroutine problems, and communicate about mathematics) and attitude (self-confidence and a disposition to question, explore, and engage in significant mathematical problems). This goal requires that prospective elementary teachers use knowledge of how students construct conceptualizations of mathematical concepts to select and use materials, develop multiple teaching strategies and instructional activities, design and utilize authentic assessment strategies, and create learning environments in which all students learn mathematics meaningfully. Prospective teachers who enroll in the methods courses are engaged in critically reflecting on mathematics autobiographies, video clips of classrooms composed of diverse learners, and field experiences in diverse classrooms. Reflections are recorded in journals and posted to an online discussion board.

METHODOLOGY

Guided by naturalistic inquiry, as the researcher-instructor involved in this ongoing, multiyear initiative, I employ a qualitative methodology to understand phenomena in context-specific settings (Lincoln & Guba, 1985) and to "make sense of phenomena in terms of the meanings people bring to them" (Denzin & Lincoln, 1994, p. 2). This approach assumes that meaning is constructed by both the researcher and the participants. Because I provide a mentoring component, the prospective teachers and I interact to influence one another. Consistent with a naturalistic paradigm, the knower and the known are inseparable. Within the context of this study, naturalistic inquiry is utilized to develop a body of knowledge, enables careful elucidation and explication of participant interpretations (Strauss & Corbin, 1990), and illuminates the experiences of the prospective teachers as they develop a disposition to teach mathematics for diversity. This framework gives voice to the prospective teachers and provides insights into their unique perspectives and orientations on teaching mathematics for diversity.

Between 1998 and 2002, 10 classes have participated in this research project. Depending on course enrollment, each semester the experiences of between 40 and 50 prospective teachers are examined. These prospective teachers are typically White women from overwhelmingly White rural and suburban communities. The data for this ongoing study are gathered and triangulated via multiple sources of evidence, including: (a) the prospective teachers' journals of reflections, (b) reflections posted to the online discussion board by the prospective teachers, (c) the researcher's field notes of observations of the methods courses, and (d) prospective teachers' final papers in which they discuss issues related to the course, including teaching mathematics to diverse learners and engaging in critical reflections. Secondary data sources in the form of the prospective teachers' mathematics autobiographies and narrative accounts of critical moments in teaching and learning diverse learners are utilized to triangulate these data (Glesne & Peshkin, 1992). Data analysis consists of a qualitative interpretative approach involving the researcher and the participants. A holistic analysis is accomplished by introspection, rereading and recontextualizing the data, and reviewing analyses with the prospective teachers, allowing them to react to and to clarify and elaborate upon their responses.

STRATEGIES FOR COUNTERRESISTANCE

It is my contention that a significant factor in helping students learn mathematics with understanding is to provide tasks and activities in which all students are actively involved in doing mathematics, thinking reflectively, and engaging in discourse. In contrast, many prospective teachers hold a rather narrow view of teaching that is based on their own experiences as learners. Educated in traditional classrooms, they are, for the most part, passive, uncritical learners who have been denied the opportunity to engage in critical reflection on mathematics teaching and learning. Because prospective teachers have typically not been challenged to think deeply, when provided with opportunities to engage in reflection, they are more likely to reflect only on technical issues (Van Manen, 1977). As the prospective teachers begin the reflective process, their initial journal entries and discussion board postings are, for the most part, literal. That is, though descriptive, their contributions present unexamined beliefs or ideas. However, as the prospective teachers begin to reflect upon their prior experiences with and attitudes about diversity, they begin to acknowledge their own beliefs about diversity (McLaren & Giroux, 1997). The prospective teachers are requested to respond to one another's postings to the online discussion board on a weekly basis. In addition to stimulating contributions that go beyond merely descriptive to reveal nuanced interpretations or analyses of significant issues, this process fosters a sense of being a member of a collaborative learning community.

In order to develop a critically reflective, transformative outlook in the prospective teachers, the participants and I examine and discuss a rubric that is utilized to determine whether reflections that are analytical, interpretive, perceptive, intuitive, or literal. Together, we utilize the rubric to assess the students' critical reflections. A copy of this rubric appears in the Appendix. I utilize reflection prompts and stems as well as modeling to encourage the prospective teachers to start the process of reflecting in their journals and on an online discussion board. Reflection prompts are based on the critical features of classrooms and include the nature of classroom tasks, role of the teacher, social culture of the classroom, mathematical tools, and equity and accessibility (Hiebert, 1997). I respond to journal entries and online postings by posing questions designed to move the prospective teachers toward reflecting on a deeper level, or to stimulate further reflection. As they work through this process, the prospective teachers' contributions become more perceptive and reveal interpretations and analyses of significant issues pertaining to the mathematics education of diverse learners.

Mathematics Autobiographies

Teachers' beliefs about mathematics, as well as the social context of the situation, influence mathematics teaching (Ernest, 1991). Because their pre-existing knowledge, beliefs, and experiences may influence the way in which learners construct knowledge (Becker & Varelas, 1995), I begin the methods courses by engaging the prospective teachers in writing their mathematics autobiographies. The prospective teachers are requested to focus on identifying and describing critical and important events in their mathematics experiences; describing how their beliefs, attitudes, and feelings about mathematics developed; and illustrating how their lived experiences shaped their particular perspectives on mathematics teaching and learning. The solo process of writing and reflection is followed by a collaborative process of in-class discussions and reflections on the autobiographies. In an effort to move the prospective teachers toward greater awareness of how their views of mathematics teaching and learning are influenced by their educational experiences, through the process of shared critical reflections they are challenged to engage critically and meaningfully with their own backgrounds, assumptions, and beliefs about mathematics teaching and learning and diverse learners. During this process, as the instructor of the methods courses, I participate by sharing my own experiences as both a teacher and learner of mathematics. The prospective teachers who enroll in the methods courses are overwhelmingly from small towns or rural communities, monolingual, and White, with very little direct intercultural experience (American Association of Colleges for Teacher Education, 1995). In contrast, my own background is urban, bilingual/bicultural with much direct intercultural experience. Because I want to demonstrate that effective teachers of mathematics do not always share their learners' language and culture, I typically choose not to share my own bicultural/bilingual background with the prospective teachers. This is connected to my goal to prepare all teachers to teach mathematics for diversity. Instead, I share how my experiences as both a teacher and a learner in diverse classrooms both in the United States and in the developing world have shaped my own disposition to teach mathematics for diversity.

For the elementary prospective teachers, the process of writing and engaging in collaborative discussion and reflection typically reveals mathematics achievement disparities that began early in the teachers' lives and influenced the educational and professional options available to them for the rest of their lives. For the majority of the prospective teachers, critically reflecting upon our shared autobiographies leads to a consciousness that what transpires in elementary mathematics classes plays out in later achievement and persistence levels. For example, the autobiographies revealed that prospective teachers who had negative experiences with elementary mathematics and mathematics teaching chose to take the minimum numbers of mathematics courses required in high school and college. A typical prospective teacher response, entered in her journal of reflections, suggests an awareness of how instructional practices embody teachers' beliefs, which are a reflection of their own experiences and background (Cabello & Burstein, 1995):

> Just as I now see how some of us didn't do well in math, myself included, not because we are inferior but because of other issues like the way the teacher treated us, how she responded to us, thinking that we wouldn't be good in math, for example. My feelings of being inferior as far as math is concerned really did affect my choices in life. Now I can understand that I will have students in my own classroom that I might come in with wrong ideas about as far as if they are good in math or what they are able to do in math. I don't want to ever hold any ideas about my students and what they can do before I get to know their backgrounds and lives outside the class

first. Understanding this will help me make learning math a positive experience for them. (journal entry, Prospective Teacher A)

In response to the process of writing and critically reflecting upon her
mathematics autobiography and those of her peers, another prospective
teacher reveals that she is beginning to reconceptualize mathematics
teaching and learning. The journal entry, written during the middle of the
semester, suggests that engaging in critical reflection contributed to her
reconceptualization of mathematics teaching and learning:

> It was interesting for me to hear how many of us lost interest in math in ele-
> mentary school because we weren't as fast as the top kids and how so many
> times the teachers focused on those kids, the ones who were the first to give
> her the right answer. Many of us came to believe that we just weren't good
> at math. It makes sense that a child who doesn't respond to that way of
> teaching will think they're not good in math. The important thing for me is
> understand my students and how they learn math and to help them under-
> stand that just because they don't learn math one way doesn't mean they are
> not good in math. I want to make my own classroom different from my own
> negative experiences. (journal entry, Prospective Teacher M)

Video Clips

Because teachers develop a greater understanding of teaching through reflection that was based on actual practice (Schon, 1983), the prospective
teachers view video clips of mathematics teaching and learning in elementary classrooms composed of diverse learners. Some of these videos were
provided as part of the Wisconsin Networking Project for Improvement of
Mathematics Education Project for use in preservice mathematics education courses whereas others were taped by me during visits to elementary
classrooms. The clips, which are shown prior to the prospective teachers'
field experiences, offer detailed images of mathematics teaching and
learning and provide the teachers with additional opportunities to engage
in critical reflection. As such, they are a tool to further develop a disposition to teach mathematics for diversity.

During the first half of the semester, the prospective teachers have not
yet had the experience to view a classroom episode and begin the process
of critical reflection, so they are provided with several points on which to
focus their reflections. For example, they are asked to examine the mathematical tasks in which the learners are engaged and to determine whether
they provide opportunities for diverse learners and encourage all learners
to participate. The prospective teachers are also asked to observe and analyze the pedagogy, discourse, and learning environment, including interactions between teacher and learners. They are then asked to reflect upon

the question, "If you were the teacher in this classroom, what might you do differently and why?" Finally, the prospective teachers are asked to discuss what they learned from the reflection process and if they made any changes to their conceptualizations of teaching mathematics to diverse learners as a result of engaging in critical reflection.

As illustrated by the following exchange, archived from the online discussion board, engaging in collaborative analysis and guided reflections on the mathematics teaching and learning in the video clips provided the prospective teachers with opportunities to consider multiple perspectives (Barnett, 1991). These postings are in response to a video episode that depicts a constructivist classroom in which a White teacher engages his linguistically diverse learners in a student-centered exploration of the properties of polygons:

> That classroom was so interesting! I like the fact that the teacher never talked down to the kids. He really seemed to think the kids could solve that kind of problem and was interested in what they had to say about the math. I felt that this was a safe place for the kids to explore without being embarrassed. Everything he did, he showed them that their ideas mattered. This is a classroom that you need to begin to work on from day one and it will take a lot of work but seeing how it helps the kids, it is worth it. (original thread, Prospective Teacher R)

> When the video started, I didn't think the kids would respond like they did. But they all had something to say! They were learning that how to use math language and the teacher gave everyone who wanted to a chance to share and ask questions. Because of this, I personally think he is a good role model for a new teacher. (response, Prospective Teacher M)

> I thought the same thing at first about the kids responding. That maybe because they were ELL they wouldn't talk. Thinking that they might not be able to respond like that, I never would have tried to ask kids to explain. But the teacher treated the kids like he knew they could do it and their ideas really did matter. I think that he set a high standard for them and believed they could do it and they did! (response, Prospective Teacher A)

A video clip that depicted a classroom dominated by traditional, teacher-centered, procedurally focused instructional practices prompted the following postings to the online discussion board. In the video episode, culturally and linguistically diverse learners are seated in rows following step-by-step instructions transmitted by a White teacher. Despite their years of apprenticeship in traditional classrooms (Lortie, 1975), the prospective teachers' posting illuminate a change in conception about what it means to teach and learn mathematics (Brown, Cooney, & Jones, 1990):

The thing I really noticed here is how the teacher just called on the one girl. He let her give all the answers! The other kids just sat there. You could see they weren't involved at all. He didn't leave any room for questions. It's obvious, he is only interested in hearing the right answer from someone and it probably only comes from that girl. It's so important for us to open it up to all students and to give them a chance to try. (original thread, Prospective Teacher T)

Don't you think that he was sending a message that all he cared about was someone coming up with the right answer? I think the one girl gave the answers that the teacher wanted to hear—the right answers. It didn't matter about other ways of doing the problem or if someone had a question. To me that sends such a negative message to all the other kids! What a way to shut down from math when the teacher doesn't even care enough about the other students to listen to their way of doing the problem. (response, Prospective Teacher R)

What I noticed right away was that the kids were packed so tight it was like they were locked in their desks! They couldn't even get out to come up to the overhead. It's like he's afraid that he'll lose control that the kids will get out of control if you give them some active role. All he had to do was to put the desks together and then the kids could talk to each other about the math. It's the same way with what he was looking for as far as one right answer. It would have been nice to see what the other children were thinking and how they solved the problem. You know it doesn't take any real effort on the teacher's part to teach like this. (response, Prospective Teacher S)

Field Experiences

Research has suggested that field experiences are often the most important component of teacher education programs (McIntyre, Byrd, & Foxx, 1996). These experiences enable prospective teachers to engage firsthand in mathematics teaching and learning on a daily basis. In order to enhance the development of teachers who are prepared to address the needs of K–6 elementary school learners living in contexts of cultural and social diversity, each of the methods courses in which critical reflections are utilized to elicit a disposition to teach mathematics for diversity has a field experience component. During their school-based field experiences, the prospective teachers are placed in elementary classrooms composed of educationally, ethnically, socioeconomically, and linguistically diverse learners. The prospective teachers' field experiences are 3 full days per week for 8 weeks. During this time they are required to observe, assist with, and teach mathematics lessons.

A challenge to facilitating teaching mathematics for diversity relates to teachers' resiliency toward (Lampert & Ball, 1998) and their tendency to rely upon traditional methods of teaching mathematics. However, an on-line discussion of a constructivist classroom of diverse learners suggests that the prospective teachers had begun the process of reconceptualizing mathematics teaching for diverse learners. These postings also reveal an element of surprise that lies at the heart of any reflective activity (Schon, 1987):

> Wasn't it amazing to see how the kids had ownership over their classroom? They were responsible for their own learning and were totally involved in the math centers. I was amazed at what those kids could do! When I walked around and listened, they were talking about math. At first I thought that they would never be able to work on the activities that they would need a lot of structure and direction from the teacher. But watching them totally changed my idea about what those kids could do as far as math. Just because a student comes from a different background doesn't mean that they can't do math. It is up to me as a teacher to make sure my classroom welcomes all children to math. (initial thread, Prospective Teacher J)

School-based observations of a teacher-centered classroom dominated by a transmission mode of instruction resulted in the reflections acknowledging the invisible pedagogy (Bernstein, 1990) that acts selectively on learners from different backgrounds:

> The worksheets the teacher gave out didn't make any sense to the students. If something doesn't have any meaning in the students' life, how can they be expected to stay interested? What really bothered me was that the teacher didn't care whether the students were understanding or not. I saw so many kids who were just left out of the learning because this teacher just moved on to the next page. I think that she didn't respect these kids and didn't hold up anything for them to reach for. I don't ever want to be that kind of teacher. This experience made a big impression on me and you will read more about it in my final paper. (journal entry, Prospective Teacher K)

> If I had a class like this one, I would think about what I could do to change things to make the math have meaning for children who didn't grow up here and who are still learning English. For example, in this class [methods course] we looked at math from other cultures. I think if this teacher had taken some time she could have come up with some activities that incorporated things that the children could recognize from their own cultures. (journal entry, Prospective Teacher A)

> I think that these children might have had difficult lives. Here they are in a new country, a new school. Maybe they haven't done so well in math before so if they start out with negative self-esteem and they keep failing in math,

it's only going to begin a negative cycle. It's important to build in success and encourage them. I want to make my classroom a place where all children can find success in math. (journal entry, Prospective Teacher R)

Reflections on Critical Reflections

The prospective teachers are required to write a final reflection paper in which they discuss how the experience of engaging in critical reflection affected their views of teaching and learning mathematics with a particular emphasis on diverse learners. In preparing their final reflection papers, the prospective teachers were requested to return to earlier journal entries and online postings These final reflection papers reveal that engaging in the process of critical reflection enables them to identify connections between classroom practices and the "wider educational, social, economic, and political conditions that impinge upon and shape classroom practice" (Beyer & Zeichner, 1987, p. 326). For example, a passage from one final reflection paper suggests the prospective teacher has developed a perspective transformation:

> This was such an important process for me. At first I thought that critical meant something negative but now I see that it is a way of looking at and thinking about teaching math and what we as teachers can do to improve it for all of our students. The experience of critical reflection has helped me to think about what is important to focus on in my own classroom, especially about making sure all students are given a chance to experience success in math. Important things are how I will respond to a child and whether I make them feel comfortable trying and making mistakes and being careful not to shut them out from math. I don't ever want to be the kind of teacher that will just pin a label on a child that they're not good in math and before that I didn't realize how easy it is to fall into that pattern of just standing up and teaching and not thinking about the impact we are having on our students. Before, I didn't recognize all of this but now I can look at a classroom and think about the environment, the math, the way that a teacher talks to her students, and how all of these things are going to make a difference to the way the children think about math and how that is going to carry out for the rest of their lives. (final reflection paper, Prospective Teacher A)

Throughout the semester, the prospective teachers collaborate on several in-class and virtual assignments. As they work interdependently, the prospective teachers take responsibility for one another's learning, develop a respect for multiple perspectives and solutions, and evolve into a collaborative learning community. Collaborative analysis extends the process of critical reflection. Responding to one another's reflections is integral to the transformative component of critical reflection. Because the process discussed here concerns collaborative analyses, it differs from that of Schon (1987) who regarded reflection as a solitary process or as a process engaged in with one mentor. Collaboration actively involves the prospective teachers and me as participants in a community of inquirers who critically reflect upon teaching and learning mathematics to a diverse student population. As one prospective teacher noted:

> Making the reflections collaborative showed me that there are different ways of looking at teaching math, our classroom, what we do as teachers, and our students. Making the reflections critical showed me that instead of just looking at something and talking about it, we do something to change it for the better. I learned that even though we have different experiences, they can be helpful to all of us. It was helpful to hear the professor's own experiences too. Sharing all of our experiences pointed out important things to me that I missed the first time but got me thinking about them. During this semester and through my own experiences and hearing about the experiences of my peers, I now understand what we mean when we talk about access and equity as a main goal of math teaching. That we want to include all children in being successful in math and how important it is to continue this reflection process when I have my own classroom. (final reflection paper, Prospective Teacher R)

CONCLUSION

The initiative discussed here; engaging teachers in critical reflections, provides some response to the question of how to prepare White teachers to teach mathematics for diversity. Over the course of each semester, these critical reflections typically reveal perspective transformations. As such, they are a first step toward eliminating the achievement gaps and ensuring an equitable learning environment for all learners in mathematics. The responses of the prospective teachers suggest that differential teaching based on learners' language, culture, socioeconomic status, or family background is not an unsolvable problem. Rather than accepting resistance to teach for diversity as an intractable problem resulting from the inflexible conservatism of the teachers, as mathematics educators, we must consider how our own teaching practices may constrain our ability to prepare prospective teachers to teach mathematics for diversity.

Prospective teachers' perceptions of mathematics, mathematics teaching and learning, and mathematics learners are filtered by their worldviews that have been shaped by their prior experiences as mathematics learners. Providing prospective teachers with experiences to challenge their preconceived notions of diverse learners and encouraging them to reflect critically upon those experiences is a first step toward restructuring and broadening their vision of mathematics teaching and learning. For many prospective teachers, the process of engaging in critical reflection requires both a paradigm shift and a period of disequilibrium as their beliefs about mathematics, teaching and learning mathematics, and mathematics learners are challenged. Though we want to facilitate a disposition to teach mathematics for diversity, "we must be realistic about what can be accomplished within the current structures of teacher education" (Zeichner, 1994, p. 7).

The initiative discussed here provides an important first step in fostering teacher educators' understanding of how prospective teachers construct an image of mathematics teaching that promotes access and equity for all learners. The next critical step will be to develop strategies to help prospective teachers sustain a disposition to teach mathematics for diversity by routinely engaging in critical reflection in their daily interactions with learners. If engaging in the process of critical reflection facilitates a recognition of the social consequences of mathematics education, it is possible that prospective teachers may develop a perspective transformation that moves them beyond their classrooms to a greater awareness of personal and social constructs to develop the capacity for self-direction (Diamond, 1991). As prospective teachers begin to realize that they play a critical role in the continuance or the elimination of disparities in mathematics teaching and learning, teacher educators must assist them in developing habits of critical reflection and a commitment to resolve inequities in mathematics teaching and learning.

REFERENCES

American Association of Colleges for Teacher Education. (1995). *Survey of teacher education enrollments by race/ethnicity and gender,* Fall 1995. Washington, DC: Author.

Barnett, C. (1991). Building a case-based curriculum to enhance the pedagogical content knowledge of mathematics teachers. *Journal of Teacher Education, 42,* 263–272.

Becker, J., & Varelas, M. (1995). Assisting construction: The role of the teacher in assisting the learner's construction of preexisting cultural knowledge. In L. P. Steffe & J. Gale (Eds.), *Constructivism in education* (pp. 433–446). Hillsdale, NJ: Lawrence Erlbaum Associates.

Bernstein, B. (1990). *The structuring of pedagogical discourse.* London: Routledge.

Beyer, L. E., & Zeichner, K. M. (1987). Teacher education in cultural context: Beyond reproduction. In T. S. Popkewitz (Ed.), *Critical studies in teacher education: It's folklore, theory and practice* (pp. 298–334). Philadelphia: Falmer Press.

Brown, S. I., Cooney, T. J., & Jones, D. (1990). Mathematics teacher education. In W. R. Houston (Ed.), *Handbook of research on teacher education* (pp. 636–656). New York: Macmillan.

Cabello, B., & Burstein, N. D. (1995). Examining teachers' beliefs about teaching in culturally diverse classrooms. *Journal of Teacher Education, 46*(4), 285–294.

Denzin, N. K., & Lincoln, Y. S. (1994). *Handbook of qualitative research.* Thousand Oaks, CA: Sage.

Dewey, J. (1933). *How we think.* London: Heath.

Diamond, C. T. P. (1991). *Teacher education as transformation: A psychological perspective.* Buckingham, England: Open University Press.

Ernest, P. (1991). *The politics of mathematics education.* London: Falmer Press.

Flores, B., Tefft Cousin, P., & Díaz, E. (1991). Transforming deficit myths about learning, language and culture. *Language Arts, 68,* 369–379.

Glesne, C., & Peshkin, A. (1992). *Becoming qualitative researchers.* White Plains, NY: Longman.

Gore, J. M., & Zeichner, K. M. (1991). Action research and reflective teaching in preservice teacher education: A case study from the United States. *Teaching and Teacher Education, 7*(2), 119–136.

Hiebert, J. (Ed.). (1997). *Making sense: Teaching and learning mathematics with understanding.* Portsmouth, NH: Heinemann.

Hutchinson, C., & Allen, K. (1997). The reflection integration model: A process for facilitating reflective learning. *Teacher Educator, 32*(4), 226–233.

Jordan, M. L. R. (1995). Reflections on the challenges, possibilities, and perplexities of preparing preservice teachers for culturally diverse classrooms. *Journal of Teacher Education, 46,* 369–374.

Kagan, D. M. (1992). Implications of research on teacher beliefs. *Educational Psychologist, 27,* 65–90.

Kemmis, S. (1985). Action research and the politics of reflection. In D. Boud, R. Keogh, & D. Walker (Eds.), *Reflection: Turning experience into learning* (pp. 139–164). London: Kogan Page.

Lampert, M., & Ball, D. (1998). *Teaching, multimedia, and mathematics: Investigations of real practice.* New York: Teachers College Press.

Lincoln, Y. S., & Guba, E. G. (1985). *Naturalistic inquiry.* Beverly Hills, CA: Sage.

Liston, D. P., & Zeichner, K. M. (1991). *Teacher education and the social conditions of schooling.* London: Routledge.

Lortie, D. (1975). *Schoolteacher.* Chicago: University of Chicago Press.

McIntyre, D. J., Byrd, D. M., & Foxx, S. M. (1996). Field and laboratory experiences. In J. Sikula, T. J. Buttery, & E. Gayton (Eds.), *Handbook of research on teacher education* (2nd ed., pp. 171–203). New York: Macmillan.

McLaren, P., & Giroux, H. A. (1997). Writing in the margins: Geographies of identity, pedagogy, and power. In P. McLaren, *Revolutionary multiculturalism: Pedagogies of dissent for the new millennium* (pp. 16–41). Boulder, CO: Westview Press.

McLeod, D. B. (1992). Research on affect in mathematics education: A reconceptualization. In D. A. Grouws (Ed.), *Handbook of research on mathematics teaching and learning* (pp. 575–596). New York: Macmillan.

National Council of Teachers of Mathematics. (2000). *Principles and standards for school mathematics.* Reston, VA: Author.

Nieto, S. (1998). From claiming hegemony to sharing space: Creating community in a multicultural education course. In R. Chavez Chavez & J. O'Donnell (Eds.), *Speaking the unpleasant: The politics of (non)engagement in the multicultural education terrain* (pp. 16–31). Albany: State University of New York Press.

O'Grady, C. R. (1998). Moving off center: Engaging White education students in multicultural field experiences. In R. Chavez Chavez & J. O'Donnell (Eds.), *Speaking the unpleasant: The politics of (non)engagement in the multicultural education terrain* (pp. 211–228). Albany: State University of New York Press.

Reyes, L. H. (1984). Affective variables and mathematics education. *Elementary School Journal, 84,* 558–581.

Richardson, V. (1990). Significant and worthwhile change in teaching practice. *Educational Researcher, 19*(7), 10–18.

Risko, V., Roskos, K., & Vukelich, C. (1999, April 22). *Preservice teachers' reflection: Strategies, qualities, and perceptions in learning to teach reading.* Paper presented at the annual meeting of the American Educational Research Association, Montreal, Canada.

Schon, D. (1983). *The reflective practitioner.* London: Temple Smith.

Schon, D. (1987). *Educating the reflective practitioner.* San Francisco: Jossey-Bass.

Strauss, A., & Corbin, J. (1990). *Basics of qualitative research: Grounded theory, procedures and techniques.* Newbury Park, CA: Sage.

Tate, W. F. (1996). Mathematizing and the democracy: The need for an education that is multicultural and social reconstructionist. In C. A. Grant & M. L. Gomez (Eds.), *Making schooling multicultural: Campus and classroom* (pp. 185–201). Englewood Cliffs, NJ: Prentice-Hall.

Van Manen, M. (1977). Linking ways of knowing with ways of being practical. *Curriculum Inquiry, 6*, 205–228.

Zeichner, K. (1994, April). *Action research and issues of equity and social justice in preservice teacher education.* Paper presented at the annual meeting of the American Educational Research Association, New Orleans, LA.

Zeichner, K., & Gore, J. (1990). Teacher socialization. In W. R. Houston (Ed.), *Handbook of research on teacher education* (pp. 329–348). New York: Macmillan.

Zehm, S., & Kottler, J. (1993). *On being a teacher: The human dimension.* Newbury Park, CA: Corwin.

APPENDIX
Rubric for Critical Reflections on Mathematics Teaching and Learning

Analytical	Provides a powerful and thorough analysis and interpretation of significant or important issues. Claims and arguments are fully justified and supported. Provides a rich context.
Interpretive	Provides an interpretation or analysis of important or significant issues that goes beyond reporting what has been observed. Claims and arguments are justified and supported. Provides a descriptive context.
Perceptive	Provides a helpful interpretation or analysis of important issues. Limited support or justification for arguments and claims. Provides a useful context.
Intuitive	Provides some insightful ideas but is incomplete with regard to analysis or interpretation. Limited support or justification for arguments and claims. Fails to provide a descriptive or useful context.
Literal	Provides a report of what has been observed but with little or no analysis or interpretation. No support or justification for arguments and claims. Fails to provide a context.

8

"Eh, Mus' Be Smart Class": Race, Social Class, Language, and Access to Academic Resources

Pauline W. U. Chinn
University of Hawaii-Manoa

I teach prospective elementary and secondary teachers at the University of Hawaii-Manoa, a second career that follows more than 20 years of teaching science in Hawaii's public and private schools. Why I became a science teacher and teacher educator instead of a research scientist is the first of several stories about power, privilege, and schooling in this chapter. The stories set the stage for my work as a teacher educator at a minority institution preparing prospective teachers to be sensitive to the ways class, culture, ethnicity, language, and gender impact on teaching and learning, particularly in science.

I use theories of narrative and social reproduction to analyze these stories from the perspective of power, status, and competing ideologies. My own understanding of science as a (multi)cultural endeavor developed over a period of years along with my growing awareness of the way my ethnicity, gender, and social class contributed to the way I became a science teacher.

OUR STORIED LIVES: NARRATIVE WAYS OF KNOWING

I am a prime example of someone who should have become a scientist but did not. My father's entire professional career was dedicated to science education. As children, my sisters, brother, and I spent many weekends in his chemistry class enthralled by demonstrations or engaged with science magazines while he caught up on his work. As intermediate and high school students, we developed science projects for school and district fairs and participated in the science enrichment and advanced-studies programs funded by the federal government in the post-Sputnik and Cold War years. As a college undergraduate, I worked in science laboratories and carried out research in organic chemistry sponsored by a National Science Foundation fellowship. But in those important college years, things began to slip and shift from science toward education. I graduated in 3 years with high honors and an honors thesis on organic synthesis, but my degree was in secondary science education. I was not the only one in my family. My older sister says she dropped out of calculus because she did not want to compete with boys or siblings and graduated as an elementary teacher, as did my youngest sister. My younger brother graduated with a science degree then went away for graduate degrees in ecology, public health, and medicine.

What happened to the girls in the family? It's not that we lacked encouragement and support to go to college. I knew from the time I entered grade school that high school graduation was just a step to a college degree, the real educational goal. We were all provided with educational opportunities, but boundaries were placed on the girls' ambitions because of our gender. I can accept now that this was done with the best of intentions, but I regretted being born a girl from the time I knew boys enjoyed more freedom. Gender-based roles seemed so natural and normal in the patriarchal, Confucian-influenced culture we were immersed in that its arbitrariness only became apparent years later as I did the research leading to my dissertation, "Becoming a Scientist: Narratives of Women Entering Science and Engineering" (Chinn, 1995). I had to learn a different language and a different way of thinking about knowledge and research to name and understand what happened in my American-educated, yet Confucian family. When I began to understand my own life, I began to understand what happened on a much larger scale in Hawaii and nationally to yield the patterns of high academic achievement for some and mediocrity or poor school performance for others.

But first I will finish a story that I now realize is not purely personal but can be understood and critiqued through the lenses of gender, culture, race, and class. Though my Chinese father never discouraged his daughters directly from studying science and was proud of our accomplishments, in terms of the good life he saw for daughters he was a man of his ancestral culture and World War II generation, still bound by considerations of Confucian ideology and gender (Chinn, 2002a). Girls could be college educated to be science teachers or nurses, careers that allowed them to be feminine and family centered. Scientists were men who did field and laboratory work as he had. He never deviated from wanting me to dress more femininely, and like my mother, also a teacher, never mentioned science as a possible career. At college, I learned that some men were disturbed that women were entering careers traditionally occupied by men. In the physiology lab where I worked, a Japanese-American graduate student told me that he would never date a woman who competed with him in science. In the chemistry laboratory, my relationship with a much older, unmarried, White male adviser was strained and distant. The concepts of mentoring and fostering a research team were foreign to this introverted, nearly wordless man. I knew more about the research of other chemistry students and faculty than the research being conducted by his graduate student at the neighboring bench.

Under these social conditions, chemistry research was indeed lonely and tedious. It took long hours to complete experiments, and as I still lived at home, I seldom was part of the evening breaks that men participated in more readily. I have good memories of the few times I joined the guys to socialize and talk about research, but when I graduated with high honors and a thesis in organic synthesis, no one in my family or the chemistry department encouraged me to continue in science. I still wanted to be a research scientist after receiving a master's degree in science curriculum. I even told my husband that when we returned from visiting his family in India, I wanted to continue my science studies. But when we came back his career took off, we bought a house, and I became a science teacher.

As I moved further from my goal of being a scientist, I wondered what went wrong. But science research taught me to be objective and to ignore the emotional and this approach merged neatly with the subordinate role of Asian females. My Chinese-American parents flatly refused to discuss careers considered inappropriate to women and I did not argue my case. Yet, when it came to personal decisions, I had internalized the American dream of individual merit, ability, and the "pursuit of happiness" I had learned at school. Only in retrospect did I realize that I held conflicting cultural narratives and ideologies in my head at the same time. I was not the only one. My older sister gave her version of the Declaration of Independence to my parents when she was a fifth grader. But nobody talked about cultural contradictions, and years passed before I studied the theories that allowed me to use my experiences to understand the underrepresentation of women and minorities in science.

My story about how I did not became a scientist reveals that I now give a privileged position to stories, or narratives, that people tell about others and themselves. Because it is through language that a person understands her place and is understood by others, these narratives, defined as stories with culturally derived plots, are a fundamental mode for creating meaning out of human experiences (Mishler, 1986; Ricoeur, 1992; Witherell &

Noddings, 1991). These reveal individual differences but draw on a reservoir of culturally familiar themes and values. Theorists ranging from philosophers to linguists think that personal stories develop out of a person's unique locus in a matrix of culture, history, social setting, physical place, and interpersonal relationships. We come to know ourselves through the lenses of culturally derived narratives that convert the chronology of what might be perceived as fragmented, discordant events into a meaningful existence. The stories we tell create a personal history, one that is constantly under construction and, potentially, reconstruction throughout our lives.

Culturally shaped personal narratives construct social reality and identities through their messages of power, rank, and prescribed ways of being and acting that establish relationships among individuals and groups (Gee, 2001). According to Ricoeur (1991), "If all human experience is already mediated by all sorts of symbolic systems, it is also mediated by all sorts of stories that we have heard" (p. 29). But stories do not have equal power; those told by high-status individuals embodying the dominant culture are accorded legitimacy and the authority to direct cultural resources that shape lives of those with less status.

As I began to understand what had happened to me through the lenses of gender and culture, I began to look at the larger picture. I wanted to understand what happened in Hawaii's schools and society that led to predictable outcomes by ethnicity, class, and gender.

THE STORY OF SCHOOLING IN HAWAII

Cultural narratives may be thought of as mental models in the form of stories or myths that guide people's thinking about others and the world. The notion of the greater power of stories told by members of the dominant culture is foundational to understanding how Hawaii's schools developed to reproduce a stratified society. Hawaii is unique among states in having a unified school system serving a population that is two thirds Asian and Pacific Islander. Slightly less than one fifth of Hawaii's K–12 students attend private schools, a higher percentage than anywhere else in the United States except for Washington, DC (*Honolulu Star-Bulletin*, August 26, 2001). Whites, Japanese, Chinese, and Koreans tend to be enrolled in middle-class public schools and selective private schools that prepare the majority of students for college. Public schools in rural, agricultural, and working-class neighborhoods tend to be dominated by Filipinos, Native Hawaiians, and Pacific Islanders from Samoa, Tonga, and Micronesia. In economically depressed rural areas, Native Hawaiians are often the largest ethnic group, standardized test scores tend to be low, and teacher turnover and dropout rates high.

What cultural narratives and ideologies contributed to these patterns of education in Hawaii? Hawaiians and other Polynesians place a high value on genealogy. The story of one's family connections through past generations establishes one's status and social location in society. In a parallel fashion, the genealogy of Hawaii's schools interwoven with my parents' educational experiences illuminates the way powerful groups construct school systems to prepare youth for particular economic niches in society.

Western education in the Kingdom of Hawaii began with New England missionaries who arrived in 1820. They converted spoken Hawaiian into a written language, translated the Bible, and taught the newly Christianized chiefly class to read. The Chief's Children's School, now known as Royal School, was founded in 1839 at the request of the chiefs. Missionaries founded Punahou, a private, Protestant school in 1841 for their children to "offer the means of receiving an excellent English education under the best moral guidance . . . kept apart from the contaminating influence of ignorant and vicious natives" (*Polynesian*, July 3, 1841, cited by Stueber, 1964, p. 62). The 1840 Constitution, strongly influenced by American advisers, established schools for commoners. Permitted to establish state schools if enrollment passed a certain threshold, Christian sects competed for both converts and students.

This genealogy reveals that from the start, Hawaii's schools were marked by differences in social class, religion, curriculum, language, and ethnicity. The tiered school system replicated caste aspects of Hawaiian society, reinforced racist stereotypes of Native Hawaiians held by the White elite, and became a vehicle for monoculturalism by "catering to the dominant or mainstream culture, providing second-class treatment or no special consideration at all the persons of non-mainstream cultures" (Haas, 1992, p. 161).

The 1840 constitution also included the foreign notion of private property, enabling the White elite to acquire choice lands for the plantations that would dominate Hawaii's economy and shape its school system for over a century. Plantation managers looked overseas for labor as the Native Hawaiian population plummeted from foreign diseases. In 1852, 293 Chinese laborers arrived, the first of a series of immigrants to occupy the lowest rung of the social hierarchy. Labor policies were racist and exploitative well into the 20th century. Planters subscribed to the 19th-century theory of polygeny that held that humans belonged to unequal races (Gould, 1993). In 1885 the Reverend Bishop proposed that Chinese and Hawaiians "being of similar social level" could produce offspring with better qualities than the parent races (Porteus, 1962, pp. 157–158).

By the turn of the 20th century, pro-American businessmen had overthrown the monarchy, Hawaii was annexed by the United States, immigrants outnumbered Hawaiians, and speaking Hawaiian was forbidden in schools. Whites patronized private schools and opposed improving public schools as only 2% of plantation jobs needed a high school degree. In 1920, less than 5% of students were enrolled in high school, sugar cost $0.22 per pound with a profit of $0.18, class size was up to seventy students, and $2 was spent per student versus $6–8 in Western states. Even so, the president of the Hawaiian Sugar Planters Association argued for the Department of Public Instruction (DPI) to reduce expenditures to "a more practical and business basis" (Stueber, 1964, p. 296). From 1924 to 1959, the DPI sanctioned English Standard schools that employed oral tests to select a small proportion of K–12 students for more rigorous academic preparation. The policy institutionalizing language as a marker for education and social class was accompanied by policies forbidding the speaking of home languages and Pidgin English, the Hawaiian Creole spoken by working-class children, in the schools (Chinn, 1999a; Stueber, 1964).

My mother came from a middle-class family. She attended an English Standard school whereas her older brother attended Punahou, the elitist, predominantly White school begun by missionaries for their own children. Her father, a contractor, mingled with Hawaii's governor and other society elites through business and YMCA activities. They were born in hospitals where doctors signed their birth certificates; she took piano lessons from a Frenchman. Throughout her life, her schooling and social life went smoothly whereas my father, son of a butcher, born with a midwife in attendance, had to carry a photo ID to prove he was a U.S. citizen. My mother's Chinese-language studies were uneventful, but he stopped his after being criticized by a teacher for not focusing on his regular studies. He told me that even as a college student, he and other non-Whites felt compelled to walk across the street from the houses of the wealthy. Records show that plantation managers viewed Chinese men in a negative light. Described as "loud-mouthed and belligerent, quick-tempered and sensuous" (Stueber, 1964, p. 215), they were thought too likely to become "townsmen, not the strong-bodied inoffensive farmers that the country needed" (Porteus, 1962, pp. 157–158).

With a graduate degree in agriculture, my father hoped to be a soil or plant scientist. But he never was hired by the plantations. Instead he became a science teacher who strongly believed education was the way to elevate one's status in society. He lobbied the Territorial legislature to increase the number of public secondary schools and taught chemistry and physics at Roosevelt, Hawaii's only English Standard high school. His students excelled in science competitions and he was recognized as Father of the Year for Education in 1959, the year Hawaii became a state. For the rest of his career, as Honolulu District mathematics and science specialist, then as a Hawaii's science curriculum specialist, he worked to move science education from the plantation era into the space age.

Hawaii's public schools now require 2 years of middle school and 3 years of high school science for graduation. But Native Hawaiians, Filipinos, and Pacific Islanders are still underrepresented in science and overrepresented in programs for academically at-risk students. As a legacy of Hawaii's colonial past, public schools are among the most tracked in the nation and 45% would be judged racially segregated by federal standards due to their association with plantations (Tobin et al., 1992). Negative stereotypes fostered by plantation managers to induce competition among different racial groups still circulate in schools and society (Takaki, 1994). Standard English is still a marker of social class and education. Hawaii's newspapers provide the forum for vigorous debates about Pidgin English and poor school performance that echo the Ebonics controversy (Chinn, 1999b; Haas, 1992; Ogbu, 1999). The issues of language and poor test scores will not disappear soon given that "15% of Hawaii residents in 1990 were foreign-born compared with 8% nationally, suggesting a greater challenge in teaching language skills tested on the SAT and NAEP" (Education and the Economy, 1998, p. 3; http://www.hawaii. gov/dbedt/hecon/he11-98/index.html).

In the following section, the subtle yet powerful role that stories and stereotypes play in shaping the way individuals think, believe, and behave is explored through a theory of social reproduction.

BOURDIEU'S THEORY OF SOCIAL REPRODUCTION

Pierre Bourdieu's (1977) theory of reproduction of social subjects is a valuable conceptual tool for understanding the roles of schools, families, and churches in developing enduring self/other identities able to withstand the evidence of competing cultural arbitraries. Bourdieu introduced the concepts of *habitus, pedagogical authority, symbolic violence,* and *cultural arbitrary* to explain how power and ideology contribute to the reproduction of social subjects. According to Bourdieu, "All pedagogic action is, objectively, symbolic violence insofar as it is the imposition of a cultural arbitrary by an arbitrary power" (Bourdieu & Passeron, 1977, p. 5).

From this perspective, all forms of teaching whether done in the context of schools, families, churches, governments, or media are power-imbued forms of symbolic violence. These teachings are arbitrary in the sense of not being grounded on fundamental truths but on claims to truth, legitimacy, and authority. Thus, the imposition of arbitrary teachings by powerful pedagogic authorities in the form of parents, teachers, media, and religious leaders wreak symbolic violence on less powerful subjects. Through long exposure, individuals may internalize these cultural arbitraries, assume them to be natural and real, and incorporate them into their social belief systems. Bourdieu called this complex ideological phenomenon *habitus*, the inculcation and reproduction of a cultural arbitrary by a new subject.

The personal stories about my family and Hawaii's schools are examples of narratives that interpret individual recollections using Bourdieu's theoretical framework. They suggest that a critical perspective presenting the potential for social change develops if individuals recognize and decide to oppose the symbolic violence of educational practices and cultural arbitraries that increase the power of dominant groups at the expense of subordinate groups.

RECOGNIZING CULTURAL ARBITRARIES AND DEVELOPING A CRITICAL PERSPECTIVE

What are the implications for teacher education and a critical pedagogy? My own experiences and research with minority women and prospective teachers suggest that stories that might pass as authoritative can be seen as arbitrary if exposed by contradictory narratives or experiences (Chinn, 1999b, 2002a). I did not realize this until I entered social worlds unlike my familiar world. My middle-class upbringing and tracked public school education allowed little interaction with nonmainstream peers. My Asian American and White friends played cello and chess, were in Gifted and Talented classes, and were 100% college bound. I only knew students like me. In college, science work stressed individual competence and teacher preparation did not include critiques of gender and language discrimination, tracking, or colonialism. As a student teacher, I taught Advanced Placement and Honors Chemistry at Roosevelt High School, which still retained the elitist culture and curriculum of an English Standard school.

I learned little from my father's occasional drives through the poorer neighborhoods of Honolulu to point out ways of life he wanted us to avoid. I did not really "see" how gender, class, and culture impacted schooling until I taught science in a low-income, minority middle school. I had just returned from 6 months in India where I saw how being born high caste led to much better options in life than being born low caste. One day as I walked with my Filipino and Pacific Islander students past an open classroom, I heard one say, "Eh, mus' be smart class—all Japs!" That offhand remark implicitly connecting schooling, race, and access to educational resources opened my eyes to cultural arbitraries and politicized my view of education.

As a teacher educator, I think it is imperative that prospective teachers become aware of their own cultural values as well as their prejudices and assumptions about other groups. Awareness of oneself as a cultural construction is the first step, to be shared with peers who are culturally different. I assign exercises to help prospective teachers become aware of *habitus*, how they were shaped at home and school, and how gender or racial stereotypes that seem to be natural and universal are, in fact, cultural arbitraries. These activities sensitize prospective teachers to issues of power, status, and access to resources in their familiar worlds. Finally, I want to provide prospective teachers with strategies to listen to those who are less powerful and whose social worlds and cultures are unfamiliar. In the next section, I provide examples of the strategies I use with prospective teachers to help them to acquire critical, multicultural perspectives in the context of teaching diverse students.

Who knows? Perhaps if my father had had experiences that contradicted his culturally ingrained beliefs about gender, he might have supported his daughters as strongly as his son in scientific arenas. It is certain that his personal experiences with race, language, and social class motivated his work as a science educator.

HAWAII'S PROSPECTIVE TEACHERS
AND STUDENTS

Hawaii's population is about two thirds Asian and Pacific Islander and one third White. Japanese, Chinese, Koreans, and Whites tend to be in higher education and income brackets whereas Filipinos, Hawaiians, and Pacific Islanders tend to be overweighted in lower brackets. The cultural mismatch between low-socioeconomic students and a prospective teacher population dominated by middle-class Asians and Whites is a compelling reason to prepare teachers to be sensitive to the ways class, culture, ethnicity, language, and gender impact on teaching and learning, particularly in science.

Most of my prospective teachers had few Pacific Islanders, Native Hawaiians, and working-class peers in their college preparatory classes. Though everyone living in Hawaii for more than a few years knows a little about the foods, traditional dress, and cultural practices of the state's major Polynesian and Asian ethnic groups, relatively few people have deep knowledge of another culture. Personal knowledge of African Americans and Hispanics is especially low, even absent, as African Americans are less than 2% and Hispanics are relative newcomers to the islands (Donnelly, 2001).

Realizing that understanding and addressing cultural issues is an ongoing process for educators, I ask my prospective K–12 teachers in both my foundations of curriculum and science methods classes to engage in assignments centering on the nexus of self-identity, cultural affiliation, and schooling. The following series of assignments involve them in examining their social location, group identification, assumptions, and projections about their future classrooms and students. Assignments 1–3 focus on self-identity, personal learning, and teaching students of diverse cultures whereas 4–6 are directly related to science.

My Cultural CD

My source for this activity is a prospective secondary social studies teacher who got it from his ethnic studies class. He used it for a microteaching assignment in my foundations of curriculum class. I modified his lesson to provide both elementary and secondary prospective teachers with personal connections and shared narratives on the topic of cultural diversity and school success. The 30-minute lesson helps them tease apart and analyze the impact of culturally determined attributes on the development of social and self-identities. Each is given a handout with a diagram of a CD of Me (Fig. 8.1) and asked to write a self-descriptive list or sentence in each of the six tracks of the CD labeled *language, ethnicity, class, gender, peer group,* and *social identity.* Prospective teachers then are asked to share their personal CDs in groups of four of maximum cultural diversity.

Following the sharing, groups are asked to discuss how and why certain combinations of cultural characteristics can lead to higher or lower

FIG. 8.1.   My cultural CD.

chances of academic success. Each group develops a CD of Success and CD of Struggle and reports back to the whole class. In this way, the knowledge and experiences of diverse individuals are elicited on an individual level, shared with a small group, then discussed by the whole class. Prospective teachers limited to middle-class experiences, as I was, are introduced to compelling personal stories that provide insight into cultural arbitraries affecting access to education. Because this lesson occurs in the first weeks of class, prospective teachers like the way the assignment simultaneously allows them to get to know new classmates and future colleagues through a lesson relevant for working with diverse students.

How I Learned to . . .

This focused free-write lesson developed out of one of my assignments in a graduate class on constructivist learning. The objective of this 20-minute assignment is to establish the fundamentally social nature of learning. It counteracts the notion that academic ability is innate and individualistic and emphasizes the critical relationship between teacher and learner.

Prospective teachers are asked to identify something they do well with the writing prompt, "How I learned to . . ." Next they are directed to write for 5 minutes in great detail about how they became interested in the subject and developed their expertise. They do not have to choose an academic area, and very few did, choosing instead to describe how they learned to cook, surf, or play a guitar or ukulele. Most of them generated half a page to a full page by the end of the writing period. Next they formed groups of three to four to share their stories of learning and to note where the stories of learning are different and where they are the same. At the end of 10 minutes of discussion, each group reported out to the whole class on the similarities and differences in the stories of learning.

What becomes evident after several groups have reported is that the differences have to do with the activity chosen by individuals, whereas the similarities have to do with the social nature of becoming interested in and learning to do something well. Most groups will conclude that developing expertise has a lot to do with persistence, practice, encouragement, and feedback from more skilled individual(s). Though a few prospective teachers may talk about developing expertise in a negative social environment to prove they can rise to a challenge, most stories are associated with supportive social interactions that encourage the ongoing risk taking that is an integral part of learning.

Following the class discussion of successful learning, I sometimes ask prospective teachers to write about and then discuss something they did not like. Interestingly, for this part of the assignment, they are more likely than not to identify a content area. Mathematics was often a topic that was disliked because learners experienced negative feelings due to poor test scores, unpleasant interactions with teachers, or inadequate support for learning. Asking prospective teachers for their negative learning experiences may reveal much that can be related to culture-based learning styles and pedagogy. The importance of emotions and communicative style is relevant to cultural expectations, such as the Asian and Polynesian expectation that children show respect by listening to adults in contrast to Western expectations that students actively engage in questions and discussion.

Another 10-minute extension of this activity involves concept mapping. Prospective teachers are asked to concept map the activity they know well then to concept map an activity described by a group member. The group reconvenes to compare concept maps of something that is known deeply and well compared to something less known. If the instructor chooses a gender-, class-, or ethnicity-based activity, such as describing how to play football or do laundry, this is a way to get the point across that learning in a variety of areas is culturally based and can be accessed and assessed. Prospective teachers find this exercise interesting because it does double duty as a personally engaging way to highlight the role of culture in learning while introducing an assessment strategy. At the discretion of the instructor, prompts that more pointedly address locally relevant issues relevant to teaching such as culture-based communication styles can be analyzed.

How I Would Teach Diverse Students

Following their examination of personal learning, I ask prospective teachers to write a short paper describing how they would teach culturally diverse students. The assignment develops awareness of their own assumptions and views about teaching and learning in the context of teaching students of diverse cultural backgrounds. Through the assignment, they explore how they feel about and plan to work with students with diverse communication and learning styles.

Many of them approach this assignment from the perspective of their own experiences as learners. They share examples of specific experiences, including the social settings and key individuals who have influenced their views of teaching and learning. By this time in the course, they recognize that personal experience has a powerful influence on shaping the way people see the world, and many of them explicitly highlight the relationships between culture and pedagogy. A prospective teacher of Korean and Hawaiian ethnicity wrote that he heard his Korean grandmother's voice stressing the importance of doing well at school when he reflected on what shaped his views of education. But when he thought of himself as a student, he heard his Hawaiian voice and those of his friends opposing learning limited to mainstream content (Chinn, 2000). These reflective exercises help prospective teachers become aware of that they may view teaching and learning from multiple perspectives.

A prospective secondary teacher who was already working as a Hawaiian-language teacher provides another example of the way cultural experience shapes views of teaching and learning. She employs her culturally shaped teaching strategies in her Hawaiian-language classes. She introduced how she learned at home through a proverb: *"Ka 'ike o ke keiki. Nana ka maka. Ho'olohe. Pa'a ka waha. Ho'opili. I ka nana no a 'ike. I ka ho'olohe no a maopopo. I ka hana no a 'ike."*

> This proverb translates as, "The learning of the child: observe, listen, keep the mouth shut, imitate. By observing, one learns; in listening, one commits to memory; by practice one masters the skill." This is a proverb that many Hawaiian families follow even today when teaching their children. I remember my parents, grandparents, and even aunties and uncles telling my brothers, sisters, and myself these things and I remember how learning was made easier if you listen, for if you began to wander or daydream you would be whacked on the knee. The whacking of the knee was based on word meaning. Deafness is *kuli*. The knee is also *kuli*. So when the old folks (teachers) get exasperated and whack you on the knee, it means you are acting like a deaf person. You are not listening.

I found her story so relevant to cultural learning styles that I developed it into an environmental science lesson that I have used with prospective teachers and high school science students (see Appendix A). The goals of the lesson are to introduce teachers and students to learning styles that have high survival value in cultures in which knowledge is transmitted orally.

What Scientific and Technological Achievements Are Credited to Your Group?

In this assignment, prospective elementary science teachers examine the relationship between subordinate and dominant cultural groups through the ways knowledge is constructed, appropriated, and transmitted. As most prospective teachers entering science have learned it largely from textbooks and laboratory exercises, few have examined their science learning from a critical perspective. First, they are asked to identify the cultural group they identify with, then research, write up, and report on the science and technology credited to their group. Chinese, Japanese, and Whites, especially men, found a large body of science and technology credited to their culture/gender groups.

A Japanese woman wrote about chick sexing, a procedure separating males from egg-laying females. Shigeru Nitta discovered it at the University of Tokyo in 1924 and brought to the United States. Her pride is evident in the following excerpt from her report:

> By raising sexed chicks, the poultry industry realizes greater gains in labor, feed, space and fuel . . . During the Depression, the hatchery and poultry industry, one of the largest in the United States, suffered heavy financial losses . . . [and] . . . turned to chicken sexing to remedy the situation . . . Through conscientious training of hundreds of chicken sexors [sic], American Chick Sexing School and Amchick, one of the nation's largest primary contractors for chick sexors gained the confidence of hatchery and poultry industry operators throughout the world . . . For his work in advancing harmonious relations between the United States and Japan through his pioneering work in chicken sexing, Shigeru Nitta was presented with a Japanese government *Kunsho* award in 1993.

Filipinos, Pacific Islanders, and subordinated Asians such as Okinawans were surprised to find little or nothing in the literature even when they requested the help of university librarians. Women of all ethnic groups found much less attributed to women than men and used their findings to critique gender stereotyping and unequal access to cultural resources. One woman reflected on her own life and what she could do as a teacher and mother:

> Another thing that got me seriously thinking of science and me was writing the paper about our ethnic background. I read a wonderful book about women in science and found one common thread was that the women who became scientists had excellent female role models themselves. Either a mother or other adult female inspired them to continue in their quest for scientific knowledge. Most of the women I read about were practicing in times when women attending college for anything besides teaching or nursing was very rare. One woman . . . had to use a basement lab to conduct her research because she was not allowed above the first floor to the lab where the rest of the department staff worked. I found myself seriously considering the message I am sending my own two daughters about science and women's roles and men's roles. Lindsey is in 1st grade and Taylor in preschool yet I know they are learning from my example every day. I want them to grow up to be young women who feel the confidence and assurance to become whatever they want to be . . . I don't want them to be "scared" to try something that makes them uncomfortable . . . I must say, I have checked out more science books from the library this semester than I have in my whole life!

The few White men in the class did not take a critical perspective on White privilege or consider the appropriation of knowledge from other cultures. They tended to be bored with the assignment, feeling it simply confirmed what they already knew, the dominance of White men in science. Their stance opened up a space for women to discuss the absence of women and minorities as an indicator of power and privilege based on the cultural arbitrary of male superiority. Women, on the other hand, learned from this assignment that persons who have been oppressed or silenced more readily perceive a social phenomenon as the outcome of a cultural arbitrary. Examining who gets credit for scientific and technological knowledge is an important topic in its own right, but gender and ethnicity patterns should also be critiqued for the unspoken message that science is the domain of dominant men. A Japanese female doctoral student in high-energy physics told me succinctly, "Physics, it's like men started it" (Chinn, 2002a).

This assignment is especially interesting for another reason. It revealed that Hawaiian activism had made a positive impact on ethnic and academic identity. Prospective teachers who identified themselves as Hawaiian have benefited from a Hawaiian cultural renaissance of the past quarter century that established the vitality of indigenous cultural practices and knowledge. They knew about medicinal and fiber plants, conservation, and agricultural and navigational practices. It pleased me as a longtime educator that many of them perceived this as a trivial assignment because it was now common knowledge that Hawaiians could build seaworthy double-hulled canoes and navigate by the stars across thousands of miles of ocean. Non-Hawaiian peers accepted this as proof of Hawaiian knowledge and technical expertise. The new generation of teachers, unlike some of their predecessors, considered Hawaiian students as academically capable as any others (Chinn, 1999b).

Did they know of young Hawaiians who wished, as one high school girl told me 20 years ago, to be able to cut out the part of her that was Hawaiian? None of them did, though they recognized that Hawaiians as a group still suffered from negative stereotypes and were still educationally and economically disadvantaged.

Interview a Child

In an assignment intended to provide prospective elementary science teachers with insights into the science understandings of children, each interviewed an elementary student to explore the child's understanding of the world and the source of this knowledge. Each interview was analyzed in light of implications for student-centered science instruction, presented to the class, and discussed. Along with introducing a qualitative method for action research, the objective was to provide age-appropriate information on the science knowledge held by diverse students. The interviewees ranged from young relatives to children in their field settings. The prospective teachers were amazed at the depth and range of science knowledge expressed by children. They found that children from middle-class families with ready access to books and educated adults could speak as experts in their areas of interest. They found that children who came from Hawaiian families who continued fishing and planting had a working knowledge of these activities. Prospective teachers also found that children held views about the world based on stories they had heard from authoritative adults. For example, one child reported that dark clouds in the sky meant that God was angry.

Overall, this was the multicultural research activity the prospective elementary science teachers liked the best and recognized as directly relevant to their work with diverse students. Being in a field-based preparation program, they were already in elementary school settings so finding a child of the appropriate age to interview was not a problem. They saw clearly how knowledge of students' lives was valuable to teachers who oriented their instruction to students' prior knowledge. Most had never talked to children about what they knew and how they learned it. They felt the activity provided insights into children's thinking and learning and were surprised at the range of knowledge and beliefs from nonschool sources. The assignment compelled the recognition of the importance of family and community as educational resources.

CULTURALLY RELEVANT, STANDARDS-BASED
SCIENCE LESSONS

The development of culturally relevant science curricula aligns with a growing recognition in the broader educational community that minority students' learning can and should be addressed in ways connected to traditional values and practices (Reyhner & Davison, 1993). Hawaii has a Science Content and Performance Standard that reflects traditional Hawaiian views of sustainability and stewardship. *Malama I Ka 'aina*, Sustainability, mandates that "students must be taught to make decisions needed to sustain life on Earth now and for future generations by considering limited resources and fragile environmental conditions" (see http://doe.k12.hi.us/standards/index.htm). To meet this science standard, curricula that include Hawaiian cultural perspectives instead of purely Western science viewpoints make sense from both a science and cultural perspective. Key differences between traditional Hawaiian and modern Western views of the natural world are outlined next.

Hawaiians recognized their lands as fragile ecosystems highly sensitive to human interference. The basic land unit, the *ahupua'a*, provided the framework for Hawaiians to relate to each other and local resources. Most *ahupua'a* ran from sea to mountaintop and included fresh water, fishing rights, croplands, and forest. Families belonged to an *ahupua'a*, unlike Westerners who belonged to villages or towns. People living upland, *mauka*, exchanged products with people living *makai*, at the shore. The *mauka–makai* exchange, including marriage, within the *ahupua'a* developed interdependence, self-sufficiency, and sense of place associated with deep environmental knowledge (Abbott, 1992). Even today, the cultural emphasis on linking generations past, *na kupuna;* present, *na makua;* and future, *na opio;* is inseparable from knowledge of the *ahupua'a* that sustains the community.

In contrast, as a science teacher, I know that school science tends to be taught as value free, impersonal, Eurocentric, and universally applicable. International research collaborations such as the development of the Space Station and the construction of telescopes on Mauna Kea in Hawaii by Canada, France, Japan, the United Kingdom, and the United States exemplify the application of laws, principles, and processes that operate anywhere in the universe. But these big Western science and technology efforts valorize knowledge seeking leading to domination over nature, not Hawaiian values of a sense of place, sustainability, and respect for the natural world.

Few prospective science teachers are aware of the great differences between the worldviews of Native Hawaiians and Western scientists. They may not even be aware of issues of underrepresentation of Hawaiians and other indigenous peoples in science. But carrying out assignments such as "Interview a Child" and "How I learned . . ." during the first few weeks of classes sensitizes them to the roles that cultural and personal experiences play in knowledge building and interest in science. These experiences provide a foundation for planning and teaching lessons that address content standards while being culturally relevant. By the time they begin lesson planning, prospective teachers recognize the importance of instruction that connects to children's cultures and communities.

Because Native Hawaiians make up about one fifth of the K–12 population and are the group most at risk of school failure, many prospective teachers develop lessons oriented toward Hawaiian children. For example, a Japanese-American woman who planned to be an elementary teacher in a Hawaiian community modified a lesson on mollusks to highlight those important in Hawaii. Her science lesson incorporated cultural uses of the *opihi*, a limpet valued for food and for its shell, used in precontact Hawaii for adornment and as a scraper. As part of her microteaching lesson, she taught her peers how to prepare and use the shell. A Native Hawaiian prospective teacher who also planned to teach in a Hawaiian community made a generic marine science lesson culturally and locally relevant. Her lesson addressed the Hawaii Science Content Standard *Malama I Ka 'aina,* which translates as "caring for the land." She localized the lesson by using place names and activities familiar to her students—swimming, fishing, and canoe paddling. The lesson on nonpoint source pollution (a concept that I think becomes more comprehensible, personally involving, and culturally relevant if presented as the people's pollution) involves students in making decisions on whether they would swim, fish, or paddle a canoe in coastal waters increasingly polluted by human activity. (See Appendix B for a version of this lesson, *"Malama I Ka 'aina*: How Clean Are Your Streams and Beaches?")

INDIGENOUS CULTURE AND THE CURRICULUM

Most public and private secondary schools now offer Hawaiian-language classes and K–12 Hawaiian-immersion public schools recently celebrated their first graduates. Every public elementary school has a program where *kupuna,* Hawaiian elders, teach children Hawaiian cultural practices. Unfortunately, the teaching of Hawaiian culture (and other nonacademic curricular content) is threatened by the No Child Left Behind act of 2001 that mandates low-performing schools to increase standardized test scores or lose federal funds. The law affects 127 Hawaii schools receiving Title I federal funds, many serving Hawaiian communities. Under pressure to improve scores in 2 years, low-performing schools are offered the choice of purchasing commercial educational programs or developing their own. The overwhelming majority have opted to select a commercial program, increasing the impact of monocultural curricula in schools with high proportions of indigenous Hawaiian students.

Where this has occurred, I already hear from teachers that they feel forced to use inappropriate curricular materials and methods with their students. What are the implications of this curricular shift due to high-stakes testing? The stories of two schools, one that ended and another that began a culturally relevant ag-science program, conclude this chapter.

Two years ago I visited a student teacher in a rural school that served a 50% Native Hawaiian student population. His agriculture students raised hogs and traditional Hawaiian crops, sold hydroponic vegetables to the community, studied horsemanship, and constructed a bioremediation system to clean and reuse wash water from the pig pens. By preventing wash water from going into the environment, the engineered ecosystem kept the hog-raising program from being shut down. It also conserved water, was a modern application of Hawaiian practices and values, and was used to teach science topics such as water and nutrient cycles.

But instead of supporting a program that integrated science, Hawaiian culture, and agriculture, the White principal, a mainlander, canceled several agriculture classes in favor of reading classes. Low standardized test scores were the reason given. But scores were good considering that 12% of adults in the community versus 21% statewide held college degrees. Open-ended reading scores of 17% above average (vs. 23% nationally) were higher than other rural schools with similar proportions of Hawaiian students. The strong support of the Hawaiian community for the program did not alter the principal's decision. Hawaiians who worked at the school told me they thought the principal's underlying motive was to eliminate classes that taught their children how make a living from the land. They feared their children would leave for work in towns and be replaced by outsiders seeking a rural, yet comfortable lifestyle. They foresaw the decline of their tight-knit, self-sufficient community and deeply resented being shut out of curricular decision making. Within a year of my visit, the hog-raising program and bioremediation system were shut down, the new teacher was out of a job, and an industrial arts teacher was teaching agriculture classes.

Ironically, at the next school down the road, a local Japanese-American principal immediately hired the displaced teacher to develop a culturally relevant ag-science program to reduce the number of Hawaiian students failing traditional, textbook-based science courses. The school's recognition that students' culture, knowledge, experiences, and interests should be part of science curriculum development echoes National Science Education Teaching Standards (National Research Council, 1996).

School stories like these show that curricular decisions can be analyzed for subplots involving race, power, class, and economics. They reinforce my commitment to provide prospective teachers with strategies that help them find out what is important to students and their communities. Action research that uncovers educational issues within their own schools can move prospective teachers out of familiar comfort zones. Recognizing how mainstream curriculum, instruction, and assessment can marginalize nonmainstream students is the first step in addressing these issues. Educators may not realize they are guilty of institutional racism (Haas, 1992), but mainstream, Eurocentric curricula can lead to the devaluation and gradual loss of nonmainstream cultural knowledge, languages, and worldviews ("The Triumph of English," 2001).

In Hawaii as in other places, Western school science puts indigenous practices and knowledge at risk (Snively & Corsiglia, 1998). Fortunately, mainstream communities are beginning to recognize that Native Hawaiian cultural practices and values provide models for sustainability and resource management. This has led to support for culturally relevant science education programs (Chinn & Sylva, 2000). However, as long as

Hawaii's schools use mainstream standardized tests as a primary measure of student achievement, there will be the risk of institutional racism and the need to provide prospective teachers with knowledge and tools to make connections between culture and curriculum and address educational inequity (Chinn, 2002b).

REFERENCES

Abbott, I. A. (1992). *La'au Hawai'i: Traditional Hawaiian uses of plants.* Honolulu, HI: Bishop Museum Press.

Bourdieu, P., & Passeron, J.-C. (1977). *Reproduction in education, society and culture.* London: Sage.

Chinn, P. (1995). *Becoming a scientist: Narratives of women entering science and engineering.* Ann Arbor, MI: UMI Dissertation Services.

Chinn, P. (1999a). Isabella Aiona Abbott and the education of minorities and females. *Teaching Education, 10,* 155–167.

Chinn, P. (1999b). Multiple worlds and mis-matched meanings: Barriers to minority women engineers. *Journal of Research in Science Teaching, 36*(6), 621–636.

Chinn, P. (2000, April). *What preservice teachers bring to the classroom: How sociocultural experiences shape future teachers of diverse learners.* Paper presented at the annual meeting of the American Educational Research Association, New Orleans, LA.

Chinn, P. (2002a). Asian and Pacific Islander women scientists and engineers: A narrative exploration of model minority, gender and racial stereotypes. *Journal of Research in Science Teaching, 39*(4), 302–323.

Chinn, P. (2002b, September). *Preparing science teachers for Native Hawaiian students: The roles of cross-cultural immersion and cultural translators in cross-cultural literacy.* Paper presented at the International Ontological, Epistemological, Linguistic and Pedagogical Considerations of Language and Science Literacy: Empowering Research and Informing Instruction Conference, Victoria, British Columbia, Canada.

Chinn, P., & Sylva, T. (2000). *Malama I ka 'aina: Using traditional Hawaiian and modern environmental practices to develop standards-based, K–12 science curricula for teachers of Hawaiian and Part-Hawaiian students* (A project to develop elementary and secondary curricular materials supported by the U.S. Department of Education). Washington, DC: U.S. Department of Education, Office of Elementary and Secondary Education—School Improvement Programs.

Donnelly, C. (2001, September 9). Delving into isles' diversity. In Keiki to kupuna: The people of paradise. *Honolulu Star-Bulletin,* p. 6.

Education and the economy, A Report from the Department of Business, Economic Development & Tourism, Hawaii's Economy, November 1998. Retrieved December 10, 2003, from http://www.hawaii.gov/dbedt/hecon/he11-98/content.html.

Gee, J. (2001). Identity as an analytic lens for research in education. In W. G. Secada (Ed.), *Review of research in education* (Vol. 25, pp. 99–125). Washington, DC: American Educational Research Association.

Gould, S. J. (1993). American polygeny and craniometry before Darwin: Blacks and Indians as separate inferior species. In S. Harding (Ed.), *The racial economy of science: Toward a democratic future* (pp. 84–115). Bloomington: Indiana University Press.

Haas, M. (1992). *Institutional racism: The case of Hawaii.* Westport, CT: Praeger.

Mishler, E. G. (1986). *Research interviewing.* Cambridge, MA: Harvard University Press.

National Research Council. (1996). *National science education standards*. Washington, DC: National Academy Press.

Ogbu, J. U. (1999). Beyond language: Ebonics, proper English, and identity in a Black American speech community. *American Educational Research Journal, 36,* 147–184.

Porteus, S. (1962). *A century of social thinking in Hawaii*. Palo Alto, CA: Pacific Books.

Reyhner, J., & Davison, D. M. (1993). Improving mathematics and science instruction for LEP middle and high school students through language activities. In *Proceedings of the Third National Research Symposium on Limited English Proficient student issues: Focus on middle and high school issues* (Vol. 2, pp. 549–578). Washington, DC: U.S. Department of Education, Office of Bilingual Education and Minority Languages Affairs.

Ricoeur, P. (1991). Life in quest of narrative. In D. Wood (Ed.), *On Paul Ricoeur: Narrative and interpretation* (pp. 20–33). New York: Routledge.

Ricoeur, P. (1992). *Oneself as another*. Chicago: University of Chicago Press.

Snively, G., & Corsiglia, J. (1998, April). *Discovering indigenous science: Implications for science education*. Paper presented at annual meeting of the National Association for Research in Science Teaching, San Diego.

Stueber, R. K. (1964). *Hawaii: A case study in development education*. Ann Arbor, MI: University Microfilms Inc.

Takaki, R. (1994). *Raising cane: The world of plantation Hawaii*. New York: Chelsea House.

Tobin, J., Allingham, B., Chinn, P., Cooper, J, Marker, N., McLaughlin, J., Pateman, N., & Phelan, A. (1992). *The 1992 Hawai'i progress report on the National Education Goals*. Honolulu: University of Hawaii-Manoa, Center for Youth Research, Social Sciences Research Institute.

The triumph of English: A world empire by other means. (2001, December 22). *The Economist*, pp. 65–67.

Witherell, C., & Noddings, N. (Eds.). (1991). *Stories lives tell: Narrative and dialogue in education*. New York: Teachers College Press.

APPENDIX A

A Hawaiian Way of Teaching and Learning

BACKGROUND

This lesson sensitizes teachers and students to Hawaiian cultural learning styles and the explores reasons for oral cultures placing a high value on the wisdom of elders. It is based on a paper by a prospective Hawaiian-language teacher.

Following is a Hawaiian proverb: *"Ka 'ike o ke keiki. Nana ka maka. Ho'olohe. Pa'a ka waha. Ho'opili. I ka nana no a 'ike. I ka ho'olohe no a maopopo. I ka hana no a 'ike."* This proverb translates as, "The learning of the child: observe, listen, keep the mouth shut, imitate. By observing, one learns; in listening, one commits to memory; by practice one masters the skill." This is a proverb that many Hawaiian families follow even today when teaching their children.

I remember my parents, grandparents, and even aunties and uncles telling my brothers, sisters, and myself these things and I remember how learning was made easier if you listen, for if you began to wander or day-dream you would be whacked on the knee. The whacking of the knee was based on word meaning. Deafness is *kuli*. The knee is also *kuli*. So when the old folks (teachers) get exasperated and whack you on the knee, it means you are acting like a deaf person. You are not listening.

Questions

1. What does this story reveal about learning in oral societies?
2. What kinds of knowledge would be important to conserve and transmit?
3. Why are elders much more respected in nonprint cultures than in modern societies? (Consider drought, famine, tsunami, 100-year storms.)
4. What are ways of transmitting knowledge besides talking, reading, and writing?
5. To preserve really deep, local knowledge, how would marriage be arranged?

APPENDIX B

Malama I Ka 'Aina: How Clean Are Your Streams and Beaches?

Time: 40–50 minutes
Class: Earth Science, Biology, Social Studies
Grade Levels: 3–8

Teacher Background

Storm drains direct runoff from yards and streets into streams leading into oceans. In Hawaii, the only water allowed in storm drains is rainwater and water from fire trucks.

I. Science Standard: *Malama I Ka 'aina*, Sustaining Food Supply and Conservation of Resources. Students make decisions needed to sustain life on Earth now and for future generations by considering limited resources and fragile environmental conditions. Driving question: What can we do to conserve our natural resources of water, stream, and coastal life and keep the environment healthy for living things?

II. Goal: Students will learn how water resources are affected by human practices and be able to suggest ways individual and society can reduce negative impacts.

III. Student Learning Objectives:

A. Students will simulate and evaluate the impact of rainfall and runoff from lands not disturbed by human activity versus those settled by people.

B. Students will suggest personal and societal solutions to water pollution.

IV. Resources and Materials:

Map of your *ahupua'a* or watershed

Four large, wide-mouthed, clear plastic jars (gallon size)

Four long-handled spoons

Source of water and sink

Four sets of small bags filled as follows: Bag 1 with leaves, twigs; Bag 2 with small items of litter, for example, wrappers, cigarette butts, bottle caps, and so on; Bag 3 with ketchup or chocolate syrup to simulate oil and food wastes

V. Instructional Procedures: Prepare four large clear, plastic jars of clean water about 8–9 inches deep to simulate the beach where a stream enters the ocean. Put a spoon and set of labeled bags by each jar.

A. Focusing Activity (5 minutes): Referring to a map of your area, ask students what they notice along streams and beaches before and after a heavy rain. Ask them how they feel about it. Tell students they will be simulating what happens to their beach using jars and materials.

B. Group Activity (30 minutes):

1. Ask groups to look at Bags 1 and 2 and compare the contents. (They should note that organic materials are in Bag 1 and synthetic materials are in Bag 2.)

2. Ask students to put the contents of Bag 1 in their jar and stir. Ask if they would swim, or fish, or paddle a canoe in water with this material in it. Ask them if they think this is bad for streams and oceans. (Most will say they might not swim but would still fish and paddle a canoe as natural materials break down and provide food for plants and animals.)

3. Ask students to put the contents of Bag 2 in their jar and stir. Ask if they would swim, or fish, or paddle a canoe in water with this material in it. Ask them if they think this is bad for streams and

oceans. (Most will say it's bad because it's not natural and will not break down.) If you have some clear plastic items, some students will know that sea turtles may eat plastic bags as they look like jellyfish.

4. Ask students to put the contents of Bag 3 in their jar and stir. Ask if they would swim, or fish, or paddle a canoe in water with this material in it. Ask them if they think this is bad for streams and oceans. (Most will say it's bad because now it's so polluted fish and seaweeds might die and you might get sick if you fell out of your canoe.)

5. Ask students what they and their families can do personally to keep streams and beaches cleaner. (Most will suggest recycling, disposing of trash properly, washing cars on lawns, cleaning up litter or another service project, and so on. Some might suggest a planting project to bind soils that wash into streams during heavy rains.)

6. Traditional societies had to find what they needed to survive in their own area. Contrast that to modern Hawaii with its reliance on imports. How does having to find everything you need on your own lands affect the way Hawaiians (and indigenous people in general) think about natural resources? What would happen to food supplies and prices if a dock strike lasted several months? Have students imagine what would be different if 1 million people lived here without outside food supplies. What can be done today to increase sustainability?

C. Follow up with a video, photos, or readings on water pollution from industries, cities, and farm runoff. A Web search will provide articles and photos.

1. Students can assess their neighborhoods for trash that could enter storm drains, streams, and ocean. A class service project might develop from this.

2. A long-term composting project to compare breakdown of natural and synthetic materials could follow.

3. This activity could be part of a water cycle, watershed, or *ahupua'a* study.

VI. Assessment: Look for evidence from discussions, writings, and so on, that students know how runoff gets into streams and ocean and know what is legal in storm drains. Look for evidence that students know steps to take to *malama 'aina*, care for the land. Look for evidence that students recognize that Western contact and changing lifestyles may cause a devaluing and degrading of the *'aina* but realize that all people ultimately depend on a healthy environment for their survival.

9

Transformative Mathematics Pedagogy: From Theory to Practice, Research, and Beyond

Joy Moore
University of Cincinnati

According to the U.S. Census Bureau, by the year 2050, 49% of the population will be non-White, with Hispanics becoming the largest ethnic minority population by 2010 ("Hispanics to Outnumber," 1993). Historically, ethnic minority students, with the exceptions of Asians, have been underserved by U.S. education. In particular, African Americans and Hispanics have performed at the lowest levels of school mathematics academic achievement (Secada, 1992; Tate, 1997). If equity and excellence are to result from educational reforms, then effective teacher preparation must include learning to teach for diversity (Rodriguez, 1998). As the K–12 student population becomes more diverse, educational reform that benefits all students demands that teachers learn to implement more culturally inclusive and socially relevant pedagogical strategies. Schooling in the United States includes social, political, historical, and cultural contexts. Yet, teacher education programs are often lacking in addressing the multicultural issues of gender, ethnic, racial, socioeconomic, and political diversity. Sleeter (2001) reviewed 80 research studies of teacher preparation for multicultural schools, particularly those that serve historically underserved communities. The majority of the research concentrates on addressing the attitudes and lack of knowledge of White prospective teachers. Yet, little research examines those strategies that prepare strong culturally responsive and socially relevant teachers by enabling teachers to develop a cross-cultural competence and heightened awareness of sociopolitical issues within the classroom (McAllister & Irvine, 2000).

Though teachers may believe that teaching for diversity promotes academic achievement for all students, teacher preparation and professional-development programs may not provide the mathematics learning and training experiences to enable teachers to practice transformative pedagogy. The purpose of this chapter is to present strategies that have been successful in supporting practicing mathematics teachers to teach for diversity. In particular, I describe the impact of transformative mathematics pedagogy in a 2-year professional-development program.

Mathematics teachers require a breadth of mathematics content knowledge, pedagogical knowledge, and knowledge of the influences of students' linguistic, ethnic, racial, and socioeconomic backgrounds and gender on learning mathematics (National Council of Teachers of Mathematics [NCTM], 1991). Often in teacher preparation programs, the mathematics methods courses are disjoint from the mathematics content courses and issues of sociocultural diversity are absent in both. Too often, methods courses are offered in the College of Education, content courses are offered in the College of Arts and Sciences, and never the twain (faculty, course content, curriculum, or pedagogical approach) shall meet. This lack of connectivity and inclusion presents challenges to prospective and inservice teachers who seek to incorporate their content knowledge and pedagogical knowledge in a classroom practice that is culturally responsive and socially relevant. As an African American, female mathematician and educator (I hold an interdisciplinary PhD in both mathematical sciences and education), I practice this particular tripartite transformative mathematics pedagogy in my courses. At the University of Cincinnati, I hold a joint appointment between the Division of Teacher Education in the College of Education and the Department of Mathematical Sciences in the College of Arts and Sciences that is intended to bridge the divide and foster collaborative efforts that will greatly improve the preparation of mathematics teachers.

In that regard, I participated in a comprehensive program for the professional development of long-term substitute teachers in a unique tripartite capacity. Within the program, I served as classroom instructor, internship field experience supervisor, and research mentor for two teachers who were seeking secondary school licensure in mathematics. The uniqueness of this role resided in my ability to impart and influence teachers' mathematics content, pedagogical, and sociocultural knowledge. I taught two mathematics content courses, not methods courses. Teachers in my precalculus and calculus courses were afforded the concrete experience of learning mathematics within a culturally responsive and socially relevant classroom environment. For five of these teachers, I was then able to provide field supervision of their practice as teachers in their own classrooms. Finally, I mentored two of these students in an action research project titled "Toward the Practice of Culturally Relevant Mathematics Pedagogy." This tripartite exposure combined content, pedagogy, and a sociocultural perspective. The strategies I implemented at each stage of the program were purposeful with the intent of developing an awareness of, appreciation for, and incorporation of the sociocultural diversity that resides in our urban classrooms, while providing a comprehensive learning experience for mathematics content and pedagogy. This type of professional development is an essential step toward improving the school mathematics achievement of all students.

This chapter relates the impact of my strategies on the professional development of a teacher-researcher who will be called Nash. It documents his journey from student of mathematics and mathematics education to developer of his own pedagogical practice to researcher of mathematics education. It gives account of a teacher who was committed to teach for diversity but felt he lacked the proper pedagogical content knowledge and training to implement effective transformative pedagogy in his classroom. It describes the strategies I implemented to help him enact his commitment. This chapter outlines specific aspects of the comprehensive program that assisted these teachers in developing their own classroom practices that support learning and school mathematics achievement for all students. It relates strategies that prepare teachers who are mathematically competent and equipped to teach in culturally relevant and socially responsive ways. The next section discusses the theoretical framework that informs my pedagogical practice and the research project. The third section provides a sociocultural context for the comprehensive program and the research project. This is followed by a description of the methodology. The fifth section elaborates on the use of reflective journals in my mathematics content course. It includes a discussion of the impact of the research project on the pedagogical practice of the teacher-researcher. The chapter concludes with a summary of the study and gives implications of the findings for successfully addressing pedagogical change.

THEORETICAL FRAMEWORK

As a mathematician and a teacher educator, I find it as equally important to include the pedagogical relevance of the subject matter as it is to provide a profound understanding of the fundamental mathematics (Ma, 1999) in my content courses for prospective and in-service teachers. As the experiences that mathematics teachers have while learning mathematics have a powerful impact on the education they provide their students (NCTM, 1991), these college students in particular need to experience their own mathematics learning in ways that are significant to the development of their own pedagogical practice. In its standards for the professional development of teachers, NCTM recommended that:

> Mathematics *and* mathematics education instructors . . . model good mathematics teaching by engaging teachers in mathematical discourse, creating learning environments that support and encourage mathematical reasoning and teachers' dispositions and abilities to do mathematics; and expecting and encouraging teachers to take intellectual risks in doing mathematics and to work independently and collaboratively. (p. 127)

Yet, content and pedagogical considerations are not enough in preparing teachers to improve the school mathematics achievement of all students. Learning and teaching do not exist within a vacuum; rather they are part of a social, political, cultural, and historical complexity of context. Teaching mathematics requires an understanding of the impact that socioeconomic background, cultural heritage, attitudes and beliefs, and political climate have on the learning environment (NCTM, 1991). Urban educators in particular need an awareness of and appreciation for this complexity that should be incorporated throughout all teacher preparation curricula. I consider that amalgamation of mathematics content, pedagogy, and sociocultural diversity the practice of transformative mathematics pedagogy. If teachers are expected to teach for diversity and understanding, then they need opportunity to develop and enhance their pedagogical content knowledge. They need to experience their own mathematics learning in an environment that reflects the environment they are expected to create in their own classroom. Transformative mathematics pedagogy affords them that opportunity and provides concrete examples of how to meet the demands of an increasingly diverse student population within our ever-changing global society.

Defining Transformative Mathematics Pedagogy

My transformative mathematics pedagogy is conceptually grounded in a constructivist learning theory combined with a sociocultural and a sociopolitical perspective (Beauboeuf-Lafontant, 1999; Ladson-Billings, 1995b; Rodriguez, 1998). It is closely aligned with a standards-based pedagogy that incorporates social relevance and cultural responsiveness for the improved mathematics achievement of all students. It acknowledges and accounts for the psychological, sociological, historical, political, and cultural factors that influence educational experiences in America. The educational experiences of African American students in particular are the focus of this chapter as African Americans are the largest ethnic group within the context of my class and the school setting of the research project.

Rodriguez (1998) posited that sociotransformative constructivism (sTc) is an orientation to teaching and learning that takes into account how social, historical, and institutional contexts influence learning and access to learning in schools. He described sTc as an interception of multicultural education as a theory of social justice and social constructivism as a theory of learning. Transformative mathematics pedagogy and curriculum within the framework of sTc would incorporate standards-based, hands-on, inquiry activities with an awareness of and reflection on how the mathematics is socially and culturally relevant and tied to everyday life. This reflection is a vital, yet often lacking, component of teacher preparation programs if teachers are to develop the necessary competencies to promote social change within the classroom.

Working from a framework involving situated cognition theory, Ladson-Billings (1997) dealt with the social context of the mathematics classroom. In particular, she identified successful teachers of African American students as practitioners of a culturally relevant pedagogy. She suggested that students learn best in an environment that acknowledges the prior knowledge the students bring to class, rather than one that focuses on what students do not know. Students' cultural and experiential knowledge is used as a bridge to attain new knowledge. With culturally relevant mathematics, students' sociocultural roots are strengthened because their (ethno) knowledge is legitimized (recognized as valuable) in the classroom (Borba, 1997).

Yet, cultural consideration is but one aspect of transformative mathematics pedagogy. As I view education as a means for social transformation, transformative mathematics pedagogy must include a sociopolitical perspective. Culturally relevant teachers understand the political nature of schooling and help students see their role in the global community (Lipman, 1995). Culturally relevant pedagogy empowers students to examine critically the society in which they live and to work for social change (Ladson-Billings, 1992). Beauboeuf-Lafontant (1999) suggested renaming culturally relevant teaching as "politically relevant teaching" in order to emphasize the political, historical, social, and cultural understandings that such teachers bring to their profession. Lipman (1995) argued that it is the pedagogical and cultural knowledge of exemplary teachers of students of color that needs to be incorporated into teacher education and professional development. Both prospective and in-service teachers need the opportunity to develop sociocultural and sociopolitical perspectives in their pedagogical and content knowledge.

SOCIOCULTURAL CONTEXT

In an effort to address the need for mathematics teachers in Cincinnati Public Schools (CPS), a university faculty member designed and implemented a 2-year professional-development program for long-term substitute teachers. The original cohort of 25 students were already certified teachers working in CPS, either as substitutes or with certifications in areas no longer in demand, such as home economics. The program consisted of a year of course work and a year-long internship experience with field supervision from a university faculty member or the CPS mathematics manager. At the conclusion of the program, participants were expected to earn either a middle school mathematics certification or a secondary school licensure in mathematics. They also earned credit hours towards a master's degree in education from the University of Cincinnati.

The racial and gender composition of the cohort consisted of nine African American women, three African American men, three White women, one White man, and one Asian man. As urban mathematics educators, these teachers needed professional development that included mathematical content knowledge as well as culturally responsive and socially relevant pedagogical knowledge. I taught precalculus and calculus during the spring and summer quarter, respectively, of the 1999–2000 academic year. The precalculus course met twice a week for the 10 weeks of spring quarter. The calculus course met Monday–Friday for 4 weeks during the summer term. Each class was a 75-minute session.

At the completion of their year of course work, I was assigned five of the teachers for the year-long internship experience. I supervised these teachers throughout the 2000–2001 academic school year. This supervision included weekly observations of their mathematics classes, bimonthly meetings to discuss progress, problems, and recommendations, and quarterly evaluations. Two of these teachers were African American women, two were White women, and one was a White man. Three of them were high school mathematics teachers and two were middle school mathematics teachers. The classroom demographics were predominantly African American students with low- to middle-level socioeconomic status (SES) backgrounds.

The research project described in the following section was developed during the first semester of the internship year and conducted during the second semester of the internship year. Nash, the teacher-researcher, taught at a high school with a student population of 1,800. African American students made up 88% of the enrollment, White students comprised 10% of the student population, and the remaining 2% included Asian and Hispanic students. The school was a magnet high school situated in an urban setting.

Nash is a White man who was in his early 30s at the time of the research. He had been teaching as a long-term substitute for 3 years, which included a year in Grades K–3 with severely behaviorally handicapped students. Upon entering the program, he had been teaching high school mathematics for 2 years. He also taught modern world history during one of those two years. All of his teaching assignments had been with special-needs students in CPS. Nash is a native Cincinnatian and a product of CPS. He has an A.S. degree in premedicine/respiratory therapy and a B.S. degree in health/physical education. Nash views education as a means for social transformation rather than a systemic maintenance of the status quo. Keenly aware that far too often teachers are unable to influence district policies for students, he is very much invested in his classroom and the potential to effect change for his students individually. Nash is philosophically committed to issues of social justice and at the time of the research project wanted to find ways to incorporate a more sociopolitical perspective in his classroom practice.

METHODOLOGY

The teacher-researcher mentor experiences are the result of a university research grant. The purpose of the grant was to support CPS teachers in collaboration with College of Education faculty in conducting action research projects. A major objective of this collaboration is the mentoring of teachers as researchers. The project was twofold in purpose: to investigate the teachers' experiences in development of their own culturally relevant mathematics pedagogy (CRMP) and to examine my role as a mentor in developing the practice of CRMP. This chapter focuses its discussion on the transformative experiences of one of the teacher-researchers only, namely Nash.

The research project was conducted during the second semester of the academic school year with project development and preliminary work beginning during the first semester of the academic school year. This preliminary work called for an introduction to the literature on CRMP. I assigned specific readings (Ladson-Billings, 1995a, 1995b; Tate, 1995) from which the teachers were to identify aspects of CRMP that they found significant. We used these identifiable characteristics to derive a working "definition" of what the theory looked like in practical application. This "definition" included constructivist pedagogy with standards-based curricular content. However, it incorporated a sociocultural perspective that acknowledged the diversity in their classrooms. For the research, the term *culture* referred to the amalgamation of race, ethnicity, SES background, and societal influences that combine to create diverse experiences for students and affect their learning in the classroom. Based on the readings, the teachers were asked to identify aspects of CRMP that they thought would be important to incorporate into their practice. As part of the first self-assessment, these aspects were set as goals of incorporation to be obtained by the end of the semester.

During the semester, the teachers performed weekly analyses of their lessons with respect to the tenets of CRMP. They recorded their thoughts, class observations, and student reactions to various types of instructional style, materials, curriculum, and pedagogy. I incorporated my role as research mentor into the field supervision I was performing as part of their internship experience. During my regular weekly observations of their classes, I maintained a separate research notebook that included my observations of aspects of CRMP in their classes. We then held weekly "debriefing" sessions where we shared our observations, reflections, comments, and suggestions about the practice of CRMP in the classroom. These research sessions were held in addition to the bimonthly meetings that were part of the regular field supervision.

At the conclusion of the research period, the teachers wrote a second self-assessment. They identified the objectives they thought they had obtained during the research period and stated suggestions for future growth and improvement in their professional development. They presented these findings at an annual regional conference as the culminating event of the research experience. Data collection included notes from classroom observations during field supervision, notes from our discussion sessions, my own reflective journal, and reflective journals from the teachers (LeCompte & Preissle, 1993; Spradley, 1979).

REFLECTIVE JOURNALS

Mathematics teachers need a profound understanding of fundamental mathematical content knowledge (Ma, 1999). Yet, well-prepared prospective and in-service teachers require an additional dimension of understanding—they need to learn how to learn mathematics (Conference Board on Mathematical Sciences, 2001). As in-service teachers, I wanted them to critically assess their own learning experience in my class and apply that experience when creating learning experiences for their students in their own classrooms. I wanted them to realize and recognize themselves as learners in order to better understand and relate to their students as learners. I also wanted them to evaluate their response to me as their teacher, so that they can critically assess themselves as teachers for their students.

Teaching mathematics entails developing a personal knowledge of oneself that combines sensitivity and responsiveness to learners with the knowledge, skills, understanding, and dispositions to teach mathematics (NCTM, 1991). Teaching for diversity requires the recognition of one's own cultural background, SES, ideological commitments, and educational experiences and how these factors influence one's classroom practice. Teacher preparation and professional-development programs must provide prospective and in-service teachers the opportunity to develop this personal knowledge in relation to the development of the content knowledge. I found the use of reflective journals in my content courses as an effective way to accomplish those objectives.

Students in my class were required to maintain journals, which I reviewed periodically. I instructed them to record any and all thoughts with regard to their own mathematics learning, comprehension, and development. I explicitly told them that these journals were to promote an examination of their own learning to help them better understand and relate to their students' learning. I also told them at the beginning of the course that it was my endeavor to teach the content course in such a way that they may adopt or adapt any characteristics of my instructional practice into their own teaching. Hence, they were at liberty to examine my pedagogy in their journal by including things I did that helped or hindered their mathematics learning. Many of the entries related the students' response to the learning environment, the curriculum, the instruction, and the reflective journal itself. All quotes in this section come from their reflective journals.

The effectiveness of requiring reflective journals to foster an awareness of diverse student learning is exemplified in the following journal entry. This excerpt also reveals this teachers' development of transformative thought, as he admits his initial resistance to pedagogical change that evolves to an appreciation for the pedagogical practices of the classroom:

> I really didn't want to be bothered with this journaling thing. I don't like writing stuff down. But I can see now that this can be good for me. It makes me think about what I am doing and how I am thinking about what I am doing. That's good for understanding how I learn. Then when someone else talks about how they worked the problem I can compare that to how I did it and realize its not always the same. I didn't like this "everybody has to talk thing" either, but I guess that's good too, or else I never would have known how one problem can spark so many different approaches and trains of thought. It's stretching me, but I guess it's a good stretch.

The importance of identifying curricula that is responsive to the students' experiences was the topic of a whole-class discussion one day. In my own reflections on the class, I realized that my examples for applications usually came from engineering, medicine, or business because those were the areas in which I possessed varying degrees of expertise or knowledge base. One of the students made note of that and made the following entry in their journal:

> My students are always asking "When are we ever going to use this?" But if they learn the content within the context of a real-life problem then that question should go away. I use contextual problems in my class, and they still ask that question. Why? I think it's because the context doesn't mean anything to them personally. It has no relevance to their own experience and so they don't make the connection. We talked in class today about if that same content is taught with respect to FUBU clothing or NIKE advertising or the music industry than they would make the connection because those are their personal areas of interest. Engineering can be sound engineering and producing, business can be marketing, advertising, and sales for SPRITE or Busta Rhymes in Do the Dew. That's what they are interested in. EUREKA!!!

An underlying component of all the previous journal entries is the importance of student discourse in the classroom. Each individual student comes with a unique contribution to the learning process and classroom discourse is an excellent vehicle for facilitating those contributions. Without the whole-class discussion, the teachers may have never received the catalyst they needed to transform their thinking about curriculum, learning styles, context, and the significance of personal relevance.

Journaling as an effective pedagogical strategy for fostering an awareness of diversity in the classroom is supported by the following journal entries:

> I really thought I understood the problem, until Terry gave her explanation for how she worked it. Now, I have a whole different perspective for looking at it. This will really help me explain the concepts to my own students in more than one way. Terry based her method in her personal experience. Different people and cultures have different experiences which effect how they think. That's important to remember when I am teaching my students. Now I know why Dr. Moore keeps saying there are many different roads to Egypt, but we will all still end up in Egypt. I see now that different people think of the same thing in different ways and that there is no one RIGHT way. Thank you Dr. Moore.

> All my life in elementary school I was told I was wrong because I didn't work the problem the way the teacher did. Now I know my way was right all along even if she wouldn't let me use it. I also remember how bad she made me feel. Like I was stupid. I will never do that to my students. If they get the right answer with a different method from mine, I promise to always

take the time to investigate their way (whether in class or out of class depending on the time) and validate their creativity the way you have done
with us. WOW!! I really am smart after all.

These two entries are indicative of the types of entries made by most
students within the first 2 weeks of class. By using the journals to analyze the learning environment I established in the classroom where multiple approaches and perspectives to problem solving were encouraged
and validated, the teachers had developed an awareness of diversity
upon which I was then able to expound explicitly. As they "introduced"
the topic in their own writings, they were open to class discussion of
curriculum, learning environment, and other pedagogical issues with regard to diversity in mathematics education. This diversity includes issues of gender, race, ethnicity, and culture. Culture refers to the amalgamation of societal influences based on one's race, ethnicity, religion,
gender, and sexual preference. Mathematics was seen by many of these
teachers as "culture-less" in that it was a "science that was accessible to
all people, based purely upon intellectual ability." However, throughout
our discussions on mathematical concepts, I would share historical facts
that situated mathematics within a context that was new for most teachers. For example, when questioned about the use of particular symbols
like Σ (sigma) or π (pi) in mathematical writing, I informed the teachers
that the old saying, "Looks like Greek to me!" was quite accurate in that
many mathematical symbols are members of the Greek alphabet. I then
asked them to consider the canonical acceptance of this practice. In particular, π is a well-used Greek representation for a geometrical measurement, yet geometry is a mathematical science with its roots in Egypt. The
identification of $a^2 + b^2 = c^2$ as the Pythagorean theorem is another example. Though the Greek philosopher, Pythagoras, is credited with "discovering" the theorem, few people recognize or realize the years he
spent living and studying in Egypt and other parts of Africa. Having
taken a History of Mathematics course during the first quarter of their
participation in the professional-development program, oftentimes the
teachers raised these types of issues throughout the daily discourse in
the class. A few of the teachers revealed in their journal writings that initially they did not see the importance of such contextualization of the
content. They thought these "asides" were trite and insignificant. My
emphasis in all my classes is that a teacher's pedagogical practice must
be student centered. By constantly connecting the "asides" to the students' perspectives and the affective domain of their mathematics learning experience, I helped the resistant teachers see the value of "politiciz-
ing" the content. Using the historical perspective as a foundation
facilitates the transition in class discussions to the current sociopolitical

relevance to students' mathematical learning. This journal entry shows one teacher's transformation of thought:

> I really wondered when that History of Math class was ever going to matter. I mean who cares about all that ancient history stuff. But I see now that it can have real impact on the self-identity and self-esteem of my kids. If they can see themselves in the world of math, then they may be more likely to embrace it . . . This whole math thing can be pretty politically charged. Culturally, too. I thought it was just pure science. I guess I need to be more aware of what and how I say and do.

Many of the teachers developed a strong sense of "culturally" critical assessment. They realized the multitude of influences (capitalism, racism, sexism, popular culture, historical, political, economical, and social) outside the classroom environment that affect student learning within the classroom environment. This process of realization, recognition, and self-revelation is foundational in the development of transformative thought.

THE RESEARCH PROJECT

Preliminary work for the research project involved introducing the teacher-researchers to the literature base on CRMP. I wanted to expose them to scholarly readings that would provide them with theoretical foundations as well as an exemplar of what the theory of CRMP "looked like" in practice. I emphasized that the readings were not meant to be "recipes" for practice, but rather a framework or "lens" through which they could focus their analyses of their own teaching and student learning. As this was a participatory action research project, I wanted the teacher-researchers to be very much involved in examining the aspects of their practice that they thought would be useful to them in improving their pedagogy. I instructed the teachers to identify two categories of characteristics in their readings: those aspects of CRMP they assessed were already a part of their practice and the tenets they thought they needed to incorporate in their practice. I believed the first category would be a necessary catalyst in developing the second. If the teacher-researchers could self-identify with some of the tenets of CRMP, then they would be more likely to embrace the process of fuller development of other aspects of the pedagogy. My intent was to increase their awareness of and appreciation for the import of a sociocultural perspective in their practice.

Nash was particularly appreciative to find his own practice and educational philosophy articulated in the literature: "Seeing myself in the readings, really gave me more confidence about what I am doing in the classroom." In his initial self-assessment, Nash identified the following elements of CRMP as part of his classroom practice: (a) a student-centered pedagogy where students were actively, productively engaged in learning, (b) students' academic needs influenced lesson planning and often inspired adjustments to be made during instruction, and (c) students initiated construction of knowledge independent of the teacher, making conjectures and connections to prior knowledge. Yet, he felt the need to improve his classroom practice and wanted to identify ways to accomplish that goal. As he sought to implement aspects of CRMP in his own classroom, his journey from theory to practice and research led to the fuller development of his transformative thought. The following accounts depict ways in which Nash identified himself as a socioculturally relevant teacher.

Evidence of Nash's Transformative Thought

In our discussion sessions, Nash provided a critique of the educational system as well as an analysis of his role in it. Nash believed that improving student attendance and attitudes toward learning could raise student achievement. He also addressed methods of assessment in determining student achievement:

> I believe our district operates under some basic flawed presuppositions. A student can be enrolled in a 10th grade math course but this does not ensure that a student has a 9th grade math education. I have a number of students who are in my 10th grade geometry class but have not passed the 9th grade proficiency test or 9th grade algebra. At the end of the year the district will administer a common exam to my students (a standardized assessment). A low percentage of passing students is not a valid reflection of their achievement, or an accurate assessment of our success as teachers. If assessments were fair then we would pre-assess every student the first week of school and then post-assess the same students at the end of the year . . . we could measure achievement in terms of growth. This is a fairer, better way of measuring the effectiveness of pedagogy.

Nash described himself as a "product of urban education." As such, he felt he was better equipped to understand, appreciate, and respond to the diverse academic and sociocultural influences particular to urban educational settings. He believed his personal experiences gave him a sense of cultural competence that improved his ability to relate professionally with his students. Nash defined cultural competence as the ability to relate to and in varying degrees become a part of a group based on a commonality shared among members of the group. That commonality may be race, gender, ethnicity, sexual preference, class, talent, skill, or ability. The commonality of the group infers a particular "cultural" identification, which is socially constructed and often in opposition to school academic achievement. For example, Nash perceived that the still widely held belief that girls "can't" do math or "shouldn't" be scientific or mechanically inclined is manifested in his classroom regularly. He gave anecdotal accounts of how the girls in his class "dummy down" so they will be more socially accepted and thereby more attractive to the boys. The same girls who score high on standardized tests and written examinations, do not display the depth of their ability in open classroom discourse, whole-class discussion, or when working in small groups on classwork. With respect to teachers mediating cultural competence for students, he related the following experience:

> I was a successful athlete who ran into some of the same stereotypes as my peers (i.e. "dumb jock" syndrome). Other athletes who were more successful academically were viewed as "over-achievers". At times I felt that it was an issue of achievement vs. acceptance. A lot educators were probably aware of this dilemma but chose not to create opportunities where cultural competence could be maintained along with academic achievement. I believe teachers who understand and demonstrate cultural competence are better equipped to work in the urban setting. For me it comes a little easier probably because I am a product of urban education/life.

During my field observations of Nash's class, I have seen him purposefully encourage his female students to openly excel and take pride in their mathematics achievement. He was aware of gender inequities in mathematics education and how male students often socially disregarded their female peers who achieved academically. Nash had a "wall of fame" in his classroom where all students could openly display work on which they had made significant academic progress. I view these efforts as his attempt to offset a socially constructed, stereotypical, negative identity with a self-esteeming, high-achieving identity.

Nash expressed strong beliefs with regard to equity and fairness. He felt a responsibility to increase students' social awareness. He admitted that students put up barriers, but believed it was the teacher's responsibility to get around them:

> If I can get kids to believe that the choices they make are going to effect [sic] their futures. If I can give them hope, then their decision can make a change. If they can discern the inequity and the social order, then they can make stands for themselves and improve their perspectives. Let them be the decision makers about what's fair or not, not what's best for me, but what is equitable and what is not. Then they can do good to society as a whole.

During the research project, the city experienced civil unrest with the shooting of a young African American boy by a White police officer. The event occurred over spring break, and many students at the school had been involved in the public uprising. Upon returning to school, Nash's team leader insisted that normal routines be maintained. She felt it would be a mistake to deviate from normal lesson plans because the students would not be able to handle any discussions without getting disorderly. Nash decided to do the following:

> Discuss with students the events which took place during our Spring Break (the shooting and the rioting). I chose to do this "lesson" because I wanted 1) to let the students know I was concerned about their feelings and opinions and 2) it would be difficult for students to concentrate on math if other things were on their mind. I predicted that some students would come back to school emotionally charged up due to the recent events. I wanted them to know that it was OK to talk about these recent (recurring) issues. In the bigger picture I was hoping to reveal a diversity of opinions and experiences among the students and to reinforce the need to respect.

Nash organized this discussion as an open forum. He laid the initial ground rules for respectful and acceptable discourse and then allowed the students to broach their concerns and opinions about recent events. He acted as moderator in acknowledging each "speaker" and facilitating the participation of any student who desired to contribute to the conversation. During our follow-up session for this lesson, I questioned Nash about the expenditure of an entire class period on a nonmathematical activity. He argued that the activity improved the learning environment and thus implicitly positively affected his students' learning. Nash expressed a concern that students were too quick to challenge authoritative systems physically, but not intellectually. He believed that the only way to influence people's views was to engage in discourse and become an active participant within the system. He viewed intellectual engagement and discourse as directly related to promoting social awareness. He considered the establishment of an atmosphere of caring as a crucial component in facilitating these objectives.

Goals of Incorporation

Issues of social justice became a focus area in Nash's action research. In his initial self-assessment, he identified three goals of culturally relevant pedagogy that he wanted to more fully develop in his classroom practice: Produce students who achieve academically, produce students who demonstrate cultural competence, and produce students who can understand

and critique the existing social order (Ladson-Billings, 1995b). In particular, he wanted to identify ways in which he could incorporate social justice issues into his geometry curriculum:

> As I continue to mature I am finding myself more concerned with social inequities. Understanding the dynamics of social inequity requires us to understand our social order. When we begin to examine our social order based on facts and truths we become empowered to become productive citizens who have the ability to promote social change. For me it is difficult to get together social order issues with math content. This part does not seem easy to me.

I assisted Nash with this goal by developing a series of questions or rubrics by which he could evaluate his lessons for strong mathematics content and the inclusion of social relevance. The questions were provocative and intended not to provide a guidebook, but challenge Nash to exercise his own creativity in modifying the curriculum for his students. We decided upon this approach after seeking resources that incorporated social justice and mathematics content. Nash believed the mathematics text lacked relevance for his students and he believed his relationship with his students qualified him to develop his own materials. He sought my guidance and expertise in validating the mathematical content and I encouraged him to think outside the box in modifying his lessons. The following two examples are evidence of how he transformed his curriculum.

During a discussion session, when I had challenged Nash about the mathematical rigor of his lessons, he realized that "we did not represent real situations verbally, numerically, or graphically." The exercise called for the solution of a proportional expression using similar triangles. The worksheet gave several diagrams of similar triangles and students were asked to find the missing side length:

> I will build on this exercise with a lesson that asks students to locate a building proximal to Davis which is x feet in height. I will preface the assignment by saying that community leaders are searching for a building locally . . . so that they can mount a radar device which will be used by the local weather officials to warn residents of local weather emergencies.

This lesson was relevant to students because of frequent tornado warnings in the area as well as flooding conditions on the riverfront that directly impacted the lives of several of his students. In our discussion session, Nash elaborated on how his verbal representation could be extended to a graphing exercise. He stated that he would use the height of the school building as a fixed standard and fix an angle of elevation between the ground and the radar. He would then ask for varying values of x and have the students make a numeric table of the resultant values. He would then have them graph these values and use them to predict future resultant values using different building heights in the neighborhood around the school. He believed this would successfully incorporate a verbal, numeric, and graphic representation of the proportion problem and incorporate social relevance for his students.

Nash was particularly frustrated by an exercise that emphasized the import of accurate, detailed written mathematical communication. The exercise required students to draw a geometrical shape on their own graph paper. They were then allowed to give written communication only to their partner in an attempt to have the partner draw the exact same shape. The exercise was then repeated with oral communication and the two drawing samples of the partner were compared to the student's original drawing. Nash felt the students enjoyed the hands-on activity but that it held little social relevance for the students. Using our developed rubric of questions, I prompted Nash to develop a different type of exercise. He spent a week creating the following exercise that included the analysis of reliability statistics. In his exercise, an unexpected interruption to the class period would occur from a "visitor" who was lost and seeking directions to a particular classroom. After the visitor left, Nash would ask the students to give a written statement describing the visitor. Nash stated his learning objective during a weekly discussion in this way:

> The lesson learned is that everyone has different/unique perceptions (what we see and take to be true may not be the case for others). In this example I would talk about communication and how it could be connected to eyewitness testimony in a court of law. I would encourage students to examine the reliability of eyewitness testimony in our judicial system based on what we learned from this lesson.

When I challenged Nash about the mathematical content in this activity, he offered this addendum the next week:

> I would make an itemized standard of accuracy like height, weight, race, clothing type and color, gender, etc. Then I would assign points for the accuracy of each item in their written statements. I would have the students score their statement and compare the class statistics of reliability with standardized reliability statistics for eyewitness testimony.

Nash was successfully developing ways to bring social awareness into his geometry class curriculum, while maintaining the rigor of mathematical content. Research findings included a heightened awareness of cultural competence and social action for Nash. He valued this awareness

and perceived it as a means to improve students' involvement and engagement in classroom learning. Nash found multiple means of assessment challenging, but believed them to be beneficial in accurately depict-
ing students' achievement. He criticized the use of state-mandated
standardized testing as the predominant measurement of student
achievement. He recognized the misplaced emphasis on the "end product" instead of on the continual journey to attain knowledge. Nash concluded that the tenets of CRMP contained the theoretical elements of pedagogy necessary for the school mathematics success of all students.
However, he noted that the practice of any pedagogy that results in academic achievement for all students, must be holistic in nature and adapt-
able in practice to meet the academic and sociocultural demands of the
ever-changing society in which we live, learn, and teach. He concluded
that practice is neither final nor finite in its implementation, but must always be analyzed and reevaluated for its effectiveness in promoting student learning and achievement. He determined the reflective journals to
be an excellent tool for such analysis. In particular, he considered my rec-
ommendation to maintain reflective journals on their pedagogical practices with respect to a particular pedagogical theory or theories an effective means to promote creativity in, provocative thought about, and
regular self-assessment of his classroom performance. He believed this
process resulted in better classroom instruction and ultimately improved
student learning.

CONCLUSION

In examining the many aspects of resistance to pedagogical change,
though prospective and in-service teachers may believe that student-
centered, inquiry-based, problem-solving, collaborative learning is most
effective in promoting academic success for all students, they also may
lack the skills, knowledge, and personal experiences in their own mathematics learning to move away from transmissive teaching. The strategies I
employed in the comprehensive program address this and empower
teachers to practice a culturally responsive and socially relevant pedagogy. Social reconstruction is initiated as teachers begin to look critically
at their classroom environment and the practitioner becomes the action
researcher, transforming theory into practice and research on that practice
cycling back to transformative theory. Nash experienced an evolution of
professional development that included the roles of student, teacher, and
teacher-researcher. He cited the strategies employed in my classes in con-
junction with the research experience as significant in his professional and
academic career. The continuity of my influence from classroom content

instruction, to field supervision, to collaborative research mentorship is an unique opportunity that is worth replication. It provides for a synergistic union of mathematical content, socially relevant pedagogical methods, and research. Being able to impact the professional development of teachers holistically is a powerful step in the quest for transformative mathematics pedagogy throughout the American educational system. This chapter has documented how strategies of transformative theory led to the practice of transformative pedagogy in the classroom and supported a teacher who desired to be culturally responsive, socially critical, and primed with potential as he continued his academic pursuits. This chapter related his journey from theory to practice, research, and beyond.

REFERENCES

Beauboeuf-Lafontant, T. (1999). A movement against and beyond boundaries: Politically relevant teaching among African American teachers. *Teachers College Record, 100*(4), 702–723.

Borba, M. (1997). Ethnomathematics and education. In A. Powell & M. Frankenstein (Eds.), *Ethnomathematics: Challenging Eurocentrism in mathematics education* (pp. 261–272). Albany: State University of New York Press.

Conference Board on Mathematical Sciences. (2001). *The mathematical education of teachers, Part I.* Washington, DC: Mathematical Association of America.

Hispanics to outnumber U.S. Blacks next century. (1993, September 29). *The Cincinnati Enquirer,* p. F4.

Ladson-Billings, G. (1992). Reading between the lines and beyond the pages: A culturally relevant approach to literacy teaching. *Theory in Practice, 31,* 312–320.

Ladson-Billings, G. (1995a). Making mathematics meaningful. In W. Secada, E. Fennema, & L. Adajian (Eds.), *New directions for equity in mathematics education* (pp. 126–145). Cambridge, England: Cambridge University Press.

Ladson-Billings, G. (1995b). Toward a theory of culturally relevant pedagogy. *American Educational Research Journal, 32*(3), 465–491.

Ladson-Billings, G. (1997). It doesn't add up: African American students' mathematics achievement. *Journal for Research in Mathematics Education, 28,* 697–708.

LeCompte, M., & Preissle, J. (1993). *Ethnography and qualitative design in educational research* (2nd ed.). San Diego: Academic Press.

Lipman, P. (1995). Bringing out the best in them: The contribution of culturally relevant teachers to educational reform. *Theory in Practice, 34*(3), 202–208.

Ma, L. (1999). *Knowing and teaching elementary mathematics.* Mahwah, NJ: Lawrence Erlbaum Associates.

McAllister, G., & Irvine, J. (2000). Cross cultural competency and multicultural teacher education. *Review of Educational Research, 70*(1), 3–24.

National Council of Teachers of Mathematics. (1991). *Professional standards for teaching mathematics.* Reston, VA: Author.

Rodriguez, A. J. (1998). Strategies for counterresistance: Toward sociotransformative constructivism and learning to teach science for diversity and for understanding. *Journal of Research in Science Teaching, 35*(6), 589–622.

Secada, W. G. (1992). Race, ethnicity, social class, language, and achievement in mathematics. In D. A. Grouws (Ed.), *Handbook of research on mathematics teaching and learning* (pp. 623–660). New York: Macmillan.

Sleeter, C. E. (2001). Preparing teachers for culturally diverse schools: Research and the overwhelming presence of whiteness. *Journal of Teacher Education, 52*(2), 94–106.

Spradley, J. P. (1979). *The ethnographic interview.* New York: Holt, Rinehart & Winston.

Tate, W. (1995). Returning to the root: A culturally relevant approach to mathematics pedagogy. *Theory in Practice, 34*(3), 166–173.

Tate, W. (1997). Race-ethnicity, SES, gender, and language proficiency trends in mathematics achievement: An update. *Journal for Research in Mathematics Education, 28,* 652–679.

10

Seeing *IT* in the Lives of Children: Strategies for Promoting Equitable Practices Among Tomorrow's Science Teachers

Randy Yerrick
San Diego State University

In a volume devoted to examining the complexities of changing prospective mathematics and science teachers' beliefs toward a more equitable treatment of science and mathematics, it seems critical to speak to how successful, White, middle-class prospective teachers can expand their notions of content, children, and pedagogy. Although some authors have attempted to speak to this issue from the construct of pedagogical content knowledge, I find that such discussions lack the sociocultural richness associated with understanding diverse educational contexts. My goal is to address issues in ways that expand prospective teachers' views of science itself in high school classrooms through ethnographic methods supported by educational technology.

Informed by social constructivist and sociocultural theories that stand in direct contrast to deficit approaches to science and math instruction, I invited my students to explore their own teaching through videotaped sessions, challenged their assumptions of minority students' abilities through qualitative teacher-researcher methods, and engaged prospective teachers in the process of examining current literature of teaching, culture, and science to provide a venue for embracing a more progressive approach to teaching science. In this chapter, I describe the strategies I use to make prospective teachers' teaching beliefs and assumptions more overt and explicit. These strategies included (a) pre- and postteaching interviews, (b) classroom observations modeling alternative pedagogies, (c) debriefing focus groups, (d) explicit summative and evaluative commentary on shared artifacts, and (e) teacher reflective journals. I emphasize the tendencies for prospective teachers to assume that their own experiences and histories are sufficient to draw upon for expert pedagogical choices and highlight instances when such egocentric assessments of learning are wholly inadequate to meet the needs of a diverse student population. By using these strategies, prospective teachers began to critique their own assumptions about science learning and teaching as they expanded their practical and cultural, as well as content knowledge.

Theory, Practice, and Reflection in the Equity Balance

As science teacher education faculty operating in a context of de facto segregation in North Carolina, I was confronted with the questions, "What are important components of a field experience that perturbs individual beliefs, enables reflection on historical experiences, and supports the construction of revised teacher knowledge? What kinds of experiences can best equip novice teachers for their future roles and what kinds of educational theory can best guide needed change in classrooms?" Even if science teacher educators could agree on universal and well-researched domains of teacher knowledge, we are far from understanding which kinds of learning experiences can be programmatically designed into teacher preparation to result in this kind of exemplary teacher knowledge. When I worked within a small group of science education faculty in a rural, Southern college of education that annually enrolled large populations of prospective teachers, we recognized that our university's teaching mission overemphasized the social efficiency approach (Gore & Zeichner, 1991) and inadequately addressed the social reconstructionist perspective of teacher education for such issues as long-standing racial inequity in the rural Southern schools. We were also aware of recent challenges to the assumptions that theoretical knowledge or practical advice offered in course readings and university campus lectures would be easily translated into practice by novice teachers and that prospective teachers would acquire professional knowledge before experience rather than in communion with experience (Feiman-Nemser & Remillard, 1996).

Research has shown that challenging prospective teachers' beliefs is insufficient for making change (Adams & Krockover, 1999). Prospective teachers must be given the opportunity to strengthen their knowledge of teaching, students, and content. Support can be provided in changing and expanding teachers' knowledge both in content as well as in pedagogical choices associated with inquiry teaching. My colleagues and I conjectured that prospective teachers must themselves be engaged in this kind of teaching as learners first before they would be able to fully embrace recommendations for teaching reforms.

Our attention turned to our students' sociocultural context, which became paramount to considerations for designing a field experience promoting reflection for our preservice teachers. Our new teachers' attrition rate for leaving the classroom was nearly one third within 3 years. To sustain the needed population of science teachers, we felt that we had to respond with efforts of recruitment or retention and development. We chose the latter. Of greatest concern to us was the tendency for teachers with minimal exposure to diverse student populations to assume that teaching science is a generic process free of any implicit teaching values. Assuming that their successful high school and university science experiences would necessarily translate into success for their students, novice teachers make pedagogical choices and are then often unaware that their differential treatment of knowledge promotes inequality. Their worldview as teachers is informed by a very narrow set of experiences with rare instances of challenges to their accepted beliefs about what school science should be. As Ladson-Billings (1999) argued:

> [Their worldviews] exist in protected cocoons. These individuals have never had to make an adjustment from home life to public life, as their public lives and the institutions they have encountered merely reflect a "reality" these individuals have been schooled in since birth. When these privileged individuals—and they are privileged, whether they realize it or not—see others who operate from a different worldview, they can often comprehend them only as deviants, pathologically inferior, certainly in need of "fixing." Even when individuals believe themselves to have good intentions, their own biases blind them from seeing the real people before them. (p. 74)

Assumptions prospective teachers make concerning diverse students are based upon very little classroom teaching experience or exposure to different home and school cultures. As many have argued, prospective teachers do not understand what they need to know (Bryan & Abell, 1999; Schon, 1987) and must be given experiences if they are to accommodate other frameworks. Without such experiences and the support to make sense of practice, their assumptions can blind novice science teachers to make accurate assessments of their own success in teaching. For example, novice teachers may be concerned for their lower achieving students' performance but may be unaware of its causes or successful strategies for addressing their students' needs. LeCompte and Dworkin (1991) argued that students' expressions of disinterest are often symptomatic of issues other than content and that teachers need to turn away from the popular child-deficit model to address such issues.

Our second concern for designing our field experiences stemmed from the notion that school science represents a cultural phenomenon all in itself (Aikenhead, 2001) and that this school science culture is often so different from out-of-school cultures that it excludes other perspectives at a cost to diverse students. The vast number of school science classrooms to which we had access were racially biased by de facto tracking policies and best exemplified by the transmission of facts and a mind-set of received knowing (Clandinin, Davies, Hogan, & Kennard, 1993). We were reminded of Rodriguez's (1997) critique that the national standards as they currently exist offer little compelling reason for teachers to change their practices. Though we were advised strongly by our college to trust our cooperating teachers as "our surrogates," we chose to collaborate with a school in which our faculty members could interact with experienced onsite and novice teachers as collegial partners in learning. Hence, faculty taught and invited others into their teaching as they conducted research on-site. As Goodman and Fish (1997) argued, promoting field experiences that support "against-the-grain teaching" may be a difficult environment to manage but an ideal setting for teacher growth.

Certainly ample evidence exists that prospective teachers may deflect and undermine courses intended to challenge deeply held beliefs (Pajares, 1992; Tann, 1993) or that prospective teachers may attend to assignments in a largely pedestrian manner while harboring a completely different set of beliefs. Bryan and Abell (1999) argued that, "teachers' preexisting views of teaching and learning are so pervasive that unless teacher educators personally engage students and directly challenge these deeply rooted beliefs, attempts to bringing about change in students' views will be ineffectual" (p. 122). For example, the research demonstrating vast differences of concerns between higher and lower achieving students (Phelan, Davidson, & Cao, 1991) can be misinterpreted by young science teachers who rely heavily upon self-reinforcing beliefs. Still we were aware of the possibility that prospective teachers would reject or otherwise misinterpret the purposes of the field-based course with lower track students.

Prospective teachers were, therefore, attending their secondary science methods course in a different venue than at the university where it had been traditionally taught. Prospective teachers attended their methods course at a school site in which the methods professor taught lower track high school students to supplement the exposure to local science students they encountered in their normal placement at a separate school. Their own school success as a learner may have had as a member of a *successful* student community (e.g., Honors classes) may have little relevance with the student population to which they are responsible. Such a mismatch could encourage a novice teacher's myopic views of lower track students, propagating myths that some students *earn* their place in school and that diverse students are *unteachable* or *lazy*. Though most teachers are not cognizant of these beliefs, these assumptions get carried into lower track classrooms (Oakes, 1985). An unfortunate result of mislabeling of this kind is that it often provides the emotional comfort to the teacher who is struggling to find blame and who thus holds lower expectations for children who are considered unteachable. Though field experiences in teacher preparation can reinforce negative and less rigorous notions of teaching (Feiman-Nemser & Buchmann, 1985), many argue that field experiences can be instrumental for confronting prospective teacher beliefs to develop a deeper understanding of teaching (Cochran-Smith & Lytle, 1993; Hollingsworth, 1989).

To counter prospective teachers' resistance or preconceptions that prevent them from teaching for diversity and understanding, our science education department decided that an intensive field experience with diverse students that engaged them in direct contact with students who had been tracked by de facto segregation policies and practices in an historically racially segregated school would provide the richest venue for exploring their beliefs. Though several attempts to provide video case studies and other vicarious exposures to diversity had been explored, we were committed to outcomes that reached beyond exposure to diversity issues for our prospective teachers. Instead, we sought to identify biased beliefs of privileged White prospective teachers towards lower-track Black students and to change the actual practices and beliefs of prospective teachers in the context of a local earth science high school classroom.

As part of the design of our teacher education program, prospective science teachers met in a 15-week field-based setting in which they would: (a) participate in focus groups with diverse students, (b) observe their methods instructor teaching lower track students, (c) plan and teach videotaped lessons to children and each other, and (d) participate in a variety of reflective activities to discuss real challenges to the teaching contexts likely to be in their imminent future.

CHOOSING SCIENCE PEDAGOGY, FOSTERING REFLECTION, AND PROMOTING SOCIOCULTURAL DISEQUILIBRIUM

What follows is an account of efforts to explore what role teacher educators can have in shaping the experiences of future science teachers so that they can address core issues of (in)equality. It is a synthesis of a variety of my experiences, conflicts, and reflections while engaging university prospective science teachers in difficult teaching contexts outside of those cultures and beliefs that represent their own histories. Each of the claims made have emerged from an ongoing analysis of videotaped data and other artifacts collected while teaching methods courses on-site over the course of 2 years.

It is a story in which I play the role of learner as well as teacher, and it should be understood as a first attempt to deconstruct the core struggles I faced in changing prospective teachers' beliefs as an Anglo, middle-class male. I make few generalizations here for larger populations of teacher educators or their students but believe that many readers will find value in juxtaposing my teaching challenges against those in their own immediate contexts—especially those who teach to explicate and work against disparities resulting from science curriculum tracking. It is a story of crossing the boundaries between universities and public schools, between privileged and underprivileged school histories, between theory and practice, and finding ways that people, though separated by their beliefs, can construct meaning to understand differences that narrow their worldviews.

It would be unreasonable to expect the reader to accept my accounts of prospective teacher beliefs, practices, and conflicts on the basis of my interpretations of events within my methods course alone. Research accounts of cultural beliefs and values require rigorous accounts, explorations, and disclosures of agendas influencing both data collection and analysis. As an instructor of both the high school earth science class and a concurrent secondary science methods course offered on-site by the university, I subscribed to a model proposed by Hutchings and Shulman (1999) of a "scholarship of teaching" in which I used dilemmas in my own practice as venues for discussing how educational theory applied to classroom practices. As an instructor engaging methods students in issues of equity, I wrote narratives explicating my goals and strategies for instruction and the educational context in which they were employed. These narratives (Hubbard & Power, 1999) were instrumental in fleshing out the obstacles methods instructors face as well as the underlying beliefs that are at odds when conflicting worldviews meet (e.g., all students can learn vs. science for the elite). From the autobiographical narratives collected in the pilot studies, issues were identified and readings and assignments were established for the prospective students of subsequent years who would work with lower track students (e.g., Ayers, 1993; Brice-Heath, 1983; Delpit, 1995).

The data presented in this chapter were collected in the second phase of our 2-year teacher education project, which was designed to enrich prospective teachers' understanding of the sociocultural knowledge of the region in which they planned to seek employment. The first phase of the project was exploratory by nature as we sought to more clearly explicate and understand the struggles and needs of the lower track high school students whom the prospective teachers of this study would be required to teach. In the first year of this project we conducted focus groups, teacher interviews, and field observations to determine the culture of the lower track classroom context and the beliefs of students who carved out their identities within them (Gilbert & Yerrick, 2001). Teachers, counselors, department heads, administrators, and even students described the earth science class as the "lowest" (their descriptor) science course with a clientele populated by students who had failed at least one science class, threatening their graduation. I was the methods course instructor as well as the earth science teacher, teaching earth science daily in the high school while advocating a strong school partnership in science, mathematics, and technology. The earth science class was overrepresented by Black students, who comprised more than 80% of the 32 students in this class in a school with a less than 40% Black population—de facto segregation based primarily on standardized mathematics and reading scores as well as discipline records.

My colleagues and I—who are mostly White and middle class—were aware of the limitations of our university's approach to adding a course on cultural diversity in an attempt to prepare our prospective students to teach in predominantly rural, nonintegrated public school contexts (Office of Planning and Institutional Research Report, 1996). In a region where more than 60% of the population was Black and less than 10% of our teacher candidates (drawn from the same region) were Black, we began to explore how and why so many of our teachers were White and what their motivations were in becoming local teachers. The courses that had been developed at our university had little to do with assisting our students in their actual teaching of Black students and reflecting upon equity issues. Courses were often one of two extremes: either strongly theoretical, cerebral exercises separated from actual contact with teaching experiences (or even diverse student populations for that matter) or purely pedestrian teaching skills that ignored the larger contextual issues that drive schools to treat students of nonmainstream cultures differently. Even the teachers we served told us that completion of our courses was a very poor indicator of whether prospective teachers could actually balance issues of equity in their teaching.

Our department wanted to do more for our prospective teachers than simply talk about equity and diversity. Moreover, the tolerance movement surely undermined the very process of understanding and valuing multiple worldviews by promoting the notion that we ought to just "put up with" one another. Because our teacher candidates did not enroll in any education courses until their university senior year, their university science lecturers were their only models of science teaching until their final 10 months of teacher preparation. Their limited view of science was exacerbated by their minimal experience in real school contexts. The result was a set of competing messages to our students. Though they needed to relearn what it meant to learn and to teach science, they were preoccupied with the practical advice they received—assuming their content knowledge was sufficient to guide their teaching.

There are no reference books telling us how to teach in predominantly Black, rural, impoverished contexts. I had read of the children of Trackton and Roadville (Brice-Heath, 1983) who attended school in communities only a few hundred miles from my university. I had paid close attention to the plights of Delpit (1995) and Paley (1989), who showed that pedagogy based in middle class, White values was inappropriate for some students. I had also read of Paley's critique of White teachers attempting to teach children of color. Though each made substantive contributions toward understanding the dilemmas of Black students, I had difficulty finding out just what to do each day in my high school class. I knew that what I was trying did not work and was not well suited to the context. One of my problems was in me—perceiving how the transparency of my own culture was affecting the judgments I made on a daily basis. Culture, after all, is not something that is recognizable as simply a physical or linguistic attribute. Neither is one's own educational history immediately apparent—that is until it comes in conflict with another.

UNDERSTANDING SCIENCE IN THE LIVES OF CHILDREN

One of the frameworks that I have found most helpful is that of David Hawkins (1974). In his essay "I, Thou, and It," Hawkins provides an eloquent argument for the centrality of content (IT) and how understanding the craft of teaching is wholly insufficient without the appreciation of the relationships among teacher (I), student (THOU), and content (IT). After 15 years of teaching experience with kindergarten to graduate students in a wide range of cultural settings, I have come to a deeper understanding of how Hawkins defined IT as I have learned to find IT in the lives of my students. I seek to share my insights regarding the deepening and broadening of my prospective teachers' knowledge of science and promote with my students how to recognize IT when you see IT.

In the next section I share some strategies I have used to incorporate Hawkins' framework into my teaching for equity and diversity in science classrooms. There are a variety of applicable frameworks for situating a science methods course, but Hawkins' (1974) seems especially appropriate as it balances the centrality of content and cultural knowledge while separating and juxtaposing the experiences, goals, and contributions of student and teacher in the context of the classroom. It is a framework that guides the science educator in identifying not only the content that the teacher desires to teach their students but also why and how important connections to content can be made—especially in the cases in which science teacher and student are so different that some kind of bridge must be constructed in order to make sound pedagogical decisions. It is such applications of theory to practice that rarely are discussed outside education classrooms or methodological texts and that this chapter seeks to explicate.

I discuss each of these strategies in nearly chronological order. Though I did not use all of Hawkins' strategies each semester, I outline a general plan for introducing my students to different kinds of thinking about science teaching and the process of finding IT in the lives of their students.

Strategies for Exploring the THOU in Science Teaching

"Who are my students?" was the first question prospective teachers were required to explore. Young teachers normally assume that students are in science classrooms because they want to learn science. If prospective teachers have not first grappled with this question, they will likely be surprised by student resistance to engaging in thinking and speaking scientifically—especially if their students have been told for years that science and mathematics are too hard for them to learn. Novice teachers must first come to a place in which old practices are challenged before they will be able to contrast them with alternatives that are proposed. Prospective teachers in these contexts must take on a disposition of inquiry in which "suddenly many of the 'sensible' ways of doing things no longer seemed acceptable" (Delpit, 1995, p. 73).

My prospective teachers were required to watch me teach in a lower track earth science class twice weekly and engage with the students as participant observers. After each lesson, I would replay sections of the videotape collected and debrief the prospective teachers on the kind of choices they observed in my teaching. To explore more thoroughly the context that the lower track students experienced in school, I assigned my prospective teachers a variety of other kinds of observations including classes of Honors students at the same school. They were to take detailed notes describing their observations in typical science instruction as well as complete an assignment of shadowing a selected student from the earth science class throughout the course of his or her normal day. This was facilitated with the students' permission and often with the agreement of other teachers as well in support of the student. During these shadowing assignments, prospective teachers were asked to document the kinds of environments and relationships their chosen student maintained throughout the day. This assignment was adapted from a description Ayers (1993) offered of an exploration strategy with the goal of compiling a more complete picture of the student. Prospective teachers learned about the treatment of lower track students within their microculture at the school. They witnessed firsthand the racial bias that tracking was inextricably tied to and they learned to take more stock in lower track students' descriptions of school that were expressed in the weekly focus groups. Prospective teachers also learned something about the role of the students in propagating their own distance from academic tasks and had opportunities to discuss this with the lower track students they were observing.

Following their observations in which prospective teachers wrote down a chronological list of events and their descriptions, they met to compare notes with another observer of the same classroom events. Their first task was to compare the descriptive events they had documented—comparing and contrasting the items included on both of their lists. Prospective teachers learned about their own lenses for viewing classrooms as they reflected on which items marshaled their attention. For example, if students mentioned a loud or disorderly student, their partner was supposed to help them understand that an organized and quiet environment was a value the prospective teacher brought to bear on their observation. Once the descriptive list was completed, partners turned to more evaluative comments characterizing what they had both observed. It was only after they had reached agreement on their descriptive comments that they were permitted to discuss whether they thought it was a "good" or "effective" lesson. Not characterizing pedagogical strategies as good or bad was a struggle for most prospective teachers. However, prospective teachers found it valuable to discuss as a group the revealed values and biases inherent in their "good" and "poor" labels. Finally, prospective teachers were required to map out their collected artifacts and observations on a Venn diagram (see Appendix) that I adapted from Hawkins' (1974) essay. These diagrams were used in a whole-class discussion to evaluate how much content taught in the day was central to the lives of the students.

The creation and revision of a Venn diagram based on Hawkins' framework required hours of interpretation but was useful as a tool for reflecting on future shared events. For example, when prospective teachers were asked to make observations, discuss them with partners, and then evaluate where these events would fall on the overlapping circles, students spent hours unpacking the meaning of observed events both individually and collectively. This process assisted them in identifying their own biases toward teaching content and what it meant to connect science to children's lives. In the following excerpt, Amanda is rethinking the placement of all questions and answers from a worksheet in the center overlap of the diagram. It is the beginning of her questioning her own assumption of content relevance for a group of students who have experienced school in ways that differ from her own:

> I learned a lot from the activity of making the diagram and engaging in the discussion with my partner afterwards, but I learned more in our session where we discussed what inquiry science really was [For example] I had placed the teacher's responses to students' questions about the homework and worksheets in the middle of the diagram as something of importance to the teacher, student and content. After we discussed it though, I thought, "Maybe these kids just wanted the answer and they really didn't care about the content?" I hadn't thought about that before. I'd want to go back now and ask if it was about the answer only, because then I would move it out of the center. It's really about school and not content relevant to students' lives. (Amanda's reflection, October 1998)

Many events were carefully orchestrated to demonstrate the richness of the culture and context they were observing as essentially outsiders. When faced with the often unpredictable nature of inquiry-learning environments, prospective teachers were uncomfortable and predisposed to maintain strong beliefs about what it meant to teach science effectively. "Why don't you just give them the answer?" they would challenge. Only half of my prospective science teachers actually made notable shifts in their approaches to teaching diverse children as reflected in their practices and reflections on their own science teaching (Yerrick & Hoving, 2003).

As a final and ongoing effort to encourage prospective science teachers to understand lower track students, I invited them to attend weekly focus groups (a nonthreatening discussion around predefined areas of interest) throughout the year in which everyone (including high school students and prospective teachers) had the opportunity to ask and answer questions and discuss how the teaching was proceeding in the earth science class. The focus groups presented an avenue to create rapport and trust with students, helping us as researchers and teachers to understand the collective identity and status within the group. Explicating the school and classroom culture was facilitated by our discussing classroom observations and requesting clarification as outsiders to the context. For example, regularly throughout the focus groups, researchers would pause the conversation and ask for clarification on specific terminology or slang, making explicit certain sociocultural knowledge to which the researchers did not have access. As White, middle-class visitors representing the university, we recognized that the students had many reasons to treat us with healthy skepticism (Chávez & O'Donnell, 1998; Howard, 1999).

Focus groups that were offered immediately following instruction and during the club hour (weekly on Wednesdays) were well attended by the lower track students, and rarely did prospective teachers miss the opportunity to listen to their students' concerns about science class and school in general. It was at these focus groups that prospective teachers learned the most about their students' lives as students often gave advice of how teaching ought to occur citing both successful and unsuccessful teachers with this group of students (Gilbert & Yerrick, 2001; Yerrick & Hoving, 2003).

STRATEGIES FOR EXPLORING THE I
IN SCIENCE TEACHING

At the heart of any culturally sensitive approach to teaching lies the question, "What has been my experience in science and how is it different from those I am required to teach?" Inappropriate decisions often result from prospective teachers simply responding to an event without a deep, reflective understanding of their personal framework upon which they draw (McDiarmid, 1999). Though their enrollment in a university course clearly demonstrated their differences from children with histories of school failure, prospective science teachers were often unwilling to admit their privileged position in society and school. In fact, prospective teachers often attributed their successes as due to "their own hard work" instead of privilege (Yerrick & Hoving, 2003).

I was very aware from 5 years of teaching experience in this region that my prospective teachers had very little exposure to inquiry teaching. My goal was to have my students be open to a variety of science teaching strategies so that they could assess for themselves what does and does not work with diverse students. Beyond the realm of content and pedagogical knowledge, the task of changing teachers' views regarding equitable science teaching for all may be doubly challenging. Not only were my prospective teachers ill-prepared to implement methods to teach scientific inquiry, they also appeared predisposed to biases against students unlike themselves. Convinced that their role as science teacher would require them to disseminate content in well-managed routines to interested students, prospective teachers repeatedly requested simple instructions of "how to best teach." It was a pragmatic, nearly mechanical approach to teaching they requested that impaired their appreciation for developing science teaching methods that could allow multiple access points to knowledge.

In order to more clearly articulate prospective teachers' beliefs about successful science teaching, I did not allow myself the luxury to assume that whatever they professed was exactly what they believed. It is well-documented that teachers can operate in opposition to the beliefs that they profess (Abell, Bryan, & M. Anderson, 1998; McLaren & Giroux, 1997).

As the first assignment of the course, prior to any readings or observations, I required all incoming prospective teachers to teach a science lesson to their peers. The lessons were 20–30 minutes long and consisted of a topic of their choice. These videotaped lessons were used in subsequent classes to explicate and expose differences between espoused beliefs and actual practice. The prospective science teachers watched their lessons individually within 48 hours after presenting the lessons, and within 72 hours of their lessons I conducted stimulated recall interviews (Calderhead, 1981) using their videotaped lessons and their written reflections. The stimulated recall interviews were flexible discursive events resembling a conversation and constructed by the agendas of both parties. The purpose of opening up the preselected portions of the video was to treat the interview as a more discursive event (Mishler, 1986). Students were also allowed to choose portions of the videotape to examine and discuss, making more transparent their own agendas and foci. Answers to questions like "Why did you start the lesson this way?" or "What were the strengths of your lesson?" provided key insights into my prospective teachers' thought processes (Calderhead, 1981).

Nearly every prospective teacher focused exclusively on their appearance, voice, or delivery. Despite their lack of formal education or experience in teaching, preservice teachers demonstrated a strong socialization toward teaching that had been developed over years prior to their methods course instruction. These novice teachers modeled a uniform representation for what constituted good science teaching at the beginning of the methods course. Regardless of their freedom to select topics, venues, and strategies of any kind, preservice teachers used their opportunities to teach in remarkably similar ways. Prospective teachers behaved as if teaching were merely a performance in which the teacher should look and sound good irrespective of student learning. When prompted for their reactions to the lessons, prospective teachers reported that they were generally pleased except for their own physical appearances or mannerisms. They rarely mentioned being either distraught or satisfied because of their students' understanding of the lesson. Rather, they gave the impression that they were the only ones involved in the lesson, as if their actions alone were an indicator of its success. I leave the remainder of the details of our analysis as well as the origins of their bias toward teaching for the reader to review according to their interest (Yerrick & Hoving, 2003).

Alongside the revelations of novice science teachers' limited ways of viewing teaching from the perspectives of content expertise, pedagogical choices, or student knowledge and culture, I was challenged to expand, reframe, and transform prospective teachers' requisite knowledge to teach for diversity. It was imperative that I make their values and biases as transparent as possible so that all could comment on and support growth among the group of prospective teachers. I routinely challenged my prospective teachers to reflect upon the relevancy of their own personal histories as learners when compared to the students placed before them in my earth science class. Readings from authors like Watson and Konicek (1990) who demonstrated some of the challenges of teaching for conceptual understanding evoked strong responses from traditionally minded prospective teachers and served as a venue to compare the advice they offered or methods they deemed appropriate. Though it was more painful for me, it was often easier to engage my prospective teachers in an educational dilemma of mine than to point the sharpened scalpel of pedagogical advice upon their own lessons. I therefore invited them vicariously into my own dilemmas, critiquing observed lessons, plans, and struggles I was facing within this lower track context. I had already required my students to write complete pedagogical autobiographies to help them explicate the kind of science experiences they recalled as learners—their fears and joys alike—and I sometimes steered the discussions in ways that drew upon the experiences of my prospective teachers to more clearly define my own misjudgments about earth science students.

Since the completion of this project, video editing technology has advanced far beyond the capabilities of copying videotapes and queuing them manually or C-Video. I now have students produce their own desktop video within the first 2 weeks to support the sharing of their autobiographies. Students are often excited about the prospect of telling their story, which they have never been asked before. Many students find creative ways of conveying successes, failures, stresses, and joys, and it serves to create a more cohesive community of learners in my methods courses. It also serves as a powerful way to learn a new technology because they do not struggle with content (the content is their own story) and can focus on applying this new tool in creative and nonthreatening ways. Overall, it is a powerful tool for exploring past science experiences and the biases that can influence future pedagogical strategies.

STRATEGIES FOR EXPLORING
THE IT IN SCIENCE TEACHING

One final question for guiding which kinds of topics, issues, and resources are most appropriate for teaching science to diverse learners is, "How do I adjust my teaching to make science more accessible to all my students?" In some important ways it is a question that speaks to issues of power in science classrooms. Deciding whose voice counts for determining the correctness of a scientific answer has been clearly documented as a core influence on classroom discourse (Lave, 1990; Lemke, 1990). Until teachers remove themselves from the role of subject matter expert (at least occasionally), the privileged role of the science teachers can inhibit classroom talk—especially efforts to promote open inquiry. When teachers assume science has a privileged role in human thinking because of its objectivity and rationality, they run the risk of excluding other perceptions of phenomena that can serve as venues to more thoroughly explore scientific thinking. In other words, if students perceive the goal of classroom talk to be the arrival at a predetermined scientific answer, students will not choose to engage, for they perceive the implicit futility of their guesses. As Ladson-Billings (1999) has noted:

> My guess is that the White colleagues and instructors of those previously quoted did not perceive themselves to have power over the non-White speakers. However, either by virtue of their position, their numbers, or their access to that particular code of power calling upon research to validate one's position, the White educators had the authority to establish what was to be considered "truth" regardless of the opinions of the people of color, and the latter were well aware of that fact. (p. 27)

As a final strategy for using Hawkins' (1974) framework for seeing science in the lives of diverse children, I required my prospective teachers to engage directly with earth science students outside of their participant observation or teaching. In one assignment, prospective teachers wrote protocols and conducted clinical interviews like those emerging from the body of conceptual change research (C. W. Anderson & Smith, 1987; Osborne & Freyberg, 1985). In these interviews they asked three different earth science students to explain or predict a real-world event. These problems and events were centered around core ideas that prospective teachers planned on teaching within the next several weeks but were sufficiently open and engaging to allow for a variety of solutions. For example, when teaching about astronomy one prospective teacher inquired, "Where do the stars go during the day? And why are there different stars in the summer than in winter?" Not only did my students transcribe and discuss with other methods students their 30-minute interviews, they also had earth science students surveying the student body at the school about such topics. In this way, prospective students were able to access the prior knowledge of students, hear some of the cultural myths, and judge the appropriateness and widespread nature of commonsense reasoning that may have been in conflict with the teachers' intended curriculum. Some of the more notable preconceptions prospective teachers needed to address included the beliefs that: (a) the sun and moon were never visible at the same time of day, (b) the same alignment that causes eclipses causes the phases of the moon, (c) seasons are caused by the close proximity of the earth to the sun, water contamination, earthquakes, disease, and other calamities that originate from spiritual causes, and (d) Black people were designed differently by God to live in different places of the world.

My prospective teachers observed me probing my students openly prior to each unit and throughout lessons in an ongoing examination of the effectiveness of my lessons. Wrong answers served as launching pads for deciding how we judge the credibility of correct answers, as opposed to being opportunities for shame and public ignorance. In addition, I kept a list of student questions that arose throughout each of the lessons for the balance of the year. No question was too insignificant to be entered, and they did not have to be couched as science prior to their submission. When a question arose, it was immediately written into the book by the student in his or her own handwriting and dated. We regularly returned to the book to see which of the questions had been answered. In this way, my prospective teachers were able to observe how my high school students' thinking about the world could guide future lessons and shape the way connections were made between students' real-world experiences and the concepts we aim to teach them.

Of course, just as I had videotaped every lesson I taught with these same earth science students, I asked my prospective teachers to tape their own lessons they taught my students. Often prospective teachers would notice superficial and egocentric aspects of their lessons first like, "I said 'um' a lot." Many students, however, graduated toward critically examining when and how correct answers, scaffolding, and providing evidence actually promoted greater understanding. Unfortunately, our reflections on science lessons were not always treated as opportunities for my prospective students to grow or challenge their knowledge about teaching. Perhaps the most disturbing was my observation of prospective teachers embracing derogatory labels for earth science students and attributing teaching difficulties to their students' perceived deficiencies (Yerrick & Hoving, 2003). I asked my prospective teachers to speak directly about videotaped lessons that had "not gone well" in the eyes of their peers. Whereas some repeatedly referred to management of student behaviors as an indicator of their successful teaching, they would attribute difficulties such as student inattentiveness or off-task talking to "undisciplined" or "lazy" students rather than weaknesses in a teacher's planning or knowledge of students.

IMPLICATIONS FOR TEACHER EDUCATION

These strategies that I have described were forwarded for the purpose of expanding the prospective teachers' knowledge about three main areas of science teaching and learning: (a) knowledge of students (Hawkins' THOU), (b) knowledge of content (IT), and (c) knowledge of their pedagogical autobiographies (I) (See Appendix) that brought them to the profession and all the values, beliefs, and predispositions that are borne out of that experience. Each strategy for exploring the meaning of science in the lives of children was a naturalistic adaptation of Hawkins' (1974) framework outlining teacher knowledge and its relationship to practice. However, these strategies were not employed separately from a careful consideration of the context in which prospective teachers were learning to teach. Hawkins seemed especially relevant given that prospective teachers and their future students were separated by vast differences in worldviews and experiences. Finding "IT" in the lives of students was an ongoing endeavor throughout the final year of these prospective science teachers' university preparation.

It was because of White privilege that nearly all my prospective teachers, who would teach in primarily Black schools, were resistant to pedagogical and ideological change, the need for which has been well documented in recent literature. If my prospective teachers had not been required to explore "IT" from a broad set of experiences like clinical interviews with students, example inquiry lessons, field trips, and other alternative practices, they would likely have embraced factual content lists from the table of contents of their text, standardized test items, or the state standards—which are all poor representations of the nature of science inquiry. Without exploring "THOU" in focus groups, interviews, school visits, and classroom observations, it would be unlikely that my prospective teachers would understand the kinds of struggles my earth science students faced both in and out of school and what necessary adjustments were timely and appropriate. For example, had my prospective teachers not had the opportunity to watch, teach, and ask for themselves what struggles lower track students encountered, it is likely they would continue to propagate unfounded and unexplored beliefs adopted from a deficit model of education. Finally, McDiarmid (1999) argued that without exploring the "I" in this teaching/learning relationship of "I, Thou, and It" through their journals, stimulated recall interviews, their overt advice to me as a teacher, and collective reflections on their actual teaching instances, prospective teachers would be likely to make very little progress shifting away from nonproductive practices acquired from their socialization as students (Cuban, 1993; Lortie, 1975).

CONCLUSION

Prospective science teachers simply have few instances in which they are required to step outside of their own experiences and view their content, the process of teaching, and the students placed before them. Higher education science methods courses offered in diverse contexts offer unique opportunities for teacher educators to stretch the traditional definitions of science teaching. These courses can also offer venues to guide prospective teachers through a safely scaffolded but difficult process of examining equity, privilege, and schools' usage of content in inappropriate ways to stratify student populations. The field of science education is lacking much substantive evidence or explicit direction on how to change teachers' beliefs about race, gender, ethnicity, and culture in science and depart from egocentric views of appropriate pedagogy. Though a few teacher educators have reported some success in changing prospective science teachers' beliefs through video case studies and other vicarious venues, I have found that the only way I can be assured of knowing my prospective teachers will continue their reflection on practice after their experiences in my class is to engage them directly with children different from themselves, provide modeling and explication of reasons for appropriate pedagogy, scaffold actual teaching experiences for them to perform and observe, and provide opportunities for both collective and individual co-construction on the meanings of teaching events. Without each of these in place in challenging contexts, I have not observed significant disequilibrium among my prospective teachers nor support for change to challenge them to move beyond the status quo. Perhaps someday our field of science teacher education will have generalizable methods for transforming prospective teachers' narrow past experiences in science into appropriate applications for successful teaching of all children. Until then, I will continue to provide for my prospective teachers rich and challenging experiences representing the on-the-job-training of equity in science education. As Hawkins (1974) so eloquently stated, "We're all in IT together" (p. 62).

REFERENCES

Abell, S. K., Bryan, L. A., & Anderson, M. (1998). Investigating prospective elementary science teacher reflective thinking using integrated media case-based instruction in elementary science teacher preparation. *Science Education, 82,* 491–510.

Adams, P. E., & Krockover, G. H. (1999). Stimulating constructivist teaching styles through use of an observation rubric. *Journal of Research in Science Teaching, 36,* 955–971.

Aikenhead, G. S. (1996). Science education: Border crossing into the subculture of science. *Studies in Science Education, 27,* 1–52.

Aikenhead, G. S. (2001). Students' ease in crossing cultural borders into school. *Science Education, 85,* 180–188.

Anderson, C. W., & Smith, E. (1987). Teaching science. In V. Richardson-Koehler (Ed.), *Educators' handbook: A research perspective* (pp. 84–111). New York: Longman.

Ayers, W. (1993). *To teach: The journey of a teacher.* New York: Teachers College Press.

Brice-Heath, S. (1983). *Ways with words: Language, life, and work in communities and classrooms.* New York: Cambridge University Press.

Bryan, L. A., & Abell, S. K. (1999). Development of professional knowledge in learning to teach elementary science. *Journal of Research in Science Teaching, 36,* 121–139.

Calderhead, J. (1981). Stimulated recall: A method for research on teaching. *British Journal of Educational Psychology, 51,* 211–217.

Chávez, R. C., & O'Donnell, J. (Eds.). (1998). *Speaking the unpleasant: The politics of (non)engagement in the multicultural education terrain.* Albany: State University of New York Press.

Clandinin, D. J., Davies, A., Hogan, P., & Kennard, B. (1993). *Learning to teach: Teaching to learn.* New York: Teachers College Press.

Cochran-Smith, M., & Lytle, S. L. (1993). *Inside/outside: Teacher research and knowledge.* New York: Teachers College Press.

Cuban, L. (1993). *How teachers taught: Constancy and change in American classrooms 1890–1990* (2nd ed.). New York: Teachers College Press.

Delpit, L. (1995). *Other people's children: Cultural conflict in the classroom.* New York: The New Press.

Feiman-Nemser, S., & Remillard, J. (1996). Perspectives on learning to teach. In F. Murray (Ed.), *The teacher educator's handbook: Building a knowledge base for the preparation of teachers* (pp. 63–91). San Francisco: Jossey-Bass.

Feiman-Nemser, S., McDiarmid, G. W., Melnick, S. L., & Parker, M. (1989). *Changing beginning teachers' conceptions: A description of an introductory teacher education course* (Research Report No. 89-1). East Lansing, MI: National Center for Research on Teacher Education.

Gilbert, A., & Yerrick, R. (2001). Same school, separate worlds: A sociocultural study of identity, resistance, and negotiation in a rural, lower track science classroom. *Journal of Research in Science Teaching, 38,* 574–598.

Goodman, J., & Fish, D. (1997). Against-the-grain teacher education: A study of coursework, field experience, and perspectives. *Journal of Teacher Education, 48,* 96–107.

Gore, J. M., & Zeichner, K. M. (1991). Action research and reflective teaching in preservice teacher education: A case study from the United States. *Teaching and Teacher Education, 7,* 119–136.

Grimmett, P. P. (1988). The nature of reflection and Schön's conception in perspective. In P. P. Grimmett & G. L. Erickson (Eds.), *Reflection in teacher education* (pp. 5–16). New York: Teachers College Press.

Hawkins, D. (1974). I, thou, and it. *The informed vision: Essays on learning and human nature* (pp. 48–62). New York: Agathon Press.

Hollingsworth, S. (1989). Prior beliefs and cognitive change in learning to teach. *American Educational Research Journal, 26,* 160–189.

Howard, G. (1999). *We can't teach what we don't know: White teachers, multicultural schools.* New York: Teachers College Press.

Hubbard, R. S., & Power, B. M. (1993). *The art of classroom inquiry: A handbook for teacher research.* Portsmouth, NH: Heinemann.

Hutchings, P., & Shulman, L. (1999). The scholarship of teaching: New elaborations, new developments. *Change, 31*(5), 10–15.

Ladson-Billings, G. (1999). Preparing teachers for diverse student populations: A critical race theory perspective. *Review of Research in Education, 24,* 211–248.

Lave, J. (1990). Views of the classroom: Implications for math and science learning research. In M. Gardner, J. Greeno, F. Reif, A. Schoenfeld, A. Disessa, & E. Stage (Eds.), *Toward a scientific practice of science education* (pp. 251–263). Hillsdale, NJ: Lawrence Erlbaum Associates.

LeCompte, M. D., & Dworkin, A. G. (1991). *Giving up on school: Student dropouts and teacher burnouts.* Newbury Park, CA: Corwin Press.

Lemke, J. (1990). *Talking science: Language, learning and values.* New York: Ablex.

Lortie, D. C. (1975). *Schoolteacher: A sociological study.* Chicago: University of Chicago Press.

McDiarmid, G. W. (1999). Challenging prospective teachers' beliefs during early field experience: A quixotic undertaking? *Journal of Teacher Education, 41,* 12–20.

McLaren, P., & Giroux, H. A. (1997). Writing in the margins: Geographies of identity, pedagogy, and power. In P. McLaren (Ed.), *Revolutionary multiculturalism: Pedagogies of dissent for the new millennium* (pp. 16–41). Boulder, CO: Westview Press.

Mishler, E. (1986). *Research interviewing: Context and narrative.* Cambridge, MA: Harvard University Press.

Oakes, J. (1985). *Keeping track: How schools structure inequality.* New Haven, CT: Yale University Press.

Office of Planning and Institutional Research. (1996). *Report.* Greenville, NC: East Carolina University.

Osborne, R., & Freyberg, P. (1985). *Learning in science: The implications of children's science.* Portsmouth, NH: Heinemann.

Pajares, M. F. (1992). Teachers' beliefs and educational research: Cleaning up a messy construct. *Review of Educational Research, 62,* 307–332.

Paley, V. (1989). *White teacher.* Cambridge, MA: Harvard University Press.

Phelan, P., Davidson, A. L., & Cao, H. T. (1991). Student multiple worlds: Negotiating the boundaries of family, peer, and school cultures. *Anthropology and Education Quarterly, 22,* 224–250.

Rodriguez, A. (1997). The dangerous discourse of invisibility: A critique of the National Research Council's national science education standards. *Journal of Research in Science Teaching, 34,* 19–37.

Schön, D. A. (1987). *Educating the reflective practitioner: Toward a new design for teaching and learning in the professions.* San Francisco: Jossey-Bass.

Tann, S. (1993). Eliciting student teachers' personal theories. In J. Calderhead & P. Gates (Eds.), *Conceptualizing reflection in teacher development* (pp. 53–69). London: Falmer Press.

Watson, B., & Konicek, R. (1990). Teaching for conceptual change: Confronting children's experience. *Phi Delta Kappan, 71,* 680–685.

Yerrick, R. K., & Hoving, T. J. (2003). One foot on the dock and one foot on the boat: Differences among preservice science teachers' interpretations of field-based science methods in culturally diverse contexts. *Science Education, 87,* 390–418.

APPENDIX

Following is an assignment from a class of methods students based in a rural Black earth science classroom in a North Carolina project:

I [I], Thou [Th], or It [IT] All that apply

1. [I, Th, IT] *Student Question*, "Where do Black people come from?"

2. [Th] *Artifact*: Methods student visitation to the local church where earth science student attended

3. [I, Th] *Teaching observation*: Standard methods make the students restless, they talk to neighbors disengage.

4. [I, Th] *Student Interview*: When they start lecturing and stuff, I don't know what I'm supposed to do so I just talk with my neighbor.

5. [I, Th] *Artifact*: Teacher is White, all but 3 students are Black

6. [I, IT] *Student question*: How did you get to be light like those people in Norway I saw on television?

7. [IT] *Curriculum*: Light rays are more direct at the equator

8. [Th, IT] *Curriculum*: More intense light rays cause a physiological response to block intense rays. This is not necessary for Anglo origin. People living north of the 45th parallel need to absorb, not block heat from the sun. They did not develop the Vitamin K response that equatorial mammals did tens of thousands of years ago.

9. [Th, IT] *Activity*: Students Survey the school to see what kids believe about how colored pigmentation is different.

10. [I, Th, IT] *Activity*: Lab activity of what it is warmer on the equator and what causes seasons

11. [I, Th, IT] *Activity*: Autobiographical essay of how their family got here.

12. [Th] *Focus Group*: This is what it is like to be Black at this school . . .

13. [I, IT] *Artifact*: You're a White teacher and all my White teachers before you have called treated me like I'm stupid.

14. [Th] *Reading*: Delpit, students may think that alternative teaching methods have little to offer them.

15. [I, Th] *Autobiograohy*: I am a White privileged teacher who has a narrow view of what successful teaching and learning is all about since I have succeeded in basically mastering but one discourse that has made me successful.

16. [I, IT] *Reading*: Hawkins & Kohl If I can't explain it so that students understand, it is not necessarily their deficiency but perhaps a sign that I need to learn more about the content.

17. [Th] *Observation*: Student talks a lot with fellow student about their own children. Students seek the reaffirmation and support of fellow mothers in the class, often at the cost of learning the content of the class.

18. [Th] *External class observation*: Teacher talked with great disrespect in another class to this student. They did not respond.

19. [I, Th, IT] *Artifact*: Collection of children's questions kept throughout the year

20. [I, Th] *Reading*: Ballanger, students will not be able to recognize the intention of rules of behavior in class if they are in conflict with basic cultural assumptions of the students.

21. [I, IT] *Artifact*: I am a successful biology student. I worked at the marine museum in the summer

22. [Th] *Focus Group*: "Ma-an, once a teacher called me lazy and asked me, 'What do you come to school for anyway . . . *lunch*?' That was ugly talkin' and made me crazy. I told my momma 'bout it and she told 'em ain't no reason to talk disrespectful and like that to kids."

23. [I, IT] *Peer Lesson*: I taught a peer lesson in which students contributed only one word answers on occasion

24. [IT] *Curriculum*: Topics include climate, seasons, migrations, and adaptations of organisms.

11

Helping Teachers Use Students' Home Cultures in Mathematics Lessons: Developmental Stages of Becoming Effective Teachers of Diverse Students

Jacque Ensign
Seattle University

In my graduate courses for prospective teachers, almost all are from middle-class, dominant-culture backgrounds, whereas the urban students they are beginning to teach as part of their field work are often from primarily low-income, nondominant cultures. One of the biggest hurdles these teachers face is finding ways to get to know their students and then to connect their classroom mathematics lessons to their students' own experiences and interests outside of school. In previous publications (Ensign, 2001, 2003) I have detailed how teachers can use students' personal, out-of-school experiences in mathematics to teach their math lessons in school. In this chapter, I focus on using this approach in teacher education courses that I teach and chronicle the steps I see prospective teachers taking as they move through denial, resistance, and later understanding of including students' cultures in classroom instruction.

For nearly a decade, I have taught courses on effective teaching in urban schools and on multicultural education. Those in my classes have been and are K–12 prospective teachers, some of whom are focusing on being mathematics and science teachers but many of whom are planning to be generalists in classrooms. Regardless of where they live—I have taught in urban areas of the Northeast, Middle Atlantic, and Northwest—all face similar challenges of finding ways to connect their students' interests with school mathematics. And regardless of where they live, I face the challenge of finding ways to help these teachers get past their fears and prejudices of who their students are, and what these students can and should learn.

On the surface, prospective teachers see me as a dominant-culture woman academic who is teaching about education of children who are different than I am. As I explain further in the fourth step that my prospective teachers take in becoming culturally responsive teachers, though I do hold a position of power and privilege in U.S. society, my identity has also been shaped by being part of the "Other," which drives much of why I care passionately about equity education.

This chapter summarizes my approach in teacher education to helping my prospective teachers learn to teach in culturally responsive ways. I argue for the critical need in teacher education to help teachers learn concrete ways of bridging the gap between school mathematics and students' own cultural experiences in mathematics. I outline the developmental steps I see my prospective teachers taking as they grapple with the need for culturally responsive teaching and summarize my teaching strategies for addressing those steps of growth in teachers, showing how prospective teachers' resistance is part of these developmental steps. I elaborate on one strategy that I have found easy for teachers to implement at all levels of mathematics instruction that has helped reduce their resistance to including students' cultures in their pedagogy. Finally, I summarize some of the action assignments I use to help prospective teachers as they move from resistance to a sense of efficacy in teaching diverse students, and suggest ways I would like to expand my support of these teachers throughout their teaching careers.

THEORETICAL BASIS

In courses on effective teaching and on psychology of learning, we in teacher education usually emphasize the importance of students' motivation (e.g., Brophy, 1998; Woolfolk, 2001). Texts and professors alike note that if students are not interested in what is to be learned, they may not learn very much and may instead exhibit behavior problems in the classroom. We note that when students feel school is relevant to their lives, they learn better. But often this is mere lip service, with professors and texts quickly moving into other theories of learning and rather generalized instructional techniques that pay scant attention to students' interests and cultures. In my experience, when instructional techniques consist mainly of generic formula of lesson plans and sequencing of lessons, culture takes a back seat (see Ensign, 2003, for an in-depth discussion of this).

Cochran-Smith (2000) quoted Ladson-Billings as saying that "the changing demographics of the nation's schoolchildren have caught schools, colleges, and departments of teacher education by surprise. Students are still being prepared to teach in idealized schools that serve White, monolingual, middle class children from homes with two parents." Having spent years teaching in schools of low-income students, I see a disconnect between what teachers are taught about discrete cultures in multiculturalism classes and what they are taught about instructional theory, resulting in an inability of teachers to use culture in instruction. When teachers do not understand that their instructional methods must relate to the cultures of their students, they make unfair assumptions about why certain students do not succeed in their classes. Those students whose cultures differ radically from mainstream teachers' cultures often literally end up in the back seat of success in schools (Gordon, 1999). Gordon warned of the "tendency to see differences between minority and majority groups as deficits to be overcome rather than as assets to be developed" (p. 4). I want my teachers to question every time they see a student in a lower level track, every time they see a student exhibiting behavior problems in school, every time they see a student who "isn't motivated." I want them to question how their teaching may be contributing to the problems they are seeing. I want them to know their students in other ways than just in academic terms, so that they know some of their students' strengths and therefore question when they see these students not doing well academically.

Wax (1993) warned teacher educators about the dangers of reifying culture as static and bounded. Seeing multiculturalism as founded on a Boas–Benedict model of culture that assumes people live in discrete cultures, Wax worried that educators miss the fluidity and dynamics of the cultures of students in the United States. He stated, "In short, the Boas–Benedict legacy of plural, separate, distinct, historically homogenous cultures is both scientifically misleading and educationally irrelevant" (p. 108). The result is that teachers carry stereotyped conceptions of the cultures of their students that may or may not have much to do with an individual student's cultural experiences. Wax contended that "our best strategy would be to envision culture in dynamic terms and to perceive our responsibilities as toward culturing not only the young, but also ourselves, throughout our lives" (p. 109). As someone who herself lives and identifies herself as a member of intersecting cultures, and consequently has experienced the nuances and blurring across what many multiculturalists consider to be lines, I have been keenly interested in finding legitimate ways for my prospective teachers to understand and to use individual students' personal cultural experiences in mathematics.

In my theoretical orientation, I approach teaching and learning from a sociocultural view in which learning occurs through cultural participation (see Kirshner, 2002, for a good discussion of behaviorism, constructivism, and sociocultural learning theories in relation to the National Council of Teachers of Mathematics and mathematics teaching). I am a cultural anthropologist of education who researches mathematics education to see how culture affects that teaching. In the case of mathematics, I see students as active participants in their out-of-school cultures as well as in their classroom culture. For all students, the more their out-of-school and in-school cultures mesh, the easier it is for them to succeed in mathematics. Resnick (1987) noted that "knowledge acquired outside school is not always used to support in-school learning" (p. 15). I see that the challenge for teachers whose students' situated knowledge outside school differs greatly from school knowledge is to find ways to bridge the two contexts to help their students be successful in school mathematics.

THIS RESEARCH

My research base from which I am drawing in writing this chapter spans 10 years and three areas of the United States—upper Middle Atlantic, lower Northeast, and upper Northwest, all in teacher education programs in large urban centers. In all cases, my students—referred to in this chapter as "prospective teachers" though in reality some were prospective whereas others were in-service teachers—were in graduate programs leading to certification and a master's degree, or a rank increase if they already held a master's degree. More than half of my prospective teachers were pursuing teaching as a second career, whereas the rest were entering teaching as a first career. During my 5 years teaching graduate classes in the Northeast, I also was a teacher-researcher in mathematics classes in local elementary schools. Vignettes included in this chapter are from my research in those elementary classrooms that has been published previously (Ensign, 2001). Unless otherwise noted, what is said about my teaching of prospective teachers applies to all three locations because I have used similar approaches in all three locations, honing my approach over time. Quotes from prospective teachers in relation to my teaching are from reflection papers they were required to write about course readings, anonymous questionnaires given during and at the end of the course, and student comments during class discussions.

A reminder: My prospective teachers span elementary through secondary grades, with only some planning to teach mathematics exclusively. The courses I have taught are not exclusively on mathematics education, but rather on multiculturalism or on effective teaching in urban schools, with my approach being to use mathematics education as a focal point.

STEPS PROSPECTIVE TEACHERS TAKE
IN CULTURALLY RESPONSIVE TEACHING

As is typical of teacher education, our prospective teachers in all three regions of the United States in which I teach generally come from middle-class homes and have led rather sheltered lives. This is especially the case in the tier one public university and in the private university, but I found it to generally be the case even in the less elite state university. Our prospective teachers' experiences with diversity have been minimal because most have lived and attended schools in mostly homogenous settings. When they begin realizing they will be teaching students who do not share the same cultural backgrounds as they themselves have, my prospective teachers' reactions follow a rather predictable pattern of moving through a progression of steps that involve denial, resistance, and understanding. I've included some of my prospective teachers' comments from reflection papers on readings, class discussions, and anonymous questionnaires to illustrate some of the stages I've observed my prospective teachers progressing through as they face how they will teach diverse students.

Deny Cultural Differences and Attribute Students' Lack of Success to Inadequate Teachers and Homes

My prospective teachers say they will involve parents and that they feel they will be the effective teachers that their students have not been fortunate enough to have had. One of my prospective teachers wrote on an anonymous questionnaire, "I plan to make my lessons interesting because that way all my students will be excited to learn." Another wrote on a questionnaire, assuming that many teachers do not do this, "I plan to foster an accepting, open environment because I feel it is vital to allow students to be successful."

Realize That Their Lives Are Quite Different From Many of the Students'

Noting how different their students are in the schools, my prospective teachers begin to wonder how to teach these students. A typical response on an anonymous questionnaire from one of my prospective teachers was, "I plan to teach with an open mind because not all students are like me."

Another wrote, "I'm still unclear how to motivate students whose culture I'm not familiar with."

Decide They Will Add a Bit of "Culture" to Their Classes

My prospective teachers begin looking for resources (books, music, food, heroes usually) to supplement how they will teach lessons. On an anonymous questionnaire, a prospective teacher wrote, "I still need to work through exactly how to make all this happen. The how is the hardest." Another wrote, "I plan to teach through the history of many art cultures because in this way students realize that all cultures use, wear, display art in their own ways."

Want a Simple Guide to Categories of People

My prospective teachers have asked during class discussions, "How do Latino youth want teachers to treat them in school?"; "What do Black youth like to do in school?"; "What subjects do girls like?"; "Who likes to do assignments in cooperative groups and who likes to do them individually?" I, however, avoid a field guide to different cultures/ethnicities/genders that is so commonly done in multicultural classes. I prefer to focus on the wide variety of experiences within each group of people while noting the dangers of stereotyping. It is my overarching concern about stereotyping, with the attendant messages of differences and deficits, as well as my experiences with the immense diversity present within groups that prevent me from giving field guides.

Because this is the stage that precedes a brief stage in which they become overwhelmed and hopeless, and quickly turns into resistance, I elaborate on my approach during this stage. I do so to show the antecedents of resistance that I later revisit in helping my prospective teachers move through their resistance toward understanding.

I move them through a brief history of racial categories in U.S. law (using excerpts from Lopez, 1996), looking at the permeability and fluidity of such categories over time. We note the pervasiveness of unequal treatment of persons depending on what category they are assigned in society. We look at the overall track record of students who have been in schools serving certain racial and class categories of students in the United States, be they mainstream middle-class students, lower-class, dominant-culture, or non-dominant-culture students.

My approach is to find ways on the one hand to acknowledge the categories into which students are sorted and treated by society, and on the other hand to move beyond those insidious categories in teaching to try to teach students as unique human beings who have their own personal cultural experiences. I want them to begin to look at students as both ongoing products of how society is treating them, and as individuals who have hopes, dreams, strengths, and needs that often transcend the very categories in which they are normally placed.

I begin by telling my prospective teachers about my own dilemma of trying to describe who I am culturally. In explaining, I relate my own cultural history. For the same reasons that I argue that teachers should not assume cultural characteristics by looking at students, I myself am not easily stereotyped by gender and ethnicity. Because of how I look, I am treated in the United States primarily as a middle-class White woman, but that is only a part of my cultural experience, in terms of both gender and ethnicity. For example, in print I am often perceived to be male and Black, and in some meetings I have been perceived to be a Black woman academic. I talk about how I have been perceived to be White, Black, female, male, gay, heterosexual, from the United States, not from the United States—all depending on contextual clues—and all resulting in my being treated very differently, and most reflecting my own identity that blurs across boundaries.

I then move from my own experience to discussing what this might mean in their teaching. I give an example of a student who is angry and a poor reader who needs to be seen by a teacher as a student who has reasons for anger and poor reading skills that may be largely the result of the environment in which this student has lived. The student may have been treated disrespectfully by citizens of another ethnicity or class, may realize how little is at home compared to what is seen on TV, may not have a home or community in which books are read, and may not have been encouraged to read well. I want my teachers to recognize and acknowledge those facets of a student's life. But I also want my teachers to be able to get to know this student as an individual, get to know what this student likes to do, get to know what "drives" this student, get to know this student's passions, and find ways to respect and care for this student as a human being. To be able to care for and respect this student, my teachers need to have ways to help this student learn well. I am concerned that my teachers get beyond blaming students or excusing students, or placating students, and instead find ways to teach all students well.

In focusing this discussion on the students whom they will be teaching, I refer them to thinkers such as Wax (1993) in emphasizing how students are "culturaling" across diverse cultures, instead of being cultured in one discrete culture. My hope is that by viewing students as richly and actively "culturing," my prospective teachers will begin to view students as uniquely rich cultural beings from whom my prospective teachers can learn as they teach them.

Feel Overwhelmed and Helpless

Feelings of being overwhelmed and helpless become prominent when I begin to really focus on the diversity of lives within the categories that schools and U.S. society often lump people. I note the wide variety of achievement within groups, while emphasizing the huge achievement differences that are currently typical in schools and asking why. We examine issues of power and privilege, and of the power of expectations. To a prompt I had written for my prospective teachers to complete on an anonymous questionnaire, "When I think of trying to successfully teach a diversity of students, I feel _____," prospective teachers responded with "overwhelmed!" and "nervous."

Using readings from theorists and researchers such as Basil Bernstein, Shirley Brice Heath, John Ogbu, Pierre Bourdieu, Samuel Bowles, Herbert Gintis, and Jay MacLeod, we examine how schools have contributed to inequities in society. I feel they have to know and understand the mechanisms enough so that when they later begin to look for solutions, we can examine those solutions to see if they are only replicating the inequities or indeed serving students more fairly. My concern is that my prospective teachers dig deeply enough into the mechanisms of categorizing and sorting students so that they cry, "Not fair! Help! What can I do?"

Feel Angry and Resistant

Before my prospective teachers cry out for help, many get angry and resistant. One student blurted out in class, "I'm angry that these people aren't taking care of themselves. My grandparents moved from the low rungs of being immigrants to now having grandchildren who are lawyers. If we could do this, others can too if they just try."

In my teaching on the education of children who have traditionally been underserved in our schools, we address issues of racism, sexism, and classism in the context of how they are socially mediated phenomena and what the implications are for educators. I've found that when prospective teachers keep this at a theoretical level, they feel safe, but when they examine how it relates to their own history and actions, they can get resistant.

In reading and discussing Delpit's provocative *Other People's Children: Cultural Conflict in the Classroom* (1995), we focus on the disconnect between teachers' and students' cultures and what implications that has for educators. I use a quote from her introduction to spark a discussion on their perceptions of what they know and do not know about students:

> We all carry worlds in our heads, and those worlds are decidedly different. We educators set out to teach, but how can we reach the worlds of theirs

when we don't even know they exist? Indeed, many of us don't even realize that our own worlds exist only in our heads and in the cultural institutions we have built to support them. (p. xiv)

As my prospective teachers read Delpit's (1995) book, they typically get quite defensive, criticizing her for being too critical of White teachers. It is during this reading that I see the most blatant resistance in my prospective teachers. Delpit pulls my prospective teachers out from the protective cloak of keeping theory at a distance, to being personal, and it hurts. While they were intrigued during Stage 4 in learning about categories, and felt helpless during Stage 5 on power relations, now they face their own possible complicity and often react by resisting. On an anonymous questionnaire, a student wrote: "In trying to bring out different perspectives it seems we were led toward a perspective of anyone who is a minority and disenfranchised has the white person to blame." One student wrote in a course reflection paper, "I felt that I as a well-off white was being attacked." The degree of anger is not contained to their writings and spills out into the class sessions, their vehemence surprising and upsetting other students. In such a situation, one student wrote in frustration about classmates who were rejecting and criticizing the readings as being offensive, "Not only was I discouraged by the views of some of my colleagues but also I was upset. I was so emotional inside that I found it hard to say anything at all. I wanted to say how glad I was that [this was written]."

At this point in a course, prospective teachers who are vehemently resisting sometimes speak up in class discussions, but often tune out in class sessions, sometimes blatantly reading other literature in class, refusing to participate in class discussions, doing only what is required in assignments. I've found it important to time my courses so that they hit the resistance stage before we have reached midterm. If this happens too close to the end of a course, they may not move past this resistance, and their end-of-course evaluations of me as a teacher reflect their resistance and distaste for what I am offering. I need ample time to allow them to soften their resistance enough to be open to moving beyond their resistance.

Move Through Resistance

It always helps to have at least a few who, recognizing themselves in Delpit's (1995) book, take it as a wake-up call and become moved to reexamine how they have related to students. Because I try to teach courses in which my prospective teachers are doing fieldwork in urban schools concurrently with my course, inevitably, after several weeks, prospective teachers begin to write in their papers and share in class discussions how much they are finding Delpit to be instrumental in helping them have new insights into what is working and what is not in their classrooms. One student wrote on an anonymous questionnaire, "Lisa Delpit's book was very eye-opening for me. She did a fabulous job of pointing out how minority cultures may not agree with the mainstream school of thought." Another wrote, "Lisa Delpit *really* made me introspective about my understanding of how to interact with people of different races and cultures." Another wrote, "Some people don't like the harshness of Delpit, but I find it refreshing. So many times cultural/diversity discussions are talked about so gingerly. Sometimes it is best to 'lay it all out there' and discuss."

After they have struggled with the facts of inequities in achievement and their desires to teach all children well, I try to offer enough success stories for them to begin to develop a sense of their efficacy for teaching diverse learners. I introduce the concept of culturally responsive teaching (also referred to as culturally relevant and culturally connected). In class I show video clips and describe the successful work of Deborah Meier with the Central Park East Schools (Meier, 1995; see also Bensman, 2000) to set the stage for exploring ways to provide quality, culturally responsive education for all students. To prepare for class discussion, students read articles, including Ladson-Billings (1992, 1997) and Levine (1994). I use materials from the Center for Research on Education, Diversity, and Excellence (CREDE; see http://crede.ucsc.edu). I project video clips from CREDE's *Teaching Alive!* CD so my teachers can see examples of instructional techniques that work well for diverse students. We discuss what they see happening in the video clips—how the classroom is structured, what teachers say and do, and how students react. We examine the clips from a variety of participants' and theorists' viewpoints. We compare the clips' classroom teaching styles to those in classrooms in which they are doing their fieldwork.

I use mathematics as an example to make the theory real and to examine how far we still have to go for mathematics to be culturally responsive. I introduce how I use math to help teachers teach in culturally responsive ways. I show samples of students' culturally connected mathematics work that I have collected in my research in urban schools. In that research, I have worked with elementary teachers to help them find ways to incorporate students' out-of-school experiences into their mathematics lessons.

A significant difficulty that classroom teachers have encountered when they have attempted to apply research on culturally connected teaching is the expense and time involved in collecting relevant materials. Whereas successful studies have employed ethnographers working in the students' communities to collect relevant materials (Civil, 1998), this is beyond the constraints of an urban classroom teacher. In my classes, I show samples of homework "home links" that students use to collect their own personal examples. For example, when asked to note one example of how they use a clock, one second grader wrote and illustrated what the clock looked like when the alarm went off in the morning and what it looked like when they had to leave the house for school. By having students supply their own personal examples, teachers do not have to spend time and money scouring the community or literature to find relevant examples of students' everyday mathematics. They can then use these problems as examples when presenting or reviewing mathematics topics or examine the math in their own samples.

The following is a vignette from my research (see Ensign, 2001, for details of the research from which this is drawn) that I share with my classes. This is an example of a teacher using students' everyday experiences. These experiences are not blatantly cultural in the sense of stereotypical foods that those who are not part of a culture may think that culture eats (stemming from a bounded view of culture), but rather are good examples of culture in the sense of how-we-do-things-around-here (stemming from Wax's notion of dynamic culture), and thus are good examples of using students' *particular* cultural experiences. I use this vignette to show an example of how a teacher drew on her students' *particular* lives and interests:

> As the second-grade students return to their classroom from recess, their teacher begins today's introductory math lesson on fractions. "Kwame, I heard you telling Deshawn about eating cake. Would you tell the whole class?" Kwame eagerly relates his experience. As his teacher draws the cake on the board, she asks these questions about the cake and Kwame's family, "Did everyone have a piece? One piece? Were there any pieces left over? Did Taishia have a piece? Did Destiny have a piece? What about Chantrelle?" And so on through the entire family, naming each family member as she shades in a piece of cake for each. As he counts the total number of pieces, she writes "8" on the board, draws a line above it, and asks him how many pieces he ate. Writing "1" above the line, she explains that Kwame ate 1 out of 8 pieces, or one-eighth. She asks the class what other foods they divide at home or with their friends. Most of the students are waving their hands in the air as they eagerly wait to add their food to the list on the board. After compiling the list of foods, the teacher redirects the students, "OK, now we have a huge list of foods you have divided. I want each of you to take out your journals and begin writing about one time that you divided food. Tell us where you were, who was there, and how you divided the food among you. Be sure to give all the important information as Kwame did."
>
> After she sees some students are finishing their writing, she asks everyone to stop for a minute, saying, "After you have written your experience, I also want you to draw the food you divided, and write the fraction of how much you ate, just as we did for Kwame's cake. Desiree, I saw you were writing about dividing a bagel. How many pieces did you have?" As Desiree says, "2," her teacher draws a bagel on the board, divides it into 2 pieces, and asks, "How many pieces did you eat?" When Desiree says she

ate one piece, the teacher writes the fraction, saying, "One of two pieces, or one-half. Were your parts equal?" When Desiree says they were almost the same, the teacher explains how in life we talk about fractions when the parts are the same or almost the same, but to be really accurate mathematically, the parts need to be equal. She then has a brief discussion with them about why the parts should be equal for fractions, and times in life when we may refer to fractions even though the parts may not be exactly equal. She encourages the students to work together on writing their fractions before putting their journals away.

She again focuses the class, asking them to look at an overhead of a workbook page. "Now that you've written and drawn about something you divided, let's see what the book has divided. Here's a square divided into how many parts? And how many parts are shaded? William, can you write this shaded part as a fraction?" After William has written the fraction on the overhead, she invites the students to complete the worksheet. Students fly through the worksheet, laughing about how easy it is. The few who have difficulty are reminded how they wrote their own fractions and urged to refer to their fractions while doing the worksheet problems.

After presenting examples of how teachers have used students' problems, to the prompt I had written for them to complete on an anonymous questionnaire, "When I think of trying to successfully teach a diversity of students, I feel _____ ," prospective teachers responded with "inspired," "excited and challenged," "encouraged," "optimistic." One prospective teacher wrote in a reflection paper that was part of a course assignment:

> How do we teach every culture that is represented in the classroom? What methods do I use to learn more about different cultures? How can I effectively teach to a specific culture without making broad generalizations about the people in that culture? These questions have left me unsettled since the beginning of this class and I have struggled to discover the answers. By intellectualizing how I might equitably teach to the culture of each child in my classroom, I became caught up in abstractions, theories, studies, and generalizations. I lost sight of the fact that it is each child that brings a gift to the classroom; I need to begin by opening the package and sharing it with the class. By connecting to the students' outside of school experience, I will most likely be able to learn about each child's cultural background and then relate the curriculum to that child's culture. In addition, I will more likely earn respect from the students if I make the effort to establish a relationship with them and—if possible—their families.

Another prospective teacher wrote in a reflection paper for the course:

> During my initial encounter with this multiculturalism, I must admit I was overwhelmed. I did not see how I was going to be able to incorporate everything I had learned about multiple intelligences, learning styles, classroom

management, and curriculum content with the issues surrounding multiculturalism. Now, however, I realize that by making a commitment to be
knowledgeable about my students I would be incorporating all of those elements . . . Each and every student deserves the chance to learn, and it is my
ethical responsibility to do everything in my ability to ensure that each student does indeed get that chance.

Develop a Sense of Efficacy

I am concerned that my prospective teachers have a sense not only of possibilities for effectively teaching diverse students, but also of some of the
hurdles they may encounter if they do this. I do this through a combina-
tion of presenting examples from my research in elementary schools and
guiding them through action assignments.

Presenting Examples From My Research. I use mathematics as an
example of what teachers face when implementing more culturally connected mathematics. I share experiences I have had in my work with veteran teachers who have tried to use students' personal mathematics problems. Classroom teachers and students sometimes have found it difficult
to focus on finding actual problems that have been experienced by the students, rather than making up fictitious realistic problems. Because I had
observed that actual problems of the students are more potent for helping
students understand mathematics concepts than fictitious realistic problems (Ensign, 1996), I have been very careful to have students use problems they have actually experienced. Once, during my research, in an effort to help the students write their problems in less time in class, a
veteran classroom teacher gave the students a sentence format on the
board with blanks for them to insert their own numbers and items. The resulting problems were hardly different from the textbook problems because the teacher had purposefully used a textbook format for the sentence format and the students' own voices did not come through in the
canned writing. Unlike their personally written problems, students did
not show interest in these problems by discussing and sharing them with
others in the class.

We discuss how having students supply their own personal math experiences has sometimes caused problems of legitimacy, with students, parents, and teachers feeling these examples are not "real" school mathematics problems. If students' personal out-of-school mathematics problems
are perceived to be using inferior mathematical knowledge to textbook
knowledge, then teachers of students who are struggling in mathematics
may fear the consequences of using students' problems because it may ad-
versely affect test scores. This was one of the concerns raised by principals
when I began my research in low-achieving schools. If state mathematics

test scores are used to judge the standing of individual schools, a principal and teachers may fear that by not focusing entirely on textbook knowledge, their school may lose what little political power it presently has. Hopefully, this will become less of a problem as teachers become aware of more research data such as that from my research (Ensign, 2001) that show the advantages of including personal out-of-school experiences in mathematics lessons.

Power relations can also be a challenge. Rather than using mathematics from received knowledge (textbook and teacher problems), using perceived knowledge (students' own personal problems) changes the power relationships in a classroom because the teacher is no longer the sole dispenser and authority of knowledge. As Weiner (1999) explained:

> When you set up your classroom so that students respect and learn from one another, and you learn from them, you contradict the hierarchical nature of the school system. When you use teaching strategies that call for your students to interpret and analyze material so that you and they critically compare ideas, you counter the "skill-drill-kill" sort of instruction that lends itself to the test-driven curricula that characterize many urban schools. (p. 61)

When a student has written a problem that requires outside knowledge (such as how to score football touchdowns), the teacher may not be the authority on this knowledge. Suddenly, a student who has not been very involved in classroom lessons may become the dispenser and authority of knowledge. For this shift of power to work smoothly in a classroom, a teacher has to feel comfortable letting students lead during portions of a lesson, such as during the following episode recorded in my field notes and discussed in Ensign (2001):

> In a fifth grade classroom in which only a third of the class would attempt more than a few problems on a textbook worksheet, when students were given a worksheet that contained only their classmates' personal problems, the students plunged into solving the problems. Once students had had time to try solving the problems alone, they were allowed to consult classmates. One difficult problem involved football scores and finally so many were still struggling with that problem that the author was asked to explain how scoring is done in football and to explain how to solve the problem step by step. The teacher listened as the student explained the problem to his classmates. Since the teacher felt comfortable taking a back seat to the author of the problem, the lesson went smoothly and students began looking for more difficult problems they could share with the class next time.

Had the teacher not been comfortable sharing the authority, students would have reverted to being mere receivers of knowledge. By being willing to share power with a student, the teacher allowed this young boy, who was often disengaged in lessons, to become intensely involved in helping his classmates solve his complex problem.

In addition to explicitly leveling power relations in mathematics lessons by encouraging teachers to involve students in sharing their knowledge and expertise with the class, I discuss with my prospective teachers how teachers need to examine how students' problems are used. Frankenstein (1997) noted that merely using students' problems to practice a particular mathematics skill may be avoiding dealing with other issues inherent in the context in which the students' problems occurred: "Knowledge is not created and recreated in the fragmented forms in which most school subjects are presented. Mathematics occurs in contexts, integrated with other knowledge of the world" (p. 13). If students' problems are presented with more of the context than just what is necessary to solve the mathematical problem, then students can discuss other knowledge that is integrated with the mathematics, such as why prices are higher in certain stores, or why some items are not sold individually. In doing so, students will learn to use mathematical knowledge to "read the world" as Freire (1993) suggested. Encouraging students to write enough of the context in which the personal math occurs can provide a springboard for teachers to discuss societal influences on the math that they experience, such as values of goods and services. This can help extend mathematics beyond the mechanics of learning to solve school mathematics problems to include a critical approach to the culture in which mathematics occurs in their lives.

For instance, in a fifth-grade class in my research, a student wrote about how much rent money her family needed. Some students in her class became very interested in the amount of the rent, noting differing rents that their families paid and what they got for the differing amounts of money they paid, noting differences between rent-assistance projects and open-market housing and location of the housing. The teacher, being sensitive to those who might be homeless or living in shelters or who did not want to reveal that they owned their house, did not solicit information from those students who did not volunteer information. A second-grade class had a similar discussion when a student wrote about buying chips at a corner convenience store whereas another student had written about buying chips at a supermarket that served neighborhoods of varying income levels. Students noted that the brands were the same but that the prices were not and their teacher helped them discuss what might influence the price differences.

Action Assignments in My Courses. I have found that once my prospective teachers see examples of how teachers have successfully taught diverse students, I need to push them to try applying and synthesizing their knowledge so they begin to feel a sense of their own efficacy. In some of my courses, I have given my prospective teachers options for projects to be completed during the course. One option is for them to spend at least 4 weeks incorporating students' personal mathematics problems into classroom math lessons in their fieldwork placements or their own classrooms. They may then analyze samples of students' work, compare pre- and postinterviews with their students to see how interests in math and perception of math occurring outside school change, and analyze students' pre- and postunit test scores. I challenge them to use the context in which the personal math occurs to discuss societal influences on the math that they experience, such as values of goods and services. In critiquing their experiences with this assignment, my prospective teachers have noted how much they got to know their students, how responsive parents were, and how their students' interests rose when they incorporated their students' personal experiences into classroom lessons.

Throughout the multicultural course at Seattle University, prospective teachers revisit lesson plans they wrote in a previous introductory course in education. This gives them a chance to apply the techniques observed in video clips and guidelines they have gleaned from readings, lectures, and discussions. I ask them to examine their lesson plans for any stereo-typing, for cultural assumptions, for amount of uniformity versus differentiation, for ways in which they may be perpetuating power inequities in their class by how they have planned to teach their lesson. Their final assignment is to work in teams to develop a transformative level of lesson plan to more equitably teach all students, incorporating many viewpoints (see Banks & Banks, 2001, for a description of the transformative level of lessons). As part of the assignment, they write a critical analysis of the strengths and weaknesses of the lesson. During class, we also critique each lesson so teams can learn from each other. After I have worked with them in transforming lesson plans to incorporate students' cultures, to the prompt I had written for them to complete on an anonymous questionnaire, "When I think of trying to successfully teach a diversity of students, I feel _____," prospective teachers responded with "confident," "happy," "fabulous!" Some elaborated further on that questionnaire, when asked what in the course had impacted their own views, attitudes, or behaviors, by stating, "I feel that it is important that we learned how to transform lesson plans"; "The transformative lesson plan is a helpful way to look at curriculum"; and "Doing the transformative lesson planning helped me see the shallowness of the additive approach (though at least a first step)." Another wrote on the questionnaire, "Those transformative lesson plans were great, and challenging to do." Another wrote on the questionnaire, noting the value of having a group do the transformative lesson plan and then have the class reflect on it, "I liked the final group project. This class taught me a lot about different people's perspectives and forced me to see the diversity of opinions, starting with the opinions in this class."

CONCLUSION

By guiding prospective teachers in examining how traditional mathematics pedagogy and content negatively affect students from nondominant cultures, and by helping them use strategies for incorporating students' out-of-school mathematics experiences and for transforming lessons, I have been able to help prospective teachers move from resistance to hope and confidence that they will be able to effectively teach all students mathematics. Ideally, I would follow all of these course activities and discussions with seminars during student teaching and with in-service study and action groups with those who are full-time classroom teachers. I see such ongoing and progressing support to be critical for sustained growth of teachers who are learning to teach mathematics in culturally responsive ways. Jennings and Smith (2002) argued similarly, noting that ongoing support is needed to really develop transformative practices in teachers.

ACKNOWLEDGMENTS

Thanks to Susan Hall for capturing the cookie fraction lesson example. Susan was a graduate research fellow at Southern Connecticut State University in 1999–2000, working with Jacque Ensign on this research.

REFERENCES

Banks, J., & Banks, C. M. (2001). *Multicultural education: Issues and perspectives.* Hoboken, NJ: Wiley.
Bensman, D. (2000). *Central Park East and its graduates.* New York: Teachers College Press.
Brenner, M. (1998). Adding cognition to the formula for culturally relevant instruction in mathematics. *Anthropology and Education Quarterly, 29*(2), 214–244.
Brophy, J. (1998). *Motivating students to learn.* Boston: McGraw-Hill.
Campbell, P. F. (1996). Empowering children and teachers in the elementary mathematics classrooms of urban schools. *Urban Education, 30*(4), 449–476.
Civil, M. (1998). *Bridging in-school mathematics and out-of-school mathematics.* Paper presented at the annual meeting of the American Educational Research Association, San Diego.
Cochran-Smith, M. (2000). *The outcomes question in teacher education.* Vice presidential address presented at the 2000 annual meeting of the American Educational Research Association, New Orleans, LA.

Delpit, L. (1995). *Other people's children: Cultural conflict in the classroom.* New York: New Press.

Ensign, J. (1996). *Linking life experiences to classroom math.* Unpublished doctoral dissertation, University of Virginia, Charlottesville.

Ensign, J. (1998). Parents, portfolios, and personal math. *Teaching Children Mathematics, 4*(6), 346–351.

Ensign, J. (2001). Culturally connected math problems in an urban school. *Connecticut Mathematics Journal,* Spring, 3–10.

Ensign, J. (2003). Nurturing mathematics learning in the classroom. In N. M. Haynes, M. Ben-Avie, & J. Ensign (Eds.), *How social and emotional development add up: Getting results in math and science education* (pp. 103–119). New York: Teachers College Press.

Frankenstein, M. (1997). In addition to the mathematics: Including equity issues in the curriculum. In J. Trentacosta (Ed.), *Multicultural and gender equity in the mathematics classroom: The gift of diversity* (pp. 10–22). Reston, VA: National Council of Teachers of Mathematics.

Freire, P. (1993). *Pedagogy of the city.* New York: Continuum.

Gordon, E. W. (1999). *A view from the back of the bus.* New York: Teachers College Press.

Jennings, L. B., & Smith, C. P. (2002). Examining the role of critical inquiry for transformative practices: Two joint case studies of multicultural teacher education. *Teachers College Record, 104*(3), 456–481.

Kirshner, D. (2002). Untangling teachers' diverse aspirations for student learning: A crossdisciplinary strategy for relating psychological theory to pedagogical practice. *Journal of Research in Mathematics Education, 33*(1), 46–58.

Ladson-Billings, G. (1992). Liberatory consequences of literacy: A case of culturally relevant instruction for African American students. *Journal of Negro Education, 61,* 378–391.

Ladson-Billings, G. (1997). It doesn't add up: African American students' mathematics achievement. *Journal for Research in Mathematics Education, 28*(6), 697–708.

Levine, D. (1994). Instructional approaches and interventions that can improve the academic performance of African American students. *The Journal of Negro Education, 63,* 46–63.

Lopez, I. H. (1996). *White by law: The legal construction of race.* New York: New York University Press.

Meier, D. (1995). *The power of their ideas: Lessons for America from a small school in Harlem.* Boston: Beacon.

Resnick, L. B. (1987). Learning in school and out. *Educational Researcher, 19*(9), 13–20.

Wax, M. L. (1993). How culture misdirects multiculturalism. *Anthropology and Education Quarterly, 24*(2), 99–115.

Weiner, L. (1999). *Urban teaching: The essentials.* New York: Teachers College Press.

Woolfolk, A. E. (2001). *Educational psychology.* Boston: Allyn & Bacon.

12

Examining the "Script" in Science Education: Critical Literacy in the Classroom

Carol Brandt
University of New Mexico

One day out of frustration, a prospective teacher came to me and said, "How much biology do I really have to know to teach this to first graders? Don't you have a lesson plan that I can put into my folder?" Though blunt in its delivery, this prospective teacher had expressed a pervasive sentiment that had simmered all semester among the class. Whenever we deviated into the complex relationships in biology, or introduced open-ended questions in science, the prospective teachers often became irritable and exasperated. They desperately wanted the "script," the lesson plans that cover the diverse range of science standards, the veritable bag of tricks that they could use for teaching in their class. Most of these prospective teachers were anxious about their mastery of science; they wanted just enough biology or chemistry to anticipate their own students' questions.

For those of us who wish to promote an inquiry-based, socially conscious approach to science, those comments from prospective teachers are disheartening. We know that following the science "script" means perpetuating inequities within our practice, that power relationships go unacknowledged and unquestioned. What strategies can we use in our science education classroom that begin to rewrite the dialogues we have with teachers? How can we bring the science "script" into question and encourage prospective teachers to improvise, critique, and become authors of their own knowledge rather than simply reactors in the public education system? How do we ease their anxieties of inadequacy and empower them to be comfortable with unanswerable questions and ambiguity?

The prospective teachers in my classes continually presented me not only with resistance to pedagogical change—that is, changing their attitude about what counts as teaching—but also with resistance to ideological change (Rodriguez, 1998). Clearly, their reluctance to experiment with strategies outside the "script" demonstrated resistance to pedagogical change. But even more deeply rooted is ideological change: notions about the nature of science, whereby the epistemology of academic science goes unquestioned. Seldom do we engage prospective teachers to ask: What counts as science?

This resistance to ideological change is even more difficult to address, as I found evidence of the default script in my own practice. Ideological resistance also includes looking at the locations, positions, and participants in science. To disrupt this resistance, we ask prospective teachers to consider: Where does science emerge in our everyday lives? Who is privileged to do science, where does this happen, and who values the results? In this research project, I was particularly interested in how different texts are used by prospective teachers to reinforce political ideologies about science at the university.

In this chapter I contribute some strategies I have used in a science content course for preservice elementary teachers, methods that focus on critical literacy and move away from science "scripts" or habitual, unconscious ways of acting in the classroom. My insights are not only the byproduct of experience in the classroom, but are also part of a practitioner research study I undertook with prospective teachers on their use of texts in our classroom. I am relatively new to teaching at the university and come to teach this course as a White, middle-class woman with an MS degree in biology. As I was teaching this class, I was a PhD candidate in education and my dissertation research led me to examine literacy practices in a variety of contexts within science education. This study helped me to see how we can work with prospective teachers to critique and break away from the "script" into which both teachers and students have long been socialized. Bringing this critical literacy to the classroom means that prospective teachers see science in its gendered, historical, political, and socioeconomic context. Critical literacy means that our reading of science texts is rooted in multiple contexts: in the classroom; in the workplace, community sites, and civic locations; and most important, in the lives of prospective teachers.

CONTEXT AND SETTING

My teaching takes places at a large Carnegie Research Extensive University in the southwestern United States. I teach a science content class for prospective teachers who are sophomores or juniors, just as they are entering the College of Education. As a prerequisite for entering the College of Education, preservice teachers are required to complete a 12-credit-hour series in the Natural Sciences Program, three science content classes designed for preservice teachers. The first course in the series is Physical Science and includes physics, astronomy, and geology. The second course, Life Science, centers on biology and chemistry, and was the focus of my teaching. The third class, Environmental Science, integrates content from the first two courses in a more problem-based approach to environmental issues. Classes are limited to 20 participants and are taught in a laboratory room with tables, cabinets full of teaching materials, a sink, computers, and microscopes.

Mirroring the composition of many elementary education courses at the university, prospective teachers in this study were mostly women. Most of the participants in the class were born and raised not far from the university. A third of the class comes from Hispanic/Latino families, two are Native Americans, whereas the remaining participants are White.

This class is structured in a way that emphasizes inquiry and hands-on activities, with little lecturing by the instructor. Our curriculum focuses on providing experiences for preservice teachers in science that allow them the opportunity to engage in inquiry, construct knowledge, and broaden their understanding of scientific principles. The content of this class is taught in a way that models how prospective teachers might teach these topics in their own classroom. Yet, this curriculum provides little instruction to assist prospective teachers in negotiating the often-difficult task of deciphering scientific literature or writing in scientific language.

My study began simply with what I thought were easily answerable questions. In my first semester of teaching this class, I found the prospective teachers resistant to using their science texts, revealed to me through their journal writing for the class. I wanted to understand this resistance and learn how I could bring the use of science texts to a more dynamic part of the class. In my third semester of teaching the course, I decided to undertake a practitioner research project that would focus on literacy practices in our classroom. The questions I explored with prospective teachers include: How do you use the textbook for our class? What is your experience when using the textbook? What role does reading the text play in your understanding of science?

THEORETICAL FRAMEWORK

Several cross-disciplinary perspectives guide this study and provide a theoretical framework for my research questions, the data I collected, and my subsequent interpretation of data. The first perspective that shapes my understanding of the science classroom is social constructivism. Advocates of constructivism argue that science is learned through experiences in the classroom where students actively construct knowledge through their participation and interaction with scientific phenomena (Knorr-Cetina, 1981; Matthews, 1994). Yet, this perspective isolates the cognitive processes of science inquiry without considering how the sociocultural context of schooling constructs and mediates learning. Social constructivism attributes learning to the connection between social interactions and higher mental functions, a perspective founded on the work of the Russian linguists, Vygotsky (1986) and Bakhtin (1981). Their research focused on the dialogic conversation, the "inter-subjectivity" between teacher and student, or students and their peers, as being the location where learning occurs. For Bakhtin "heteroglossia," or multiple voices, engaged in a conversation means that language carries multiple meanings and interpretations, and consequently plays into the process of learning for those speaking and listening. Recent studies of language in science classrooms use a social constructivist framework to explore how students use dialogue to negotiate meaning and what linguistic resources they bring to the process (Ballinger, 1997; Duran, Dugan, & Weffer, 1998; Gallas, 1995).

My theoretical framework also draws on research in critical language studies (Gee, 1996; Lemke, 1990; Luke, 2000; Luke & Freebody, 1997). This body of research examines how students come to "read" various texts and the power structures among individuals, groups, and institutions that influence how students think about and use the text. Luke and Freebody argued that ways of reading are not impartial, but "are indeed correlated with issues of identity and cultural and political power, access to capital, and contemporary configurations of gender, ethnicity, class, and citizenship" (p. 191). Critical language studies contend that reading practices and the selection of texts in schools are not accidental or random, but rather serve to support the organizational needs of the institutions and the interests of stratified cultures (Luke & Freebody, 1997). Therefore, Luke advocates a literacy approach that is not only cognitive and assists students to make meaning from texts, but also guides students in an understanding of how the text is used as a source of power and persuasion. His strategy of Four Resources plays a central role in how I have come to consider scientific texts and their integration into my classroom.

The Four Resources model (Luke, 2000; Luke & Freebody, 1997) is not another cognitive approach that claims to offer a one-size-fits-all reading strategy. Instead, the Four Resources model focuses on the steps of: (a) coding practices, (b) text-meaning practices, (c) pragmatic practices, and (d) critical practices. The first two steps are reading comprehension strategies where prospective teachers learn the meaning of individual words and phrases, come to understand the conventions of academic writing, and make meaning from the scientific text. Some prospective teachers need explicit instructions to "crack the code" of writing in science textbooks and understand cumbersome scientific terminology. Luke argued that meaning making, however, is situated in cultural, community-specific, and gendered contexts. Reading is a profoundly social and cultural experience as well as cognitive, and prospective teachers must be brought into a conversation about the pragmatic and critical processes of reading science as well, the last two steps of the Four Resources model.

The pragmatics and critical processes of reading science texts are connected to an awareness of how texts, writing, and reading are used and tied to the exercise of power within social systems. For prospective teachers, portraying science texts as a cultural construct can transform their understanding to see how writing functions to support political aims, economics, and institutions. Freire and Macedo (1987) elaborated on this type of literacy as a source of empowerment, as rooted in the possibility of people to understand and transform their society. Rodriguez (1998) also took a transformative approach and linked a multicultural perspective to social constructivism to look at the historical, social, and institutional contexts of science education. Rodriguez differentiated his method from other forms of constructivism, calling it sociotransformative constructivism, a repertoire of strategies that engage prospective teachers to understand how power is exercised through the study of science.

Critical literacy in my teaching takes on this transformative agenda and means that I work toward assisting prospective teachers to understand the political and social context of "texts" (written word, talk, and action) in science and understand how these texts are generated. Equally important, as prospective teachers read and write, they bring their own experiences, linguistic proficiency, and cultural experiences to the process of making meaning. I am interested in understanding how prospective teachers recognize the differences between their own world and that of the academy. My hope is that through the positionality of these conversations, we can come to understand the hidden curricula in our "texts" and develop more democratic strategies for access and ownership of science (Barton, 1998).

RESEARCH DESIGN AND METHODS

This research involves 18 prospective teachers who participated in a life science course that I taught at a 4-year college in the fall of 1999. All of the prospective teachers are preparing for entrance into the elementary education program, and five of them will focus their endorsement area in science. This qualitative research is based on practitioner research methodology described by Anderson, Herr, and Nihlen (1994), whereby the teacher and her students (in this case, university-level students) collaborate on research that evaluates the effectiveness of pedagogy and students' experiences in the classroom.

Data collected in this practitioner research included in-class written assignments structured around effective use of the text, reading comprehension strategies in science, and writing (laboratory reports, research reports, and reflective pieces). Also during the semester, prospective teachers kept reflective journals about classroom activities and their involvement in the course.

The textbook that was used for this course was *The Living World* by George B. Johnson (1997), a text designed for college-level students who are not majoring in science. The textbook typifies the new effort publishers are making for scientific literature to be more accessible to college-level students. Each page had color illustrations, diagrams, Web sites for more information, and an end-of-chapter summary of key concepts and key terms. In addition, the prospective teachers in this class accessed a wide variety of science nonfiction for various class projects. They used readings from the Internet, articles from popular science magazines, newspaper clippings, academic journal articles, and books from our university library.

In the spring and summer of 2000 following our class together, 9 of the 18 prospective teachers in the class met for focus group discussions and one-on-one interviews, all of which were taped and transcribed. Key themes were identified and categorized from the artifacts, journals, and transcripts through a constant comparative method of analysis (Glaser & Strauss, 1967). These categories were brought back to the participants and were explored in subsequent interviews and through electronic correspondence (e-mail).

I also kept a research journal in which I constantly explored my dual roles of teacher and researcher in the classroom. My journal writing not only was an attempt to examine the motives of these prospective teachers, but was an opportunity to challenge my own approaches to, and assumptions about teaching science.

EMERGENT THEMES

As I analyzed the transcripts from interviews, the focus group, and prospective teachers' papers, reoccurring themes emerged as important elements in understanding their resistance and the script of a science classroom. Some of these themes may not be surprising to veteran instructors, but nevertheless, we need to understand how these emotions and experiences come to play in prospective teachers' resistance to both ideological and pedagogical change.

Anxiety

All of the prospective teachers who participated in this study expressed their anxieties about learning and teaching science competently. Most of the class members had actively avoided college-level science and took this class only as a requirement. Their journal entries were laced with references about test anxiety, confusion, and past difficulties with learning science in high school. As the semester progressed, some prospective teachers became more positive about their mastery of chemistry and biology, but the anxiety of adequately teaching science to their own students lingered. When faced with difficult textbook passages filled with technical terms, particularly when we studied respiration and photosynthesis, these anxieties surfaced and dominated prospective teachers' discussions.

Resentment

As prospective teachers described their progress in the educational system to me, they often expressed their resentment to what they perceived as meaningless academic hoops or exploitive traditions at the university. For example, the following quote betrays bitter resentment to the institutional custom where university students buy expensive textbooks for college classes at the beginning of each semester:

> I always . . . every year, every semester, I make the vow: I am *not* going to buy a textbook unless I need it this time. Because I buy it and throw it in the corner and then I don't use it. But then I always get paranoid as soon as they assign that first reading: "Oh my god, I've got to read it!" But I still end up not reading it, and I do fine in the class. *And* they don't buy it back. (Rhonda, focus group discussion)

Without a doubt, Rhonda's experience with required textbooks was an impediment to her using the text in our class together. I was embarrassed to learn that the textbook I required for our class together was a brand-new edition with a CD-ROM, meaning prospective teachers could not buy less-expensive used versions of it. The text cost upwards of $90 at the university bookstore, who in turn would buy the book back for a mere $15 at the end of the semester. Here I found myself complicit in an oppressive practice that pushed prospective teachers to spend large portions of their student aid on textbook purchases. Textbooks are just one of many of ways the institution and instructors like myself collude in the publisher's exploitation of students at the university, often without much thought or malicious intent. Three prospective teachers communicated their dislike of textbooks in our one-on-one interviews, citing this reason and it also consumed more than 10 minutes of our focus group discussion.

Like most science instructors at the university, I went through the motions that precede a class: developing my syllabus, ordering the textbook, and selecting passages, often entire chapters, intended to support each lesson or activity. And all this was done with little thought on my part, or an awareness of how prospective teachers are "coerced" to buy increasingly larger textbooks for higher costs.

The resentment toward textbooks that prospective teachers articulated also surrounded their frustration in the pace of reading impenetrable text. In the interviews, each participant talked about how the scientific terminology was overwhelming for them when burdened with long passages; the pace of reading was beyond what they could reasonably retain. Rather than try to keep up, they found other avenues for obtaining information: notes from class, a Web site, their classmates' notes, or questioning me during office hours. Likewise, I had conversations with faculty who used the text to measure the pace and progress of the class in covering the established curriculum. For example, as another lecturer and I traded anecdotes at the beginning of the semester, a question from him made me pause. "How many chapters are you going to cover in the text this semester?" he asked. One prospective teacher wrote about this phenomenon in her journal that accurately described my own situation. Josie wrote:

> So many professors choose a book, but it seems as if they pick the book that seems clear to them. They fail to think about our (the students) stage of learning. Unlike professors, we don't have all of the extra information on a particular subject that makes the reading more understandable. It's almost like it happens at a subconscious level. (Josie, journal entry)

Authority and the Text

As we talked in our focus group and in one-on-one interviews, prospective teachers dismissed the relevance of their own experience and the text as an authority, as a source of knowledge in the context of our class. This insight did not appear to me until I began reading transcripts and noticed that as often as they referred to the text, they were also talking about my "lectures" and me. I found this disconcerting because in my own mind, our class was structured with very little or no lecturing.

Our 105-minute class together was often broken up into activities, experiments, and presentations, but I always had a 10-minute "wrap-up" that focused on bringing the day's lesson together. I felt that this course had modeled what a constructivist class might look like and yet, prospec-

tive teachers continued to focus on my daily summary, as well as on traditional forms of assessment such as the exams (which contributed only 30%
of their grade) as an indication of their proficiency in the course. I found
these types of comments throughout our interviews and in their journal
writing:

> After a while I just stopped [reading the text] because I could understand it
> and pass the test off the notes I was getting from you. The only time I ever
> referred back to it was when I missed a day, so I would take what I got from
> you and I would say, oh gee I don't remember that term at all. Not to take up
> your time to re-teach it to the class just because I wasn't there, then I'd used
> the book. (Rhonda, focus group discussion)

Prospective teachers, like Rhonda, felt that a teacher's primary responsibility is to direct students' attention to important information and help
them separate the endless amount of detail from foundational concepts
that define chemistry and biology. Apparently, I reinforced these notions
when I handed out review sheets for exams that summarized key topics
from each unit that we studied in our class together.

As we discussed the use of texts in science teaching during our focus
session and in the interviews, I asked prospective teachers to speculate on
the role different literature might play in their own teaching. Several participants in this research adamantly expressed that their own science
classrooms as elementary teachers would include very little reading, and
would instead focus on only activities or hands-on experiences. These
prospective teachers were unclear how other literature could be included
in their science teaching or why a teacher might want to include reading
activities with their own students as they taught science:

> Basically, I think, especially for students who aren't interested in science,
> reading is not going to help them. They are going to get the most of what
> they know from the teacher because the teacher knows more and so they are
> going to able to explain it better than the text. If you have a question while
> you are reading the text, the text isn't going to be able to change for you.
> Whereas to a teacher if you say: "I don't understand this." Then they'll ex-
> plain it a different way for you or they'll draw pictures for you. (Mandy, fo-
> cus group discussion)

Implied in the preceding quote is the teacher's role as authority over
students' experiences or the text in generating an understanding of science. Participants in this research saw the teacher as being vital in providing explanations and clarifications, or offering alternative ways to approach science. In this light, no wonder prospective teachers were so
anxious about their mastery of science concepts. Despite all our efforts to

provide a constructivist classroom for prospective teachers, they still perceived the teaching of science as a didactic, teacher-centered process. In my own research journal I reflected on my frustrations with this attitude:

> A student didn't like it that I had to "look up" information I didn't know in the textbook. Universities perpetuate this idea of the instructor as walking encyclopedias, full of knowledge and information, as omniscient. I want them to be comfortable with the gaps . . . comfortable with ambiguity and the idea that they and their students can collaborate on finding the answers together. (The author, journal entry, midsemester)

Similarly, some prospective teachers had difficulty in seeing how their journal writing was part of learning science. They expressed reluctance to reflect on and write about how biology enters into their daily experiences. Although the prospective teachers had appropriated the constructivist mantra (e.g., hands-on, minds-on), their perception of science teaching was still couched in classical terms of direct instruction. My interactions with them led me to believe that they still saw science as a mastery of facts and information rather than a process of constructing knowledge through reading, writing, experimentation, activities, and discussion. The awareness of journal writing as part of scientific literacy was missing for these prospective teachers; they did not see writing as a way to position oneself in the context of science or writing as part of the inquiry process.

Bringing the Text Into a Social Practice

In our one-on-one interviews, I asked prospective teachers to describe their experiences with learning from reading as opposed to learning from conversation. I asked them to describe how constructing knowledge from reading is different from (or the same as) talking about science. Why wasn't reading science equally useful to them as talking about science? Their answers brought to light the importance of inter-subjectivity, the dialogic relationship between speaker and listener through discourse, as opposed to reading alone. The isolation of reading silently was a hindrance to those prospective teachers who described their abilities as being "weak readers." As they confronted obstacles in the text, these prospective teachers had few resources for tackling dense passages. For them, the book excluded any possibility of dialogue—its static nature was problematic, and the participants pointed out how the text did not reflect the dynamic qualities of scientific inquiry that we promoted through other activities in the class. In our interview Josie emphasized this point: "If you're a poor reader and you pick up a science text that has all these other words . . . it's, it's like, a brick wall."

Together the prospective teachers and I realized how reading a science textbook could be enhanced through a social practice, how the text could be brought into the classroom: This was perhaps the most positive aspect of my research. By bringing the reading into a social context, prospective teachers felt their knowledge was extended. As they worked on decoding the text together, difficult passages became less frustrating and they could practice vocabulary with each other. From conversations about the text, prospective teachers could glean new meanings from the text, and could bring more skills to reading alone.

While our class was together, I wanted to experiment with different ways of bringing the text into the classroom. In the most difficult portion of the class, the unit on photosynthesis and respiration, I asked prospective teachers to bring their textbooks to class. The class formed small groups and used concept mapping (Czerniak & Haney, 1998; Davis, 1990) to organize the processes of photosynthesis and show relationships of structures and functions to each other. Using markers on large sheets of paper, they drew line-and-bubble diagrams.

Each group produced concept maps that were slightly different, emerging from their varying interpretations of the text. Using their concept maps, the prospective teachers debated what should be the key elements of photosynthesis and also recognized that the two-dimensional nature of the concept map didn't allow for representing the light and dark reactions very well, especially in specialized plants where these reactions are temporally separated. In their journals, prospective teachers wrote about their experiences with using the text in this social collaboration. Ted wrote: "We also made concept maps which I found very helpful. It was a good way to learn new ideas and put together everything we've learned about photosynthesis. It was also helpful because if we forgot to address something, it was most likely to appear on someone else's map" (Ted, journal entry).

But Mandy in her journal disagreed and found the maps confusing. She opted for redrawing the concept map that her group had done, drafting it in a way that made more sense to her. She wrote in her journal:

> When we started out this unit the concept map really threw me off. I felt like all these things were thrown together and the only thing I knew was that they all related to photosynthesis. It also probably had to do with my learning style. I'm use to things being very organized and clearly laid out. Things just seem to work so much better for me when they are taken step by step. (Mandy, journal entry)

Here was a strategy that brought the textbook to a new social location in the curriculum. In their groups, prospective teachers were reading aloud to each other, diagramming, and arguing about meaning. And this process of evaluating the meaning of the text continued into their journal writing. Through this activity, prospective teachers were practicing important literacy skills at many different levels. Clearly, participants were mastering the first two important steps of literacy: decoding and making meaning. But in my mind, the activity was missing the next step where liberating science can take place. Where was critical science literacy in the concept map? Were prospective teachers able to critique the text and see it in its social, gendered, and political context? As we conducted the concept mapping, I immediately recognized the value of using the text with concept mapping, but in retrospect, I missed that "teachable moment" where I could have extended their reading of the text to be critical literacy.

COUNTERRESISTANCE: WRITING NEW DIALOGUES FOR THE CLASSROOM

Through this practitioner research I was able to see more clearly which strategies reproduced old scripts in science and perpetuated resistance, and those activities that encouraged prospective teachers to improvise, to take risks by acting outside the "norms" of being in a classroom, and to practice sociotransformative constructivism (Rodriguez, 1998), a socially and culturally conscious process of inquiry in science. I found that my syllabus was rife with elements that heightened prospective teachers' anxieties and resentments, as well as resulting in teacher-centered learning. Like most science instructors, I assigned textbook readings each week, and on Fridays I conducted an open-book quiz. My intention was that the quiz would encourage the prospective teachers to read their textbook, but I found exactly the opposite; no amount of quizzes encouraged those already resistant to the text to read. Also, despite the exam's minor role in their final grade, testing became a focus of inadequate feelings among the prospective teachers and heightened their dependence on me. Even though the remainder of the course was inquiry based, turning to the default script, for even 10 minutes at the end of the class, thwarted all constructivist learning in the other 90 minutes together.

Those elements of my curriculum that proved to be effective in diffusing prospective teachers' resistance revolved around critical literacy and discussions of bioethics. Throughout the entire semester, we spent time each class exploring science in the news. In another part of the class, nearly a month of course work revolved around a research project on a human disease or disorder that is presented to their classmates. And finally, during our genetics unit, I introduced open-ended discussions of bioethics and the politics of scientific research. In each of these situations, prospective teachers take on new roles of authority and learn how to critique knowledge, looking for inequalities in power relationships at local, institutional, and national levels. They also come to acknowledge the default science script that governed most of their experiences beginning in the primary grades through their experiences in college.

Science in the News

Our time to talk about epistemological issues in science was focused especially on a daily feature that I called "Science in the News." Prospective teachers took turns bringing in an article from the news, magazines, or the Web that related to biology. Prospective teachers were asked to summarize the news item, discuss its importance to our society, and then discuss with the class about any biases that might exist in the research or reporting of the data.

At the beginning of the semester, most prospective teachers would enthusiastically embrace the report and claim that there were no biases. "After all, this article simply has data reported by scientists and so it's got to be unbiased." In their eyes, the supremacy of White-male science should never be questioned. To them science was value-free, and never wrapped up in politics. This was happening, even when one prospective teacher brought in articles clipped from the editorial pages of the news. Another student became suspicious of possible biases when she brought in a magazine article on diabetes followed by an advertisement for a major pharmaceutical company mentioned in the article. As we talked about it week after week, prospective teachers began to question the relevancy of research, identify power relationships of corporations or national research institutes, and ask: "Who benefits?" Often they found that women and people of color were the ones who benefited least from scientific discovery. By the end of the semester, prospective teachers were critiquing news reports without my prompting and had finally come to realize that no research is unbiased.

One of the news items we discussed was the use of DNA evidence in the Innocence Project sponsored by the Benjamin N. Cardozo School of Law, where death-row convicts were allowed to use DNA analysis to support their appeals for a murder conviction. In her journal Carmen wrote: "It's crazy how DNA is so powerful in such critical situations. Do you know when the use of DNA in trials first came around? Can you imagine how many people could have been wrongfully accused or not accused at all before the use of DNA verifying such conditions?" (Carmen, journal entry).

These kinds of journal entries are encouraging because they indicate that our class is fostering critical literacy that looks at the power attributed to certain kinds of data, in this case DNA evidence. Carmen spent an entire page describing her new awareness of how many people didn't have access to DNA testing, and how she might react if placed on a jury where DNA is used as evidence.

Creating New Texts

The portion of our class where prospective teachers were the most intensely engaged revolved around research projects on human disease and disorders. Participants drew upon information from a variety of sources to make their presentations to the rest of the class. Almost every prospective teacher chose a topic that had impacted themselves or a person in their life. Their own experience of living with an illness, or with the illness of a family member was an important element of their presentation, along with the scientific information that they had gleaned from a wide variety of literature. For example, Mandy wrote in her journal: "I have been doing research on my disease (Lupus) . . . My mom has an auto-immune disorder, that's why I chose Lupus, so I could better understand her disease." Another prospective teacher amazed herself at the amount of material she compiled and her continued interest despite the quantity of information she was finding on schizophrenia. Laurie writes about her research project in her journal: "I'm finding it very interesting and I keep wanting more . . . I never thought that I would write that I have *too* much information for a paper. That usually doesn't happen to me [with science]."

Prospective teachers wove together their own knowledge derived from their experiences with illness together with information gleaned from a wide breath of materials and presented it in a narrative style. Prospective teachers took large risks in this project, presenting their own lives to each other, talking about emotional issues, and sharing information that they hope would help others who might confront similar situations. This was the one portion of the class where I felt prospective teachers took on the role of authority and competence in the subject matter. In this portion of the class, prospective teachers were able to draw information out of a variety of texts, including technical journals and textbooks as part of their research. Despite the technical nature of some of the literature they used, with some help prospective teachers were able to extract key information and place it into the context of their presentation. In their journals, prospective teachers juxtaposed these narratives about disease that were presented against the dry readings of the textbook.

Bioethics

In our genetics unit we spend several days focused on bioethical dilemmas. In this lesson, prospective teachers realize that these scenarios are true dilemmas: No right answer or solution exists that will satisfy each person involved. I have the class break down into small groups of four. Each group has a different case study taken from Web sites on ethics or from legal case law. All of the cases revolve around gender, race, and class issues in science.

Among these scenarios is the attempted patenting of genetic material from an indigenous South American woman, whose blood was taken without consent during the Human Genome Diversity Project some years ago. Another case involves the patenting of a gene from a small rural community in Italy that bestows a lower risk for heart disease. Rather than prospective teachers simply discussing whether the court decision is right or wrong, and choosing sides through a war of words, I have a protocol that they must follow. First, they have to identify all the stakeholders in the issue, including those that might not directly be mentioned in the case. For example, prospective teachers often forget about identifying the pharmaceutical industry that paid for the research done by the scientist in the case. Second, prospective teachers have to try to anticipate what view each group would take by asking: "What would they lose or gain?" Third, prospective teachers need to look at larger issues of social justice and how science is used to justify power and influence. These issues include: the right to privacy, the right to control and own our bodies, the rights for safety, the right to access our own personal medical information, and so on. Prospective teachers are fascinated to hear about the cases that each group discussed, and they raise fundamental issues about gender, race, and class in science. We also spend some time looking at the code of ethics for different national research organizations, looking at what they value and how they determine research should be conducted.

The bioethics discussions linked to the Science in the News portion of our class. Many prospective teachers saw parallels between recent news items and the dilemmas we examined together. As we brought up the bioethics cases and the Science in the News articles, I asked prospective teachers to consider the perspectives of each person involved in the article. Josie wrote in her journal: "I had heard about 'bio-ethics' but I wasn't really sure how it affected all of us. Having the chance to go over the various cases and ask how they affect all kinds of people was a great learning experience. I really never thought of all the 'stakeholders' in different bio-ethical issues" (Josie, journal entry). Josie went on to explain that she had never stopped to consider the different points of view in an ethical conflict, some of which, she noted, are not presented in the media or in discussions.

IMPLICATIONS FOR PRACTICE

What began as a deceptively simple study looking at literacy practices in my classroom actually connected with much larger issues related to teacher preparation and prospective teachers' resistance to both ideological and pedagogical change. This practitioner research project also opened my eyes to many aspects of my own practice and allowed me to question features of my teaching. Troubling for me was the realization of prospective teachers' reliance upon teacher authority and how this reliance was perpetuated through my own practice. In many ways, I was practicing a science script that perpetuated inequalities in my classroom. Despite a nagging at the edge of my consciousness, I was unaware of how the text, prospective teachers' experience, and my voice competed for authority in the classroom. Not until I paused to listen to prospective teachers' interviews did I realize how my own voice determined scientific knowledge among the prospective teachers. Also, I can see how different aspects of my practice are complicit in perpetuating this attitude in my class: my willingness to explain rather than encouraging a collaborative search for answers, my exam review sheets, and even the very structure of my syllabus, and of course, my routine use of the textbook when creating my syllabus.

Like Eisenhart, Finkel, and Marion (1996), my experience has shown me that simply offering a constructivist environment will not result in reforming science education. Prospective teachers in this study were well aware of how our class together differed from a "typical" science course at the university. Our class offered prospective teachers many different ways to access knowledge and to demonstrate their skills in mastering the content. And yet, I found prospective teachers reverting to the model of direct instruction when they talked about their own teaching and the future role of as a teacher. If we want prospective teachers to move from "received knowledge" into the authority of "constructed knowledge" that is more socially aware (Belenky, Clinchy, Goldberger, & Tarule, 1986), then we must work with prospective teachers to deconstruct the texts (e.g., textbooks, literature, media, data) they confront. In this way, prospective teachers can be authors of their understanding, rather than surrendering their authority to the textbook or the teacher. Prospective teachers had a brief glimpse of this process in our unit on human disease and disorders when they were able to blend together their lived experiences with information gleaned from many different sources.

Luke's (2000) model of Four Resources in literacy helped me to understand the shortcomings of my teaching methods. Many of my activities with scientific literature functioned on only two levels, what Luke called the decoding and the meaning-making practices, and stopped short, ending there, and served to uphold the text as unquestionable authority. As Luke put it, "We are taught and like to think of textbooks as authoritative sources of knowledge, as clear bodies of 'truth' and 'facts' written objectively, dispassionately, and free of bias" (p. 456). And without the pragmatic and critical practices, I reinforced notions of the science textbook as invulnerable—and often impenetrable. Ironically, I could have used the concept-mapping exercise to show how each group came to "read" the text in different ways, depending on their perspective, their experiences, or their understanding of photosynthesis in a larger social context.

When reading science text is extended into pragmatic and critical practices (Luke, 2000), prospective teachers come to recognize text "genres" and understand the partial knowledge (Kumashiro, 2001) that each type of text espouses. Prospective teachers become "text participants" when they are able to see how texts are used in various sociocultural contexts. We had used similar strategies for analyzing and deconstructing popular magazine articles on science that prospective teachers brought into the classroom during their Science in the News segment, both activities that built pragmatic and critical competence with texts. But, I never considered doing the same with the science textbook, data that we used for various activities, or films that I showed.

By imposing routine textbook readings, teachers assume that students have the skills to utilize the text in a productive way. And yet my study showed that many prospective teachers resist using the textbook, and may not develop the abilities needed to read this literature unless it is brought into a more social context. Are we reinforcing already negative attitudes about scientific literature through assigned textbook readings? Using texts in a social context supports the research of Lloyd (1995) and Donahue (2000), who advocated moving reading from a solitary activity into the social realm of the classroom. Donahue found that reading could be a social activity that empowered students in his science class to exchange ideas, and become an active process that facilitates meaning, one that mirrors the processes of hands-on or inquiry-based learning. Donahue advocated that reading in a science course be expanded beyond the standard textbooks and instead include a wide array of literature, including popular fiction. Similarly, Lloyd found that social processes were an important element in helping students to decipher scientific text, moving students toward a "critical literacy" in their reading of scientific literature.

With more consistent use of texts in my classroom, perhaps prospective teachers would develop more reliable strategies for decoding thick scientific literature and approach the text with less anxiety. Mastering these basic skills is a fundamental step in their comfort with scientific literature. I want to emphasize that their apprehension is not a small issue. Relieving prospective teachers' unease is the first step toward being authors of their own knowledge, and without this sense of confidence, they will never step outside the old script of science education. This social context for reading and using texts also offers teachers opportunities to examine the historical, social, gendered, and political influences on a science text with their students.

In my own teaching, I want prospective teachers to be able to access and to evaluate a wide variety of scientific literature, from lesson plans, to textbooks, to articles on the Internet. Luke's (2000) model of literacy practices has given me a way to approach scientific literature, rewrite the "scripts" we narrate in the classroom, and implement practice that is socially responsible and that can have transformative power in our science classrooms.

Granted, this study was limited to only one semester, a short 16-week period, with prospective teachers. Would I have found the same results if I had met these prospective teachers a year later, after their teaching field experience? How will the participants understand literacy in science education a year or two after having their own classroom? At this point, my answers to these questions would be pure speculation. As a qualitative research project, this study was not intended for drawing generalizations that we can extend to other classrooms or expand to a different point in time. My intent was to explore my own practice and to better understand the motivations and experiences of the prospective teachers in my classroom. I felt that this study allowed me to "disrupt" unconscious habits in both teacher and students. This research also allowed the prospective teachers and me to consider more broadly what constitutes literacy in science education, and how we can examine written texts in new light. Sharing these ideas and discussions with prospective teachers helped me to better design strategies for counterresistance, and hopefully, encouraged these future teachers to think about how they might use scientific texts in a more socially conscious way in their own classrooms. By disrupting these old habits, we can rewrite the scripts to consider new and more democratic ways to speak, write, and read science in our schools.

ACKNOWLEDGMENTS

This research was completed with assistance from the staff in the Natural Science Program at the University of New Mexico and the New Mexico Collaborative for Excellence in Teacher Preparation (NSF DUE 9653973). I also want to thank Kathryn Herr and Ann Nihlen for their conversations and feedback on practitioner research.

REFERENCES

Anderson, G. L., Herr, K., & Nihlen, A. S. (1994). *Studying your own school: An educator's guide to qualitative practitioner research.* Thousand Oaks, CA: Corwin Press.

Bakhtin, M. (1981). *The dialogic imagination.* Austin: University of Texas Press.

Ballinger, C. (1997). Social identities, moral narratives, scientific argumentation: Science talk in a bilingual classroom. *Language and Education, 11,* 1–14.

Barton, A. C. (1998). *Feminist science education.* New York: Teachers College Press.

Belenky, M. F., Clinchy, B. M., Goldberger, N. R., & Tarule, J. M. (1986). *Women's ways of knowing: The development of self, voice, and mind.* New York: HarperCollins.

Czerniak, C. M., & Haney, J. L. (1998). The effect of collaborative concept mapping on elementary preservice teachers' anxiety, efficacy, and achievement in physical science. *Journal of Science Teacher Education, 9*(4), 303–320.

Davis, N. T. (1990). Using concept mapping to assist prospective elementary teachers in making meaning. *Journal of Science Teacher Education, 1*(4), 66–69.

Donahue, D. M. (2000). Experimenting with texts: New science teachers' experience and practice as readers and teachers of reading. *Journal of Adolescent & Adult Literacy, 43*(8), 728–740.

Duran, B. J., Dugan, T., & Weffer, R. (1998). Language minority students in high school: The role of language in learning biology concepts. *Science Education, 82,* 311–341.

Eisenhart, M., Finkel, E., & Marion, S. F. (1996). Creating the conditions for scientific literacy: A re-examination. *American Educational Research Journal, 33*(2), 261–295.

Freire, P., & Macedo, D. P. (1987). *Literacy: Reading the word and the world.* Westport, CT: Bergin & Garvey.

Gallas, K. (1995). *Talking their way into science: Hearing children's questions and theories, responding with curricula.* New York: Teachers College Press.

Gee, J. P. (1996). *Social linguistics and literacies: Ideology in discourses.* London: Falmer Press.

Glaser, B. G., & Strauss, A. L. (1967). *The discovery of grounded theory.* Chicago: Aldine.

Johnson, G. B. (1997). *The living world* (2nd ed.). New York: McGraw-Hill College Division.

Knorr-Cetina, K. D. (1981). *The manufacture of knowledge: An essay on the constructivist and contextual nature of science.* Oxford, England: Pergamon.

Kumashiro, K. K. (2001). "Posts" perspectives on anti-oppressive education in social studies, English, mathematics, and science classrooms. *Educational Researcher, 30*(3), 3–12.

Lemke, J. L. (1990). *Talking science: Language, learning, and values.* Norwood, NJ: Ablex.

Lloyd, C. V. (1995). Scientific literacy in two high school biology classrooms: Considering literacy as a social process. *Journal of Classroom Interaction, 31,* 21–27.

Luke, A. (2000). Critical literacy in Australia: A matter of context and standpoint. *Journal of Adolescent and Adult Literacy, 43*(5), 448–461.

Luke, A., & Freebody, P. (1997). Shaping the social practice of reading. In S. Muspratt, A. Luke, & P. Freebody (Eds.), *Constructing critical literacies: Teaching and learning textual practice* (pp. 185–225). Cresskill, NJ: Hampton Press.

Matthews, M. R. (1994). *Science teaching: The role of history and philosophy of science.* New York: Routledge.

Rodriguez, A. J. (1998). Strategies for counterresistance: Toward sociotransformative constructivism and learning to teach science for diversity and for understanding. *Journal of Research in Science Teaching, 35*(6), 589–622.

Vygotsky, L. S. (1986). *Thought and language.* Cambridge, MA: MIT Press.

Author Index

A

Aaronsohn, E., 111, *114*
Abbott, I. A., 175, *178*
Abell, S. K., 205, 206, 214, *220*
Abraham, J., 48, *54*
Adams, P. E., 204, *220*
Ahlquist, R., 6, *10*
Aikenhead, G. S., 64, *84*, 89, 90, 111, *114*, 121, *139*, 205, *220*
Alberts, B., 62, *84*
Allen, K., 144, *157*
Allingham, B., 165, *179*
Anderson, C. W., 217, *220*
Anderson, G. L., 248, *261*
Anderson, J. R., 63, *84*
Anderson, M., 214, *220*
Anderson, R. D., 7, *10*, 66, *84*
Apple, M. W., 34, 46, *54*
Armento, B. J., 90, *115*
Atwater, M. M., 6, *10*, 103, 104, *114*, 127, *139*
Atweh, B., 37, *54*
Au, K. H., 120, *140*
Ayers, W., 208, 211, *220*

B

Bakhtin, M. M., 19, 24, *31*, 246, *261*
Ball, D., 152, *157*
Ballenger, C., 61, *86*
Ballinger, C., 246, *261*
Banilower, E. R., 7, 8, *16*
Banks, C., 4, 6, 7, *10*, 36, *54*, 240, *241*
Banks, J. A., 4, 6, 7, *10*, 36, *54*, 88–90, 93, 97, 104, 113, *114*, 240, *241*
Baptiste, H. P., 38, *54*, 104, *115*
Barba, R. H., 103, 104, *115*
Barnes, M., 71, 73, 80, *84*
Barnett, C., 151, *156*
Barro, S., 43, *54*
Barton, A., 27, *31*, 247, *261*
Beauboeuf-Lafontant, T., 186, 187, *201*
Becker, J., 148, *156*
Belenky, M. F., 258, *261*
Bell, B., 66, *84*
Bensman, D., 234, *241*
Bernstein, B., 149, 153, *156*
Beyer, L. E., 154, *156*
Bibby, N., 48, *54*
Bishop, A. J., 48, *54*
Bitter, G. G., 95, *115*
Bleicher, R. E., 37, *54*

Subject Index